CUBA

OFFICIAL GUIDE

A. G. Gravette

Ⅿ CARIBBEAN

cuba

NATIONAL INSTITUTE OF TOURISM

First published 1988
Reprinted 1989, 1990, 1992, 1993, 1994

Published by THE MACMILLAN PRESS LTD
London and Basingstoke
Associated companies and representatives in Accra,
Auckland, Delhi, Dublin, Gaborone, Hamburg, Harare,
Hong Kong, Kuala Lumpur, Lagos, Manzini, Melbourne,
Mexico City, Nairobi, New York, Singapore, Tokyo

ISBN 0–333–42703–3

Printed in Hong Kong

'. . . the development in tourism is the natural outcome
of the policies we have adopted.'

'Tourism is one of our more remunerative
labour-intensive industries.'

'It is one of our great possibilities . . .'

'There is a growing demand in Cuban tourism.'

Excerpts from speeches made by
Commander in Chief, Dr. Fidel Castro
Ruz, First Secretary of the Central
Committee of the Communist Party of
Cuba, President of the Councils of State
and of Ministers.

Acknowledgements

The author and publishers wish to acknowledge with thanks, the following photographic sources: Anne Bolt; Cuban Tourist Board, London; Richard ffrench; G W Lennox; S A Seddon; P D Stiling; Ian F Took.

The publishers have made every effort to trace the copyright holders, but if they have inadvertently overlooked any, they will be pleased to make the necessary arrangements at the first opportunity.

The author would like to acknowledge that several of the pictures in this guide are not his own work and that credit and thanks are due to Raymond Harrison who accompanied him on an early tour of Cuba and Martha Viebock the celebrated Austrian underwater photographer. He would also like to express his thanks to the Cuban Tourist Boards, both in London and Havana who supplied further material. His thanks are also extended to Bernardo Nievares and his wife, Mary Luz and the staff of the Cuban Embassy in London, Raquel Saavedra for her dedicated work on the manuscript corrections and Gwen Lowman for the editing. He is especially indebted to Rosa Escandell Perez for her continued assistance and to those Cubatur guides and drivers who provided valuable details. Encouragement from Stuart Hamilton, Bill and Hazel Derbyshire and many others provided impetus during the compilation of his book.

For unswerving support and patience my particular thanks are owing to my wife, a constant source of inspiration.

Contents

Introduction

Cuba is a smile

When you decide to vacation in Cuba, you opt for a balmy tropical climate and a chance to see something or, in some cases, to return to a place you already know and love.

In either case, you won't be disappointed. The Cubans and the National Institute of Tourism will see to that. For Cuba is more than you've heard about or seen in snapshots: palm trees bordering a warm, blue sea; beaches backed by mountains; Old Havana; great food; delicious rum; rhythmic music; fine, white sand; a green-blue-golden landscape; the blue sky and pure air. Cuba is also the hospitality and charm of the people. Cuba is a smile, it is youth, it is love.

Look for this little island on the map. There it lies, between North and South America, in the middle of the Caribbean Sea, stretched out like an alligator.

In Cuba, you'll find just the spot that suits your needs and desires, the place that stirs your feelings and imagination.

Villas and hotels await you. Varadero, Cuba's best known beach, is cosmopolitan. The East Havana beaches are popular with all those who love watersports. At Camagüey's Mayanabo Club, cays and seashells invite explorers and collectors. Rancho Luna, near Cienfuegos, unfolds its tropical splendours. Holguín's Guardalavaca Beach is a lush and intimate garden. The Sierra Maestra Mountains rise majestically behind exuberant Baconao Park in Santiago de Cuba. On virgin Cayo Largo, you'll find solitude and silence amidst birds and fish.

Fly to the light, to the smile, to Cuba. Enjoy living for a while without clocks or obligations, without tension or crowds – open, free uninhibited. Recharge! Find health and happiness. Beautify your body and your soul. Cuba awaits you with open arms, to welcome you and make your visit a smile.

As a start, this guide provides information on all points of interest in Cuba, with the details you need presented in a simple, objective way. We hope you'll find it useful.

Lic. Gary González
General Director
Publicitur
President of the Cuban
Tourism Journalists' Club

Preface

After making landfall on Cuba Genoese explorer Christopher Columbus named the long, green Caribbean island after the Spanish sovereign's daughter, Juana. A wooden cross was erected to mark the spot of the discovery.

Having spent eight weeks in search of the 'Indies' and briefly encountering the Lukka-cairi natives on what is now the Bahamas, the Spanish mariners called Cuba's friendly inhabitants, 'Indians'. The first proper Indian settlement the sailors were to see after leaving the Spanish port of Palos was known locally as 'Cubanacan'. The adventurers believed this to be the site of the Japanese Emperor's court, but found, to their dismay, that it was the native name for a primitive colony established at the centre of the island.

Returning to their three small caravels, the *Santa Maria*, *Niña* and *Pinta*, the exploratory expedition recounted their visit to the Indian's town in the interior. Cubanacan, the first Indian settlement ever seen by European eyes, subsequently gave its prefix to Spain's key acquisition in the Caribbean ... Cuba. Many maps drawn up in following years however, show the island marked as 'Isabella' after the Queen of Spain.

The tropical islands of the Caribbean have since lured travellers from every corner of the globe. Each has its own individuality. Every island offers its own special flavour. From expeditions into luxuriant scenery, water sports on exotic beaches to excursions through historic halls and trips to fortresses of past ages, each island is unique.

One island, as Columbus discovered, proffers more than its smaller neighbours. Its unspoilt beaches are more varied, its

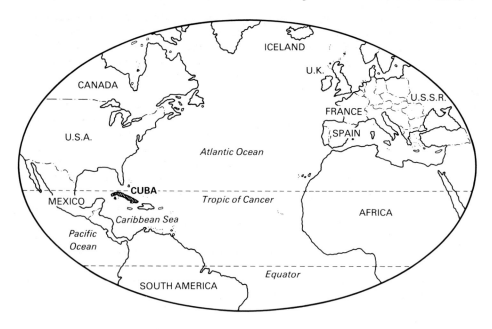

A mid-nineteenth century Carnaval in Cuba

mountain ranges and forest glades more prolific and its history more chequered and exciting.

This is Cuba – the pearl at the heart of the Caribbean – an island which fascinates as much for its enigmatic quality as for its variety. It intrigues as much for its romantic past as for its future realism. Cuba's development owes a lot to its past, but holds a great deal in store for the coming years. Many of the country's urban areas are living museums or examples of the nation's new society. Its rural regions are often a testament to the endeavours of past decades, or symbols of the progress made since the triumph of the Revolution and birth of the Republic.

Today, Cuban people feel that the successful efforts of her revolutionaries and the achievements attained over recent decades should be shared with the rest of the world through tourism. Cuba's doors are open to the sightseers and travellers, sportsmen and tourists, who are now flocking to this newly-discovered gem in the Caribbean Sea. There is as much to see and do in Cuba's towns and cities as there is to enjoy in its peaceful countryside or on its extensive shores. Many of its spectacular beauty spots are national monuments and certain towns are preserved as historic

treasures, cameos of ages gone by. Modern facilities and amenities are provided for the growing number of demanding visitors. An excellent road network has opened up the country's stunning mountain ranges and her wonderful beaches – little wonder Cuba's titles include – 'Queen of the Antilles', 'Gem of the American Seas' and, with typical Spanish flourish 'La Seimpre Fiel Isla de Cuba'.

Known world-wide for its distinguished rum and superlative cigars, this island invites the visitor to sample its diverse tastes as well as the nation's sights and sounds – remember Guantánamera?

A warm and friendly welcome awaits the traveller to Cuba's shores – as it did five hundred years ago. Whether you are an explorer, fisherman, golfer, diver, hunter, yachtsman, bird watcher or just a relaxing sun-seeker Cuba caters for everyone. So varied is the country, and so legion are the activities for visitors to this abundant Caribbean gem, that a volume of encylopaedic proportions would be needed to do justice to it. The following chapters are intended to serve as an introduction – a guide to whet the traveller's appetite and provide basic information on the more frequented areas of Cuba – the Caribbean's oldest yet most recent discovery.

Columbus discusses the future of Cuba with a
native Chieftain. A rare engraving from the
author's collection

CHAPTER 1

An Exotic Background

Ship's Log – *Santa Maria* **– off the Island of Cuba**
'I have never seen a more beautiful place:
[the island] . . . has such marvellous beauty that it
surpasses all others in charms and graces as the day doth
the night in lustre. I have been overwhelmed at this sight
of so much beauty that I have not known how to relate it . . .'

Christóbál Colón
[CHRISTOPHER COLUMBUS]
27–28 October 1492

Geographical location

The Republic of Cuba is the largest tropical archipelago in the western hemisphere and the seventh largest island in the world. It is the most important of the Greater Antilles group and quite different from its southern neighbours, the Lesser Antilles. Because of its size and location, just touching the

An eighteenth century map of the Caribbean region

Tropic of Cancer to the north, it is unique in many respects. This long, narrow island lies at the mouth of the Gulf of Mexico, where the waters of the Caribbean Sea meet those of the Atlantic Ocean. Its strategic position earned Cuba the title of 'Key to the New World', its commerce gave rise to the phrase 'The jewel in the Spanish Crown'; and the island's beauty was rewarded by that ultimate of accolades 'Pearl at the heart of the Caribbean'.

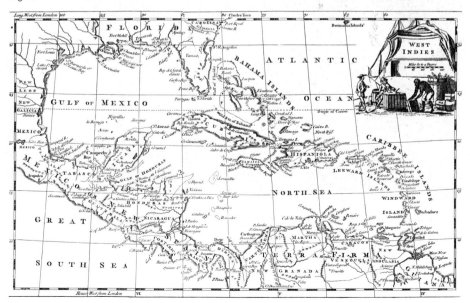

1

Haiti is Cuba's nearest neighbour – 77 kilometres to the east – and is visible occasionally from the highest point of the La Farola viaduct, Alto de Cotilla, in Guantanamo Province or from Maisí Point. Jamaica is 140 kilometres south of the island, the Yucatan peninsula of Mexico is 210 kilometres due west and, 145 kilometres north, lies Florida's Key West. The tiny islands of the Bahamas are close to Cuba's Atlantic coast and the Cayman Islands are tucked under its southern sweep of bays.

About 6500 kilometres north-east of Cuba is Europe and the United Kingdom whilst the Canadian capital, Ottawa, is about 3500 kilometres due north.

Area and features

The first map of Cuba was probably drawn up by Juan de la Costa, Columbus' pilot on his second (1493 – 1496) voyage. Cuba's entire coastline length is estimated to be nearly 6000 kilometres. The total area of Cuba is around 111 000 square kilometres – about the size of England. It has more than 1200 cays and islets; the largest island, lying off its Caribbean shores, is the oyster-shaped Isla de la Juventud (the Isle of Youth), formerly the Isle of Pines.

A long, narrow island, Cuba has been likened in shape to a scythe blade, a shark, a lizard or a crocodile. From Cabo de San Antonio in the west, to Maisí in the extreme east, the country is about 1250 kilometres long. In places the Atlantic shores are only 32 kilometres from their Caribbean counterparts and, at its widest point, the island is about 191 kilometres across.

Almost three-quarters of the country consists of low-lying plains carpeted with sugar, citrus, tobacco and vegetable crops, divided by more than 500 river basins and five mountain ranges. The elongated island's south-east region is dominated by the peaks of the Sierra Maestra. Pico Turquino is 1972 metres above sea level and is the highest mountain in the country. It is flanked by impressive peaks over 1700 metres in height, which are shown on the map. Gran Piedra (Huge Rock) is a particular attraction of the Sierra Maestra, with a sheer face to its summit at 1226 metres. Other high peaks are found in the Sierra Baracoa in the south of the island and in the far east are the Sierras Nicaro and Maguey. At the north-eastern 'nose' of the island are the folded ranges of the Sierra de Nipe.

In the centre of Cuba's south coast isolated summits run for 80 kilometres

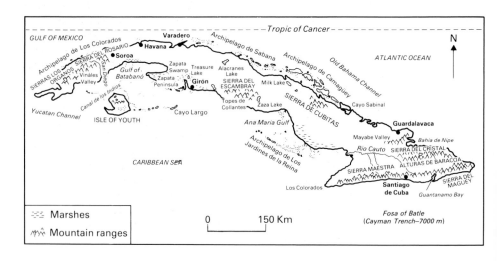

A verdant, fertile island at the centre of the Caribbean

along the coast and extend 20 kilometres inland. A popular resort region, the highest peak, San Juan commands a fine view across the Caribbean Sea. This range, the Sierra Escambray, originally named the Sierras de Trinidad – Sancti
is noted for its fine lakes and rivers. North-centrally located are the cave-riddled Sierra de Cubitas.

In the far west of Cuba is the Sierra Guaniguanico with two mountain ranges. The Sierra de los Organos (Western Organos) and the Sierra de Rosario comprise the Organos Cordillera and create a spine of moderately high peaks rising to 728 metres. This formation, across low, rich, flat plains, shapes the western 'tail' of the island. Of special interest in the Sierra de los Organos are the famous limestone caverns, karst 'haystack' hills and bizarre shapes created by the exposed conical columns of prehistoric collapsed caves.

Two features of the island's south coast are of particular interest, the Isla de la Juventud lies to the south-west. This fertile, 2220 square kilometre island lies in

one of Cuba's four coralline archipelagoes. The vast swamplands of the Zapata (shoe-like) peninsula, are also of considerable interest, but more for the fauna and vegetation than their geological structure.

The many pocket bays, or 'bolsas', along the coast have had a great influence on Cuba's economic . development. Its numerous beaches, rocky coves and tranquil lakes have promoted tourism.

The country's wealth of physical features also includes its rivers. The largest, the Rio Cauto, describes an arc around the south-western 'fin' of the island, flowing about 370 kilometres, and entering the Caribbean Sea in the deep Guacanayabo Gulf. The other 40 main rivers which are quite short, often fuel reservoirs (29) and man-made, or major natural lakes of which there are ten. Tropical forests, wooded outcrops and coastal swamplands complement the scenic beauty of Cuba's broad, sandy beaches and picturesque bays.

Cuba's seas are as varied as its terrain, each with its own peculiarities from coral reefs to deep sea caves. Fishing, diving, marine archaeology and zoology are specialities in the island's waters. Its several tidal currents provide a rich abundance of maritime life. Not

French map of Cuba by M. Bonne, from the author's collection

30 kilometres from the southern coastline, between Cuba and Haiti, is the notorious Paso de los Vientos (Windy – or Windward Passage). To the south of the island, in the volcanic sea bed, is the 7000 metre deep Fosa of Batle (Bartlett Trough) or Cayman Trench, one of the deepest stretches of water in the western hemisphere. Along Cuba's northern coast runs the famous 'Old Bahama Channel' and between the peninsula of Guanahacabibes and Mexico is the Yucatan Straits.

The combination of these varied physical and geological attributes has created a country with a diversity of terrain, coastal formations and climate unrivalled in the Caribbean region. Cuba's beauty and contrasts, together with its varied vegetation, its people and their heritage of chequered history, has produced one of the most interesting islands in the world.

Pre-history and archaeology

Many of the native Indians of Cuba, before the advent of the Spanish, took refuge in caves wherever it was possible. Others constructed rude dwellings from natural materials at hand. It is in these caves and nearby primitive camp sites that modern archaeologists have found most evidence of the life-style of the island's early inhabitants. Traces of structured villages have also been discovered in coastal and lakeside regions where caves did not exist.

Historians and archaeologists have collected remains from cave-dwelling tribes which date from about 3500 BC until about 1250 AD – the pre-Ceramic tribes of Ciboney and Guanahatabey and the following Tainos who arrived about AD 1200. The first two lately inhabited the westernmost province, now Pinar del Rio, having been ousted by the Tainos from their traditional grounds. Cueva Funcha is Cuba's most westerly cave with possible Indian connections and another 200 archaeological sites have been uncovered. These caves have produced some of the best examples of primitive tribal life. Highly developed domestic artefacts are still being uncovered in caves once occupied by the Mayarí Indians.

In the Santo Tomás Range, part of the Western Organos mountains, almost 30 kilometres of limestone caverns show evidence of tribal shelter and today provide a spelaeologist's paradise. Closeby, in Viñales Valley, the Indian Cave, discovered in 1920, is of significance as a former shelter of bygone tribes. The cave which passes through a *mogote,* or limestone hillock, contains an underground river and has produced artefacts of exceptional historical value. Not quite so spectacular is the Cave of San Miguel in a nearby cliffside, although it is a regular tourist attraction. A little further south-west of Viñales are the famous caves of Sumidero.

Three caves, which were probably Indian sites, La Virgen, Cuevas de Jaruco and Cueva Garcia Rabiou are all within a short

Indian cave wall decorations

Rita Longa's sculpture of a Taino Indian hunting Jutia

distance of Havana City. In 1985, near the Canímar River in Matanzas Province, a significant discovery of aboriginal habitation revealed evidence of bones and implements from a tribal group dating back 4000 years. West of Matanzas are the sites of La Pluma and Simpson Caves. Close to Matanzas city is Bellamar's Cave. This was discovered in 1850 whilst a worker was recovering a sheep from a deep cleft. It is two-and-a-half kilometres long and contains sensational stalactites and

stalagmites. It also probably served as an ancient Indian refuge. About 30 kilometres north is Ambrosio's Cave on the Varadero beach peninsula. Indian wall paintings and pre-Columbian tools, pots and artefacts were found on the site.

Another significant find was on the Isla de la Juventud, where three caves sites, which have been occupied for long periods by Indian tribes were discovered. These were Cueva de Finlay, de Indío and that of Punta del Este which revealed pictographs representing magical signs and charts of the heavens. These drawings have been reproduced in the local museum and in the Museum of Natural Sciences – Felipe Poey – Havana. A wealth of artefacts were also discovered in these caves.

The only location that has produced good examples of skeletal evidence from Indian occupation, together with tools, pots and artefacts, is the hillside region around Trinidad in the south-central area of Cuba. Some relics from this spot date from 2000 years ago and are now in the Guamuhaya Museum. Indian pictographs have recently been discovered in nearby Santa Clara Province.

In the Sierra Jatibonico, Ciego de Avila Province, two cavern dwellings have been located near Punta de San Juan, not far from Chambas. Clues of Indian settlements have also been uncovered in the large caves of Puntas Judas, again on the north coast. These are near Yaguajay in Sancti Spiritus Province, within a few kilometres of Chambas, and are still being investigated.

One Indian tribe, which appears to have only used caves for ritual purposes, lived near the six caverns located around the Cubitas Valley in Camagüey Province. The El Indio, Las Mercedes, Maria Teresa, Matias, Pichardo and Munoz, or Cave of the Generals, near Sola, show no clear evidence of habitation. Here, cave-wall pictographs illustrate the Indians' first encounter with Spanish conquistadores. However, all around the site were found shell, stone, bone and clay utensils and certain areas seemed to have been designated as burial grounds. These are being excavated by the Institute of Social Sciences of the Academy of Science of Cuba.

In Banes, on the far north-east coast of the island, are the remnants of an Indian settlement where shell, ivory and gold objects and ornaments have been discovered. A burial ground and a quantity of tools and pottery shards were also uncovered there. Also near Banes on the province's north coast is another famous Indian cave – the Cueva de las Cuatrocientas Rosas (400 roses).

Further south, near Santiago de Cuba, are a number of famous cliff caves where shoreline Indians set up home. Relics from these primitive tribes are now exhibited in the Bacardi Museum in the City. A 5000 BC pre-Ceramic site uncovered at Farallones de Seboruco is one of the oldest discovered in the Caribbean region.

Most famous of all the relics found in Cuba is the intricately carved, pre-Columbian 'Holguín Axe'. This treasured artefact, discovered by a Spaniard in 1860 near the south-central city of Holguín, is now a prized exhibit in the city museum.

The best examples of reconstructed Indian dwellings and sculptured figures enacting typical Tainos life, are at Guama, on Treasure Lake, in Zapata National Park. Enough traces of early native inhabitation were found here at the turn of the century to piece together a remarkable scenario of ancient Indian life. This is now one of Cuba's most popular resorts for day visits or even longer stays, with a taste of the natural ways of olden times provided in mock-Indian accommodation.

Investigations into the pre-Columbian period of Cuba's varied history, including excavations on both pre-Ceramic and Ceramic sites, are expected to reveal much more of the pre-historic life of ancient Indians in the planned programmes of archaeological discovery.

Hernando Cortéz

Early history

Before the Genoese explorer Christopher Columbus sailed from Palos, Spain, to discover Cuba with the crews of the *Santa Maria, Niña* and *Pinta*, cinnamon-coloured Amerindian tribes had roamed the island. Carib and Arawak, or Tainos natives, numbering about 350 000, were the main inhabitants of the Caribbean before the arrival of the Spanish. Their staple diet was cassava and fish, or hunted meats. They farmed maize and enjoyed festivals and primitive games.

The Proto Arawak and Arawak tribes had migrated to Cuba from the Guyanas and Venezuela region of South America in dugout canoes. The Ciboney Indians had also migrated to Cuba, apparently from the north. These tribes met Yucatan Indians who had arrived from the Mexican peninsula. The generally peaceful existence of these mixed tribes was shattered towards the end of the fifteenth century by the arrival, from South America, of the murderous Caribs, (named after the Indian word for cannibal), whose habit of preying upon the Arawak was, in turn interrupted by the arrival of the Spaniards in 1492 AD.

The Tainos had pushed the fishing groups of Ciboney, and the hunter-gatherer tribes of Guanahatabey Indians, to the far west of the island. The Spaniards hunted the Indians for sport, and to use as labour. Although, during early occupation, the aborigines were decimated, many Indian names and words survived.

'Cuba' itself may derive from the ethnic word 'Coiba'. It is also often asserted that the word comes from 'Cubanacan', the Tainos word for the 'centre of the island'. Spanish sailors adopted the Indian 'hamoc' in preference to the bunk, (hence hammock). 'Tabac', the local word for the forked reeds, or 'tobago', used by Indian Shamans to smoke tobacco through the nostrils, became the accepted word for the plant. 'Cohiba', the native name for tobacco, was adopted by the national cigar-makers as the name for one of the most excellent of Havana cigars. Even the word cigar, or 'cigarros', comes from the Amerindian word for smoking – 'Sik ar'. The word 'canoe' is a Carib name and 'potato' and 'hurricane' are both Arawak Indian words.

'Batos' was a ball game which had been played throughout the Tainos region since before their migration from the Orinoco area of South America. The name gave its prefix to the word 'bat' and its development evolved the game now known as baseball. Many other modern words are derived from those of the indigenous Cubans, like 'barbecue'. Jamaica, as heard by Columbus from the Indians of Cuba, was referred to as Xayamaca – the isle of woods and water (translated by the Spanish to mean 'the isle of gold'!).

The Tainos' social structure was quite advanced and each region was ruled over by a 'cacique' or chief. Their style of thatched houses of palm are still in use in certain isolated outposts, maintaining the ancient name of 'bohios'. The Indians also believed in deities, with a heaven called 'Coyaba'.

Tainos culture also was not without acclaim. Gold amulets, shell and coral beads, and carved statuettes adorned their persons, and, for everyday use, the rich clays of Cuba provided materials for jars and pots whilst the hard, grey-green peridotite rock was formed into elaborate knives, axe-heads and tools. Cave paintings in three provinces demonstrate the expertise of their artists and the sophistication of their perception of the earthly and extra-terrestrial worlds.

Legends also persisted, including that of the famous Ciboney chief, Hatuey – now the name of a popular beer. Hatuey, who reigned, with his comely wife, in the northern corner of what is now Guantánamo Province, had seen the slaughter of his brethren in the name of religion. In 1512 AD, by order of Governor Diego de Velázquez, he was himself burned at the stake for not embracing the Christian faith. He is said to have remarked, before his ordeal, 'If torture and murder are the wishes of your God, I cannot be part of that religion and I cannot see myself enjoying heaven with such men who obey the cruel wishes of such a God. Are there any Spaniards in Paradise? . . . In which case I have no wish to be seen there myself!'

Landing first on the north-east coast of Cuba, at Cayo Bariay, Columbus (Colon in Spanish) explored the coast from what is now Baracoa, to Gibara Bay. Notes in his captain's log indicate that he was most impressed by his initial five weeks on the island, and returned to Spain on December 5, reporting back to the sovereigns Ferdinand and Isabella.

The next year, 1493, on his second visit, Columbus, with seventeen caravels, ventured further afield. They made an exploratory trip along Cuba's southern coastline from its extreme tip to the farthest point west – a journey of more than 2000 kilometres. Columbus died in 1506, ten years after his last visit to the island.

Two years after the death of Columbus, the adventurer Sabastian de Ocampo circumnavigated the island, but it was not until 1511 that about 300 followers of Diego de Velázquez, from nearby

Diego Velázquez

Hispaniola, erected the initial, temporary settlement in Cuba. A year later, the first permanent town was founded at Baracoa. This was followed, over the next four years, by six more settlements at Bayamo, Sancti Spiritus, Puerto Principe (this town was later moved inland and re-named Camagüey), Santiago de Cuba and Batabano (later removed to a site on the north coast and named San Cristobal de la Havana – now Havana).

There were many stories of violence at this time of colonisation. Panfilo de Narvaes, founder of Havana and Velázquez' lieutenant, although supposedly on a peaceful mission, once massacred a complete Indian township. The relationship between the Spanish and Indian inhabitants deteriorated, and disillusionment set in with the settlers as the promises of vast treasures in Cuba were unfulfilled.

Some precious metal, copper, and other useful minerals were found, however, and gold discovered in the Escambray Mountains prompted Velázquez to establish the township of Trinidad. The year before this, from 1513–14, slaves began to be shipped from the African

9

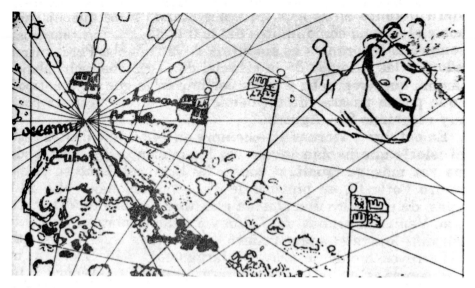

Attributed to Juan de la Costa, Columbus' pilot
on his second voyage, this 1500 map was
drawn on an oxhide

continent. Cuba's original Indians were
slowly being decimated as related in Father
Bartolomé de la Casas' tome *Brevissima de
la Destruccíon de las Indios*. The remaining
Indian labour force was supplemented by
these slaves, to work on the fields or in
mines. By this time the cash crops of
cocoa, coffee, indigo and sugar cane had
been introduced.

During 1514 Velázquez established his
base at Santiago de Cuba, made an
expedition to Mexico on behalf of the
King, Charles V of Spain, and, on his
return in 1515, constructed the settlement
at Batabano. It is from this point that the
history of Cuba, as an established country,
began to unfold.

Important Dates and Events

1514   San Cristobal de la Havana
       established
1515   Santa Maria del Puerto del
       Principe founded
1516   The oldest existing house in Cuba
       was built for the explorer
       Hernando Cortéz in Santiago de
       Cuba

1517   Governor of Santiago de Cuba,
       Diego de Velázquez, sends the ill-
       fated Cordoba quest to Yucatan.
       The Spanish Crown permits the
       importation of more slaves
1518   Under Juan de Grijalva, a second
       expedition goes to Mexico from
       Santiago de Cuba. Hernando
       Cortéz amasses 620 men for
       another Mexican foray
1519   Cortéz sets out from Trinidad, in
       February, to search for more
       Mexican gold. The first Mass is
       said in the Plaza de Armas to
       inaugurate Havana city
1521   Juan Ponce de Leon discoverer of
       Florida, dies in Cuba
1523   Holguín city established
1527   Los Indios revolt at San Salvador

10

de Bayamo and at Puerto del Principe

1528 Puerto Principe moved to near its present (Camagüey) position

1533 Revolt of Minas de Jobabo

1536 Pirate Franceses attacks Havana several times and also Santiago de Cuba

1538 A pirate raid devastates Havana. The foundations for Havana's Castillo de la Fuerza are laid by Hernando de Soto and the Cathedral in Santiago de Cuba is begun

1544 Francois le Clerc, known as Pie de Palo, or Peg Leg and Jaques de Sores, sack Havana and the country's capital, Santiago de Cuba. Havana's Castillo de la Fuerza is completed later that year

1547 Hernando Cortéz dies in Spain

1548 Sugar cane is first cultivated commercially

1550 Plaza Vieja constructed in Havana

1553 Velázquez becomes Governor of Cuba and moves to Havana

1554 Corsairs, including Jaques de Sores' ships raid Santiago de Cuba

1555 Jaques de Sores and privateers capture Havana with two small ships and 100 men. The city is fired and the Castillo de la Fuerza razed. Cojimar settlement is attacked

1558 Havana officially becomes the nation's capital and its battlements are finally completed. A new Castillo de la Fuerza begins construction

1561 Havana is established as the centre for all Spain's trade to and from the Americas

1563 Governor Diego de Mazariegos orders the construction of a military camp on the headland opposite Havana

1564 January, and the Isthmus fleet put into Havana, followed in March, by the Mexican flota. Both treasure fleets prepare for convoy to Spain, establishing the harbour as the key location guarding the Gulf of Mexico, the mainland, and its wealth of gold and silver

1568 Menendez de Aviles, Cuba's new Governor, defends the walls of

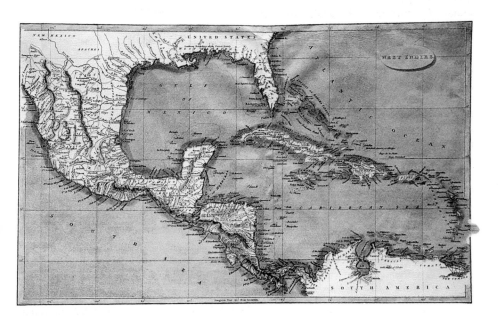

Havana and Santiago de Cuba, but Richard, the French corsair, continues to plunder north coast shipping

1570 Havana holds the first popular election

1571 Virtually all aborigine Indians are wiped out

1575 Pirates raid the north coast and Santa Cruz de Porcallo

1576 Puerto del Principe town is relocated

1577 Havana's Castillo de la Real Fuerza is completed and new fortifications are begun

1578 Santa Cruz de Porcallo is relocated as San Juan de los Remedios del Cayo

1580 Tobacco is first cultivated on Cuba in commercial quantities

1582 Trench fortifications are constructed in Havana

1585 Gilberto Girón, the French pirate, haunts the coastal shipping from hideouts in the offshore cays

1586 Sir Francis Drake, the English sea rover, is repulsed from attacking Havana with his fleet of thirty ships

1587 Santiago de Cuba's Morro castle is constructed

1589 Havana's El Morro Fort, or Fortaleza de los Tres Reyes del Morro begins construction

1592 King Felipe II confers the status of municipality on Havana

1597 Battlements of El Morro Fort in Havana are completed

1600 Castillo de San Salvador de la Punta is built in Havana

1603 Cristoforo de Roda, the Italian engineer, submits a design for a chain harbour barricade for Havana, to the King. Pirate attacks in the south by Gilberto Girón

1608 Silvestre de Balboa writes the first major Cuban literary work, *Mirror of Patience*, about the kidnapping of Cuba's Bishop Fray Juan de las Cabezas Altamirano, by the pirate Gilberto Giron

1609 Mercator Atlas includes the first artistic impressions of Havana City

1610 Havana's El Morro Fort is completed

1622 The English launch an unsuccessful attack on Havana

1623 Again the English attempt a storming of the capital

1628 Piet Heyn, commander of the 31-sail Dutch West India fleet, captures the entire Spanish treasure fleet off Matanzas. He is said to have buried the treasure on an offshore island

1630 Improvements and extensions to Havana's El Morro Castle are built

1633 The first attempts are made at constructing Havana's city walls

1638 The English again make an unsuccessful attack on Havana

1640 In Santiago de Cuba the construction commences on the El Morro Fort

The era of pirates

Since the big silver strikes had first been made in the New World, by Spain's conquistadores, Cuba had become a target for every seaborne element in the region which operated on the fringes of the law. From 1541, until the turn of the century, an estimated 200 million ducats' weight of gold, silver and jewels had flowed from the newly-discoverd lands of Central and South America. This figure increased to 250 million ducats over the following fifty years, presenting glittering prizes for the seafaring filibuster.

This vast treasure was shipped across the Gulf of Mexico, to Havana and from there through the treacherous cays of the Bahamas, up the American mainland's east coast, across the Atlantic, to Spain. It was a long, arduous, and often fatal journey for sluggish, treasure-laden galleons relying on a following wind, fair weather and sheer luck, to escape the attentions of the hordes of plunderers scouring the Spanish Main.

Captain Henry Morgan

Many hundreds of ships out of Havana fell foul of either ferocious pirates or the foul weather. Among those lost were many laden with vast riches, New World-minted Spanish coin, doubloons, pieces-of-eight and pieces-of-four, gold and silver ingots and discs, religious artefacts of precious metals, gems and jewellery. Typical was the 550-ton *Nuestra Señora de Atocha*, one of 28 Spanish treasure ships which sailed from Havana on 4 September, 1622. She was wrecked in a hurricane, together with others of the 'flota', on the coast of Florida. The *Atocha* carried 901 78-pound silver bars, 300lbs of gold in 161 bars, 255 000 silver coins, a fortune in jewels and many precious artefacts. Some galleons failed even to clear Cuban waters before disaster struck, others cleared shallows and reefs, only to be driven on to the myriad Bahamian cays or Bermuda's treacherous coves.

Lying at the mouth of the Gulf of Mexico, and guarding the 'Blue Stream' passage between Cuba and the mainland of Florida, Havana's position made it one of the most important ports of the Caribbean region. The city was the first landfall for Spain's treasure ships – a place to hole-up until hurricanes had blown over, and to be joined by other vessels forming a convoy for the homeward leg. Both Havana and Santiago de Cuba offered safe harbours for the fleets, or flota and also supplied provisions and information on the whereabouts of seaborne bandits.

The female pirates Ann Bonney and Mary Read

Both cities became increasingly wealthy as a proportion of the Aztec, Mayan and Incan booty came into the hands of Cuba's thriving populace. Smuggling and illegal barter ate away at the treasure, bound for the Royal coffers in Spain. Cuba's prosperity gave the freebooters alternative targets to the sea-going flotillas and, up and down the coast, towns and cities were regularly raided. The ports, as well as the ships, had become fair game to pirates, sea-bandits and maritime marauders.

During the hundred years since the first treasure shipment sailed from Havana, more than five attacks were made on the capital and almost every other settlement in Cuba, including Santiago de Cuba, had attracted the unwelcomed attentions of pirates and plunderers. Many towns actually 'upped-anchor' and moved inland to avoid these attacks, some even being forced to shift location on several occasions! The varied coastline of bays, cays, islets and inlets paradoxically offered excellent haunts and safe harbours for the bands of freebooters. The Pirate Coast on the Isle of Youth, and Coxon's Hole on Holguín's north coast, are typical examples of the buccaneer's retreats.

Morgan sacks Puerto del Principe

The word buccaneer possibly originated on the Cuban coast of the Spanish Main. Marooned sailors, shipwreck victims, felons, deserters and runaway slaves took refuge on the island's hospitable shoreline. Bands of these rejects from society made a living by smoking strips of meat from the herds of feral cattle and hogs roaming the countryside. The cured meat was sold or exchanged with passing maritime traffic and the process of meat preservation became known as 'boucan' – hence 'bacon' and 'buccaneer'. These motley crews were derived from just about every race whose ships plied the Main. French influence was, however, increasingly evident and, by the mid-1600s, the French forces were actually commissioning gangs of buccaneers to harass the Spanish shipping and isolated Cuban settlements.

As early as 1522, the French had recruited the services of the Florentine, Giovanni da Verrazano, to capture two Spanish treasure ships and one laden with hides, pearls and sugar from Cuba. The following years became a nightmare for shipping in and out of the Cuban ports. French raiders based themselves in the islets and cays of the Bahamas, and organised plundering was the sport of the day. Buccaneers formed themselves into bands for the systematic harassment of any likely prize on land or sea, sacking, looting and pillaging at random. Outstanding among the pirate element of these years were François le Clerc, known by the Spaniards as Pie de Palo, or Peg Leg, Jaques de Sores and, later, the French pirate, Gilberto Girón, following in the footsteps of another of his countrymen, Richard the Corsair. Some specialised in picking off shipping leaving Havana with treasure, and those arriving from Spain with fabricated goods, steel, weapons and cloth. Some plundered the towns and cities and preyed on travellers on the roads. A little later, the semi-official English adventurers and sea-rovers, Sir John Hawkins and Sir Francis Drake appeared on the scene, encouraged by the English Queen Elizabeth I, to waylay the Spanish

Edward Teach

shipping. The Dutch also joined the chase and in 1628 Piet Heyn, captured an entire treasure flotilla not 100 kilometres from the capital.

By this time the inhabitants of Havana and Santiago de Cuba had taken measures to defend their cities and protect the vulnerable shipping. In the 1570s the Governor of Havana, Menendez de Aviles, had build a fort opposite the city, in Florida, in order to command the straits. Defences had been constructed around the cities and castles and were being erected overlooking the harbours. A chain barricade blocked Havana's port, but still the pirates made persistent raids. Aviles had introduced escorts for the flotas or armadillas, in 1560, which were also intended to defend the two ports. Repeated attacks on the capital by the English navy and various pirate bands let to elaborate fortification plans. Drake, on his 1586 sortie, attempted to capture the Spanish fleet bound for Havana. He put into San Antonio, in the far west of Cuba, for refitting, and then made an unsuccessful attack on the capital. Around 1642–3, a special type of escort boat was being built in Havana. These heavily-armed, fast ships, were designed as warships. They were named the Armada de las Islande Barlevento y Seno Mexicano.

By the middle of the seventeenth century the activities of pirates, privateers, freebooters, filibusters, corsairs and buccaneers, had heightened and the period romanticised by subsequent poets, writers, and filmmakers, had arrived. This was the era of Captain Henry Morgan and Captain Mings, Edward Mansfield, Laurens de Graaf and Chevalier de Grammont, privateers who commanded large bands of semi-wild buccaneers on organised raids. Men like Bartolomeo el Portugues, the privateer, Babord-Amure, known as 'Port Tack' (because of the angle of his smashed nose!), the ruthless Dutchman, Roche Braziliano, Montbars the Exterminator, L'Olonnais (Jean-David Nav), Louis le Golif (known as 'Borgne-Fessé, for the missing part of his hindquarters, struck off

15

Captain Roberts

by a cutlass blow!), Pierre le Grand and 'Red Legs' Greaves, all vied with each other for rich pickings around the Cuban coast. Raids on townships, cattle yards and food stores were rife. Marauding bands often preyed on each other from the hidden coves and cays around Cuba's shores.

By 1701, a fleet of ships had been fitted out in Havana to protect the coastal settlements. This was called the Guardacostas. Although formidably armed and fast, they were no match for the wily privateers who had almost reduced the shipping in the Spanish Main to the one annual flota.

Edward Teach, known as 'Blackbeard', haunted the waters of the Caribbean, John 'Calico Jack' Rackham set up a hideout with the infamous female pirates, Mary Read and Anne Bonney, on the north coast of Cuba, and the privateer, Charles Vane, persistently plagued the northern and southern settlements on the island. Charles

Bellamy, Howell, and Jamaica's John Davis, Edward England, Bartholomew Roberts and John Taylor, roamed the seas. The latter based himself and his band of pirates in the cays off the Cuban coast. Howell lurked around the waters off Coxon's Hole, a favourite buccaneer's hideout, and even the famous Captain William Kidd was thought to have participated in plundering the shipping around Cuba.

By 1720 the spoils were becoming fewer and farther between. The loot from Central America began to diminish, as mines ran out, and more careful timing and plotting of flota's journeys to Spain, together with heavy protection, made pirates think twice about attacking shipping that was not 'easy meat'. The days of the pirates were fading fast and organised warfare in the shipping lanes by political powers diminished the number of hit-and-run, privateer raids. By the time the English naval force had taken Havana in 1762 the pirate bands had all but dispersed. Many resorted to smuggling and gun-running, some joined the 'legitimate' navies, others retired completely from the sea, and many were brought to justice. Some pirates even set up homesteads on the island, to become neighbours to those that they had plundered and looted!

Important Dates and Events

1646   La Chorrera Tower in Havana commenced construction. San Lazaro Tower, also in the capital, completed. Cojimar village was established near Havana

1647   La Chorrera Tower was completed

1648   Fortifications to Havana city re-commenced. A Yellow Fever epidemic thwarted building efforts

1654   Further attempts were made to complete the capital's walls

1655   Slaves and Spanish colonists escape to Cuba from the English takeover of Jamaica

1662   Captain Henry Morgan and Captain Mings sieze Santiago de Cuba from a landing at Aguadores

Beach, on behalf of the British Crown, under Jamaica-based Lord Windsor

1665   Peter Legrand, pirate, attacks Sancti Spiritus

1667   Captain Henry Morgan pillages Puerto del Principe, the original Camagüey. Francisco Nau (El Olonés) attacks in Villa Clara at San Juan de los Remedios

1674   Havana's city walls are once again reconstructed. They were not completed until 1797

1677   Bartolomeo el Portugues, the privateer, captures a 20-gun Spanish brig, off Havana, from a small piragua

1689   Santa Clara town was founded

1692   The town of Remedios was finally established after several moves, evading pirate attack, since the granting of land rights by the Spanish Crown in 1514

1695   Matanzas town was founded

1699   Pinar del Rio town was established 150 years after land rights had been granted to the Indians

1700   Tobacco is regarded as the main export

Ancient cannon bristle around Cuba's many fortresses

1701 The Guardacostas naval defence force introduced

1702 Pirate Grant attacks Santisima Trinidad

1704 Havana Cathedral begun; it was completed 73 years later

1719 Howell Davis, the privateer captures two French ships in eastern Cuba

1720 Pirate John 'Calico Jack' Rackham, former quartermaster of the buccaneer, Charles Vane, set up a temporary home with the female pirates, Mary Read and Anne Bonney, on Cuba's north-east coast, near Guardalavaca

1722 Pirate John Taylor escapes capture off the African coast to haunt Cuba's shipping lanes. Governor Dionision de la Vega establishes a shipyard in Havana

1728 Havana University was founded

1732 One of Havana's oldest existing houses, that of the Count and Countess Jarvco, was built

1734 Governor Juan Fransisco Guines y Horcasitas established the country's first Post Office

1740 Admiral Vernon, with an English naval force, attacked Havana

1750 Cuba's trade was monopolised by the Compania de Commercio de la Havana. The capital's city wall foundations are extended

1759 Census estimated the entire Cuban population at 150 000

1762 Admiral Lord Rodney, the Earl of Albemarle and George Pocock captured Havana for the English Crown. 'La Habana', golden statue was purloined from the Fortaleza de la Fuerza during the English occupation of eleven months. Trade increased fifty-fold. Charles III of Spain cedes the territory of Florida and trade rights, in return for the relinquishing of Cuba

1763 Castillo de San Carlos de la Cabana and Havana's Atares Castle both begun, and the La Punta Fort was reconstructed. The Spanish bring the last remaining 200 Indians from Florida to Cuba

1764 Overseas mail inaugurated and permission was given for the establishment of the first official rum distilleries

1767 El Principe Castle was completed in Havana

1770 The English introduced 11 000 slaves from Africa for sugar plantation work, and coffee and cacao trade exceeds tobacco

1771 Marques de la Torre became Governor

1773 Castillo de la Cabana was completed in Havana

1776 Earthquake hit Santiago de Cuba

1780 Palace of the Captain of the Generals was built in Havana

1783 Spanish introduced 100 000 more slaves from Africa

1791 Haitian revolution exiled 27 000 French planters who settled in Santiago de Cuba

1792 Sugar became the country's main produce

1797 Spanish law made free trade in Cuba legal

1806 Census put the slave population at 500 000

1812 Principal Theatre was constructed in Havana. Minor slave revolt

1816 Tobacco monopoly was dissolved

1818 Madrid conferred freeport status on Havana

1819 Carlos Manuel de Céspedes y de Castillo was born in Bayamo. Original site of El Floridita restaurant 'Pina de Plata' founded in Havana

1820 The Torre de Iznaga, a watchtower on a sugar plantation near Trinidad, was constructed – then the tallest structure in Cuba

1823 First evidence of a slave uprising in Cuba

1828 El Templete of Havana was built in the Plaza de Armas

1837 Scottish company built the first

railway from Havana to Bejucal. Garcia Lorca Theatre, Havana, was constructed

1841 Census found that 60 per cent of 162 500 population is negroid

1844 H. Upmann tobacco factory opened in Havana

1845 General abolition of slavery not accepted by Cuba

1849 Bartering of the country between Spain and North America led to a national uprising

1852 Second recorded earthquake struck Santiago de Cuba

1853 José Marti was born. First telegraph service commenced

1859 Population estimated at one million and the number of estates at 14 000

1863 Havana's city walls were removed as the capital expanded to the west

1867 Cuba's National Anthem was written in Bayamo

1868 Carlos Manuel de Céspedes led a rebellion by freeing and arming his slaves against Spanish forces, 10 October Cholera epidemic hit Havana

The next ten-year period, until Cuba signed the armistice with Spain in 1878, heralded the rise of a new Cuba from its uneasy existence under Spanish rule. Céspedes died during the revolutionary wars in 1874. New names, like Antonio Maceo, his brother José, and Máximo Gómez, were added to the roll of great Cuban heroes during this period. By 1878 the skirmishes had died down and, under the leadership of José Marti, the revolutionary forces regrouped for a concerted effort against colonialism.

Slavery was abolished in Cuba in 1880 and, 400 years after Columbus discovered the island, Jose Marti founded the Cuba Revolutionary Party, marking the turning point from early to modern history. In 1892, tobacco workers formed the first worker's assembly.

Modern history

On 24 February, 1895, the battles for freedom were resumed. José Marti, with Antonio Maceo, 'the Bronze Titan', and his brother, landed back in Cuba after exile and, in April, war once again wracked the country.

Marti was killed that year but the Cubans

fought on. In the following year, 1896, Maceo was killed after fighting more than 900 battles. The Cuban forces were within sight of victory when, on 15 February, 1898 the US battleship, *Maine*, was mysteriously detonated in Havana Bay, bringing intervention from North America.

Spain had lost 1 million dollars and 80 000 lives in the years since 1868.

1901 US Government made a rejected bid to seize control of Cuba from Spain

1902 20 May, The Republic of Cuba was declared and a puppet administration serving mainly foreign interests was set up under the Presidency of Estrada Palma

1903 US Government negotiated for the naval base at Guantánamo

1906 José Miguel Gomez led a revolt and became President

1908 1st Worker's Party formed

1912 Negro insurrection by workers

1915 Mario Garcia Menocal became President

1920 'Dance of the Millions'

1924 Communist Party of Cuba was formed

1925 Gerardo Machado took over the Presidency

1926 Fidel Castro Ruz was born in Oriente Province

1931 Main arterial highway (Carretera Central) was constructed

1933 Machado regime fell due to the revolutionary struggle. General Strike

1934 US Government took a 99-year lease on Guantánamo

1940 New Constitution was ratified

1944 In the anti-fascist, post World War II climate, President Fulgencio Batista lost the elections and sought exile in Florida. Popular Socialist (Communist) Party was founded

1947 Santiago de Cuba was hit again by an earthquake

1952 Batista returned from Florida, seized power in a military coup and formed a dictatorship.

For 60 years since the foundation of the Cuba Revolutionary Party by José Marti, the people had struggled against oppression, tyranny, corruption, betrayal and domination by external powers. The time had become ripe to strike the final blows for a true freedom and genuine independence. The people began to step up their harassment of Batista's malicious forces. The spark of revolution was fanned by a core of brave young people dedicated to the cause and established in the Sierra Maestra mountains in southern Cuba.

1953 26 July, Fidel Castro and 67 young revolutionaries attacked the walled barracks of the Moncada garrison and surprised Batista's troops on Carnival Day in Santiago de Cuba. The attack was defeated and many revolutionaries were murdered or assassinated at Siboney Farm. Those who survived were tortured and imprisoned on the Isle of Pines – now the Isla de la Juventud

1955 After an amnesty the majority of young revolutionaries re-grouped in Mexico

1956 2 December, Fidel, with 81 comrades, including Ernesto 'Ché' Guevara and Camillo Cienfuegos, landed from Mexico at Las Coloradas, on the south of the island, in the cabin cruiser *Granma*. After suffering severe bombardment, just 15 eventually reached the Sierra Maestra to renew the fight against oppression

1957 July, Frank Pais was assassinated

1958 US withdraw its support of the Batista dictatorship

1959 1 January, Victory. Fidel Castro and his revolutionary troops entered Havana after two years of bitter struggle against US-backed troops and Batista's henchmen. The Revolution of the Cuban people had finally triumphed.

A corner plaque in Havana celebrates the statement of Cuba as a Socialist country

from external agitators, by means of germ warfare, anti-Cuban propaganda, physical and psychological assaults, have had a reverse effect on the triumph of the revolution. The people of Cuba have only consolidated and the concerted efforts of the Revolution have become stronger.

Today, the history of the nation is still being created, but with a difference – today, there is a positive target for the people which is evident to all those who visit the Republic of Cuba – 500 years of heritage in the heart of the Caribbean.

Since then, there have been a series of sporadic attempts of aggression against Cuba by US-backed forces. In 1960 there were a succession of sabotage attacks in Havana. On 17 April 1961, the attempted invasion at Playa Girón or the Bay of Pigs, by US-backed troops was repelled by the revolutionary forces under the command of Fidel Castro. Later that year the US instituted an embargo against the people of Cuba. During the 1962 'Missile Crisis' attempts were made to undermine Cuba's international relations and, for the next fifteen years, a spate of landing attempts by foreign insurgents kept the Cuban people on the alert. In 1965 the Communist Party of Cuba was newly formed and, by this time the last privately-owned business had been nationalised.

These aggressive attacks and interference

Divisions and provinces

Historically the island was divided into the regions of Oriente in the east, Camagüey, Las Villas and Occidente. The names are retained now only in song or to identify national baseball teams. Today the country comprises 14 provinces – from east to west, Santiago de Cuba, Guantánamo, Holguín, Granma, Las Tunas, Camagüey, Ciego de Avila, Sancti Spiritus, Cienfuegos, Villa Clara, Matanzas, the Province of Havana, the City of Havana and Pinar del Rio. There are 169 municipalities, one of which is a special division, the Isla de la Juventud. Havana, population two million, is the nation's capital city and Santiago de Cuba is the second largest city. The population of Cuba now exceeds ten million inhabitants.

The Mariposa is Cuba's national flower

Government

The Republic of Cuba, has since 1976 been governed by elected representatives of the People's Power. The Island of Cuba is now celebrating its third decade as a Socialist Republic. Elections are held on national, provincial and municipal levels and Havana is the seat of government. Head of State is Dr. Fidel Castro Ruz, Commander-in-Chief of the Armed Forces, First Secretary of the Communist Party and President of the

The Capitol in Havana, now the Academy of Science of Cuba

José Marti (1853–1895)

Antonio Maceo (1845–1896)

Council of State and of the Council of Ministers.

Arms and the flag

The Coat of Arms of the Republic of Cuba consists of a shield in front of the rods of Justice which are surmounted by the cap of Liberty decorated with a lone star. The shield is divided into three parts. The upper third describes the mouth of the Gulf of Mexico as two land masses with a sunrise above the sea.

Cuba is represented by the image of a key – the link commanding the entrance to the Gulf. Below, and to the left of the shield, two white, diagonal bars run across a blue ground down to the edge of the Arms. The right hand third of the shield describes a mountain scene featuring a Royal Palm (*palma real*), the national tree and the official name of the Arms, 'Escudo de la Palma Real'. Olive and oak boughs embrace the Coat of Arms. The olive is on the left and oak is to the right. Both are in fruit – symbols of 'peace' and 'strength'.

The national flower is the Butterfly Bloom or *Mariposa*. Cuba's flag has undergone slight transformation since Carlos Manuel de Céspedes' 1868 original which divided the ground into a white half above and blue below. A white five pointed star on a red ground dominated the top left corner. Today the flag consists of two white, horizontal bars on a blue ground. A white, five pointed star on a red, equilateral triangle is projected into the flag from the hoist side. Both flags are flown at official Meetings of State.

The shield of the Royal Palm

The flag of the Republic

CHAPTER 2

A Cultural Melting Pot

*'What really counts is man, what really counts is the people.
Wealth exists in ourselves, in our intelligence, in our skill,
in our determination, in our discipline, in our organisational
ability. Our resources lie within ourselves.'*

FIDEL CASTRO RUZ

The people, language and customs

The aboriginal Cuban was Amerindian, and belonged to island Arawak tribes known as Tainos. These had pushed the ancient tribes of Ciboney and Guanahatabey to the westermost extremes of the country by the time of the first Spanish landings in the late fifteenth century. Decimated by the European invaders the Tainos are now considered to be an extinct race.

The Spanish replaced Indian labour with large numbers of negroes captured along the western coast of Africa. Throughout the country's earlier, chequered history the bloods of many African races have been mingled with those of every European country, but predominantly with that of Spain. A new race evolved which could claim true Cuban identity and from a melting pot of races the Cuban people developed. Today more than half the 10 million population of Cuba are white. The other 50 per cent are mainly negroes and mulattos.

Cuban people have a reputation for being warm, friendly and hospitable. They vigorously defend their identity and are intensely patriotic. Cuban solidarity was cemented with the triumph of the Revolution and each Cuban individual demonstrates a pride in his country's

achievements. To visitors Cubans are help-ful, eager to please and attentive. They often go out of their way to assist and can be almost over-enthusiastic in their generosity. An outstanding characteristic is that Cubans always appear to be busy with some work, or involved in some animated conversation, but are never too

engrossed to extend a greeting or to help with directions. School children and youngsters seem to fill each square – not surprising since half Cuba's population is under twenty.

The official language is Spanish but many Cubans have studied English, French or Russian which are the commercial languages. English-speaking staff are generally available to assist at tourist shops, hotels and cultural houses. It is most rewarding to have learned a little basic Spanish, and a few words in greeting or in asking directions can be a gesture which produces a pleasing response.

Cubans usually address each other as 'Compañero' but visitors usually prefer 'Señor'. Professional titles should be used, followed by the surname, in business trans-actions. In Cuba, when two surnames follow a given name, the first surname is the correct one to use. Often surnames are used in conversation as reference and occa-sionally 'Señor', followed by a given name. Handshakes are an accepted form of greet-ing and the more intimate the relationship the more elaborate the handshake.

A form of enthusiastic appreciation has moved from the baseball field into everyday conversation, which is expressed by smacking the palms of the hands together and joining in shouting 'Entra'. This can be quite an effective way of making a very positive point in general conversation with a good friend, although it looks a little extrovert.

A hangover from pre-Revolutionary days, the Cuban society still maintains a 'macho' image, although the workload is now equally divided and women work alongside men in every field. The people also have a great respect for healthy living and, for a stranger to step too far out of line, a stern frown or disapproving glance will quickly indicate the tolerance level. Cuban appreciation of the female form may be thought, at times, a little overt but is meant in good-natured lightheartedness and should be treated as such.

The Cuban's contented attitude is almost

synonymous with that ubiquitous item of furniture seen on verandas, in drawing rooms and outside the front doors of almost every home – the rocking chair.

Religion and faiths

Once the Spanish raised the cross of Roman Catholicism in Cuba the pagan beliefs of the island's Indians were doomed.

Another system of religious practice was introduced however, with the development of slave labour in Cuba. African spirit worship and magic practices emanated from the Calabar coast, Nigeria, the Cameroons and Dahomey. West African religions mingled with the country's adopted Hispanic beliefs tinged by influences from the French Catholic/ French African and English/Jamaican/ African sources. These sects often merged to create a special kind of religion. Among those faiths which were evolved by African slaves in Cuba the best known are those of Abakuá, of Chango and of Santería. This last powerful religion, for example, mixes Cameroon, Yoruba and Haitian beliefs with those of the French and Spanish Catholicism. Its various deities are represented by the colours: Blue = the female goddess of beauty, love and fresh water, Ochún, or the Virgen de las Caridad del Cobre (the patron saint of Cuba); Red = the male/female saint associated with war, virility, lightening, power, Changó, or Santa Barbara; White = the female saint of saltwater, vengeance and the rainbow, Oyá,

or Santa Theresa; Yellow = the female saint linked to festivities; Red and Black = the patron saint of travellers who carries a crooked stick with which to tap out secret codes and is identified with Saint Peter. One woman saint, supposedly from Africa, was known as 'Vodun' or 'Voodoo'. The slaves from Calabar introduced the Abakuá sect, and closest to voodoo is probably the Regla Mayombé, or Palo Monte sect although the 'Ñañigos' version of the Santeros sect was rife with magic. From the coasts of Nigeria, came Santería or that sect derived from the Yoruba tribe. The Afro-Cuban language, often heard in dance and song, is known as 'Ñañigo', derived from the secret societies of the West African jungles and mixed with Spanish and French. In early times, the 'illuminedo' of the sect believed that they could hear the voices of their African ancestors mixed with those of the Catholic saints.

These religious beliefs are still preserved as traditional, folkloric heritages in dance,

From its Afro roots. . .

Cuba's faiths merged . . .

26

song and dramatic arts. The carnivals and literature of Cuba have also done much to save the dying mythology of the Abakuá and Buyeria cults. African and Old World religions survived alongside each other from the sixteenth, well into the twentieth century when Roman Catholicism reached its peak on the island.

In Cuba today religious tolerance is well respected and although the primitive and pagan practices have faded into the past, Christianity is an accepted part of Cuba's heritage. Today, services of many denominations are held throughout the island on a regular basis and recently several international religious seminars have been held in Havana.

International Cuban personalities

Cuba has had its share of illustrious and notorious residents and visitors. From the ruthless conquistadores under Hernando Cortéz and Panfilo de Narvaez, to the

. . with traditional ties.

romantic buccaneering of Captain Henry Morgan and Blackbeard. Famous names throughout the panoply of history have visited and ventured, resorted to and retired to the 'Pearl of the Antilles'.

Among the illustrious have been the writers Ernest Hemingway, Jean Paul Sartre and Graham Greene. Stage and screen luminaries included Errol Flynn, Ava Gardner, Spencer Tracy, Gary Cooper and Katharine Hepburn. Sportsmen of every kind, scholars and politicians have savoured the delights of the island's balmy climate and basked on its exotic, tropical beaches.

Cuba itself has bred its fair quota of international figures. Artists and dancers, architects and musicians, literary giants and internationalists have woven the rich tapestry of Cuba's heritage. Even from the days of Spanish colonialism there were the religious writers of the sixteenth century, the seventeenth century documentalists of conquests and discovery, through many centuries to the famous authors such as Alejo Carpentier and the national poet Nicholás Guillén, both born in Cuba in 1904, and the great poet Elisio Diego, born in 1920. The names of poets such as José Zacarias Tallet, Felix Pita Rodríguez and Jesus Ruiz (Indio Nabori) are legend in Latin America and also throughout the world. Other luminaries include Cirilio Villaverde, José Lezama Lima and Miguel Barnet.

Talented artists have included José Nicholas de la Escalera, born 1734; Vincente Escobar, 1757; Miguel Angel Melero, 1836; Eduardo Laplante, 1818; Esteban Chartrand, 1840; Valentín Sanz Carta, 1849; Armando Menocal, born 1863; the great José Joaquín Tejada and Guillermo Collazo of the same era. By the end of the last century and the beginning of this, there were such artistic geniuses as Eduardo Abela, Victor Manuel Garcia, Fidelio Ponce de Leon and Carlos Enríquez, through to the later painters, Rene Portocarrero, Jorge Arche, Marianao Rodríguez and the new wave of recent artists, Angel Acosta León, Raúl Martinez and Antonio Vidal.

The names of the great exponents of the dramatic arts are legion, but none so deserving of mention as that of Prima Ballerina Alicia Alonso, Cuba's 'ambassadress' of leading ballet. In the musical field there are a thousand famous names to conjure with: Chano Pozo, Rosendo Ruiz, Enrique Jorrin, Pablo Milanes, Sindo Garay, Arturo Sandoval, Jesus (Chucho) Valdes and El Grupo Moncada immediately come to mind, as, in the cinematographic world, does the name of Tomas Gutiérrez Alea.

Folklore

Cuban folklore is inextricably mixed with that of many West African tribes, voodoo and pagan beliefs plus interpretations of European religions and traditional tales.

The negro element in Cuba endowed most stories with magic or religious significance translating ethnic tales into song, dance and ritual. Indian, Spanish, French and African traditions are now being studied by the Conjunto Folklorico Nacional which supports groups throughout the country. The Folkloric Museum at Guanabacoa describes the evolution of Cuban folklore in exhibits and tableau form and many groups recite and re-enact the traditional heritage of Cuba in the cultural houses, in theatres and on celebration days.

Cabildos dancers celebrate in costumes of African tribal dress

Religious deity worship often involved doll-like images

Primitive magical signs enliven the paving stones of La Rampa, Havana

Cuba's performing arts are legendary. Exponents of Cubana music include Leo Brouwer, José Loyola, Jorge Gómez Labraña, Beatriz Márquez and Carlos Fariñas. Others who have done much to promote the traditions of Cuban folklore and its messages are the band Irakere, founded by Chucho Valdés, Pablo Milanes, Benny More, Silvio Rodríguez, Arturo

Sandoval and Carlos Puebla. Los Papines and Juan Formell are among the most popular musicians in Cuba and nobody could ever forget the legendary song by 'guajira' singer Joseito Fernández – 'Guantánamera'.

Music

'. . . I am a sincere man from the land of the palm trees . . .'

from 'Guantánamera' by
JOSEÍTO FERNÁNDEZ

Cuba's music owes much to its African origins. Running through the country's musical vocabulary the influence is evident: Bongo = the small drum of Africa; Changui = ritualistic song of African origin; Chequeré = seed-filled gourd-like instrument shaken with both hands and prevalent in African dance; Claves = two short hardwood sticks clapped together to create a beat complementing the African drumbeat; Ekkue = sacred drum of African origin; Firma = African religious signs often used in conjunction with musical performances; Guayo = ribbed, wooden instrument stroked with a small stick and reminiscent of similar instruments used in West African combos; Rumba, Conga, Mambo = Afro-Cuban dances; Son Bembe = Afro-Cuban rythmic composition; Tumba Francesa = a dance form of French-African origin, a society founded in 1862 and also the name

Whether a Spanish serenade . . .

. . . or a group rendering of Guantánamera . . .

. . . Cuba's people are 'to the music born'.

given to a particular type of drum, many of which are referred to as 'tumba'.

Other traditional musical instruments have their origins elsewhere, like the fife, snare, batal and bass drums, but have become truly Cuban in their adaptations. One instrument has even been named after the sacred Santa Barbara of the Santería sect.

The ubiquitous guitar, variations of which appear to be limitless in Cuba, is undoubtedly a legacy of Spain. A local miniature version of the guitar is called a 'requinto' and a six or nine-stringed favourite is commonly named a 'tres'. The three-stringed Cuban guitar is the 'marimbula' – of Bantu origin. The gourd also figures significantly in the nation's musical heritage, as it does in most tropical climes. The maracas are known internationally as percussion instruments and are made from pebble-filled gourds attached to short wooden handles. A similar instrument, also made from the gourd, is the local guiro. Instruments of Afro/Haitian origin include the melé, chachás, bulás, cata, premier and seconde.

Cuban music appears to be divided into four main categories. Although they overlap, the elementary form, lending more to its African heritage, is based on folkloric roots. It comprises such ingredients as the Changui, and similar ritualistic themes of African origin. Traditional troubadour's music, harking back to those ballads of medieval Europe, is the most common form of expression in song.

Most cities in Cuba have a trova house, 'Casa de Trova', where the trova, or classical ballad, is sung by trovadores. Many performances are purely spontaneous, and passers-by often join in with the singing or accompaniment. The most revered of all Cuban trovadores was Sindo Garay and the oldest, Pablito Alminan, is still entertaining at the trova house in Santiago de Cuba. Well-known artists in this style are the Matamoros Trio. El

Grupo Moncada are famous for their performance of a post-revolutionary style of song, the nueva trova, a recent variation of the classical trova, which uses revolutionary motifs as its theme. A blues version of the trova is known as filin.

Another category of Cuban music can be found in the countryside and at local carnivals. This form owes much to Spanish traditional music, combined with that of nineteenth century France. Often the decima, old Spanish poetic style, can be detected in this type of song, which is referred to as punto campesino, and the accompanying dance – the punto guajiro or zapateo. This, in some areas, is performed at the weekly outdoor concerts, or retreta. A mixture of instruments is used in this musical form, from guitar and violin, to trumpet and barrel organ.

Musical instruments usually range through percussion and brass, from maracas, to souzaphone, but conformity is never a by-word of Cuban musicians.

The more recent of Cuban musical variations are those of the big brass band and the combo. Synonymous with the name Cuba are the dance forms which the music inspired – the conga, the rumba, the mambo, the guaracha, and the bolero. Everywhere in Cuba, from the dance floors and concert halls to the local country meeting rooms, the sound of the combo can be heard live, or on record. Nor can anyone forget the strains of Cuba's international hit song, 'Guantánamera'. From clubs and tenements, bars and reception rooms the salsa and jazz bands sound out the vibrant life-blood of a nation devoted to music.

Classical music is regularly performed throughout Cuba, and the many symphony orchestras attain a particularly high standard. Entrance charges to first-class concerts are minimal.

Dance and drama

As with the country's music, folkloric dance owes a great deal to the heritage derived from Africa. Most famous of these ancient, ritualistic dances is of Abakuá origin. It is the dance of Iremes, or small devils, which appear in this secret society religious dance with painted faces and pointed hats. This form originates on the Calabar coast, and similar dances can be traced back to the Congo's Bantu tribe and West Africa's Yoruba mythology. Black magic plays an important part in many of

A film set

these highly sophisticated, yet primitive dances, which often contain elements of the voodoo rituals of neighbouring Haiti, such as those of cobrero, mason, tahona and yuba.

Some of the country dancing and traditional dance styles can be directly traced to those of Spain and France. These are known as contradanza – introduced from Haiti as a variation of a French dance. A slower Cuban version is called danzon, and the carnival version is called carabali.

Influence from European dance has kept these Cuban adaptions as formal as their nineteenth century counterparts, but it is the other face of Cuban dance which has fired the imagination of dancers across the world.

Today the nostalgia of yesteryear's dances can be experienced first-hand in Cuba's dance halls and ballrooms. The cha-cha-cha, conga, guaracha, mambo, rumba and tango, are internationally

31

famous, as is the obviously Spanish bolero which Cuban dancers have adopted and transformed. There are now limitless variations on these basic Cuban creations, and it appears that a new twist is invented at every celebration, or street performance, by local or national groups.

The inherent Cuban instinct for dancing is displayed at the annual carnivals and fiestas. This can be seen throughout the year, at its peak, in the flamboyant shows at Varadero's International Hotel, or at the world-famous Tropicana night club. Most of the show dancers are trained at the national ballet schools, which have produced some of the world's leading international ballet dancers.

Ballet in Cuba takes a high place among the arts and the country's reputation for excellence in this field is renowned. The National Ballet of Cuba exists alongside the Cuban School of Ballet, the Ballet of Camagüey, and the School of Dance. The country's many theatres also put on modern and classical plays, opera, operetta, plays, musical comedies, dramatic productions and shows. A travelling theatre takes the dramatic arts to the far outposts of the island.

Cuba's ballet is recognised as one of the world's foremost. Among exponents of the art are the legendary names of Alicia Alonso, Jorge Esquivel, Josefina Méndez, Mirtha Plá and Aurora Bosch. Actors and actresses include, José Antonio Rodríguez, Salvador Wood, Reinaldo Miravalles, Sergio Correiri, Mario Balmaseda, María de los Angeles Santana, Silvia Planas, Veronica Lynn, Raquel Revuelta and Susana Peréz.

Arts and crafts

Almost every city, town and village, has its own Cultural House which displays the works of local artists. Art galleries are numerous – there are more than a dozen in Havana City. Most galleries display a range of arts, from paintings and etchings, to sculpture and ceramics. There are also

The island has inherited the treasured gift of painting and developed a wealth of art

the localised art forms like the unique red earthenware pottery display in Camagüey, where potters can be seen at work, and fine examples of their art can be purchased.

Cuba itself is a living gallery for those with an eye for the graphic arts. Cuba's political posters are an integral part of life and express the national identity, at the same time as extolling the virtues of the silk-screen and lithographic printer. A museum of lithography, and a working print shop, are open to the public in Cathedral Square, Havana.

Large, dynamic billboards have become part of the Cuban scenery, since the triumph of the Revolution, and they appear on the sides of buildings, street corners, on the highways and even on rural country lanes. Some have been developed to a high degree of sophistication with the use of different forms of lighting – they have become an art form in themselves.

The National Union of Writers and Artists of Cuba (UNEAC), does much to assist in the promotion and development of all forms of artistic expression. Cuban fashion and photography also have a special place in the national artistic field, as does the film industry. INTERTV of the Cuban Radio and Television Enterprise is active in this field, and the Cuban Institute of Cinematography (ICAIC) has received international acclaim for its work in the film world. The National School of Art has international recognition for its high standard of training in all art forms. Modern Cuban architecture has also developed its individual style, which can best be seen in the dramatic design of the Palacio de las Convenciones de Cuba in Havana.

Folk art and craft is the responsibility of the Fondo de Bienes Culturales. This group is reviving and preserving many early art forms such as basket weaving, pottery, wood carving, furniture making and local home crafts. Jewellery design, for 350 years a hallmark of Cuban artistic skills, is also undergoing a revival.

Perhaps the most interesting of all examples of art and craft work is to be found in the massive renovation programme being undertaken in Old Havana. Artisans, specialists, and experts in woodwork, painting, glasswork, metalwork, masonry, tiling, etc. have been drafted in from the far corners of Cuba to restore, under the auspices of UNESCO and the National Institute of Tourism, many old colonial-style houses which are a part of the country's cultural heritage.

Among the island's most famous artificers are the sculptors Rita Longa and Jose Delarra, the painters Carmelo Gonzáles, René Portocarrero, Amelia Peláez, Eduardo Roca and Mariano Rodríguez and the designers Alfredo Rostgard and Héctor Villaverde. Earlier artists include, Vincente Escobar, Esteban Chartrand and Valentin Sanz Carta. Cuba's art collections are unique.

Sport

Cubans are avid sportsmen, excelling in their national sport, baseball – thought by some to have evolved from a game played by the Indians and possibly named after the ball, la pelota, or the Indian name batos.

Baseball stadiums are situated centrally in almost every town; youngsters can be seen practising everywhere and the national teams are world champions. Luis Giraldo and Victor Mesa have an international

Souvenir hats are crafted from palm fronds

33

Children pore over giant chessmen

reputation. The World Amateur Baseball Tournament, 1984, was held in Havana and Santiago de Cuba.

Also in a world class are the Cuban boxing, and women's volleyball teams. Boxing has become a traditional pastime and Teofilo Stevenson was three times Olympic Champion between 1972 and 1980 and twice world heavyweight champion. Basketball is also a widespread favourite. Sports encouraged in schools include tennis, squash, wrestling, water polo, diving, handball, cycling, fencing, weightlifting, swimming, shooting, sailing, rowing, etc. Football is also becoming popular, and Cuba is well-known for its superiority in field, track and table games.

The national teams have held first place in the Central American and Caribbean Games for many years, second place in the Pan American Games, and the country

Golf is a growing pastime particularly popular at Varadero and Havana's Diploclub

Baseball is Cuba's national sport

Game fishing has a great following as this early picture of tournament champion Fidel Castro and Ernest Hemingway shows

Sport fishing and boating excursions are favourite activities around Cuba's 6000-kilometre coastline

took fourth place in the Olympics of 1980, holding several world records. In the athletics field Cuba's Olympic status has been assured with stars such as Alberto Juantorena, Maria Caridad Colon and Luis Mariano Delis, champions of the track, the javelin and the discus.

Visitors are invited to watch all forms of sporting activity. All athletic events are free, and Cubans delight in showing the visitor a local or national baseball game. The finals, played between the national provincial teams of Havana, Oriente, Matanzas and Las Villas, are held in April.

Sport is almost a national preoccupation in Cuba, and, wherever possible, there are sporting facilities available. Most hotels have a games room and a few have a gymnasium or gym facilities. Many of the larger hotels have Olympic-size pools – all pools are watched over by a lifeguard.

Beach hotels and resorts offer a gamut of aquatic activities, parasailing, scuba diving, snorkelling, windsurfing, jet-skiing, sailing, canoeing, pedal boating, motor boating, surfing and water skiing. Some hotels offer harpooning excursions, and, near lakes, hunting and fishing trips. Games fishing expeditions can also be organised on the Caribbean Sea, the Gulf of Mexico, or the Atlantic Ocean, from dozens of harbours and quays around the coast.

Resorts and hotels provide tennis, badminton, golf or squash. Some offer aerobics and dance classes, and many can organise horse riding, climbing, or walking expeditions and boating trips on river, lake or sea. One great sporting attraction in Cuba is the rodeo, which is becoming a major event in the visitors' calendar. Often, whilst driving in the country, small rodeos can be seen as part of a local fiesta or at carnival time.

CHAPTER 3

An Effective Economy

'. . . our country does not have the scourge of unemployment – no beggars, no illiterates or prostitutes; no gambling or drugs; . . . over 90 per cent of the children between six and sixteen years old are in school, social security covers the entire population, food is available to all and nutritional levels are really among the highest in Latin America, health conditions already command world admiration, the infant mortality rate is already down to about 15, . . . the greater the surprise and amazement of visitors when they see what our country has really done.'
'Our situation is incomparably better than that of any of the sister nations in this hemisphere.'

FIDEL CASTRO RUZ

Each year the cream of Cuba's students compete, like this selected class, for a valued visit to the Soviet Union.

Education

Education is free at all levels in Cuba and illiteracy has been eradicated. Primary schooling is compulsory for elementary tuition, and the national system includes junior and senior high schools, technical institutes, professional establishments, adult education systems and universities. Under the state scholarship scheme all students receive free education, transport, clothing, school equipment, materials, books and food.

University students also get an allowance. There are 43, recently built, higher education faculties in the country and the main universities are located at Havana, Santiago de Cuba, Camagüey and Santa Clara. Branches of these universities are situated in every province. All provinces also have technical and professional tuition facilities.

Each town and city has its own library. A system of mobile libraries is also being introduced in order to provide educational material in more out-lying districts.

Advanced education facilities exist in every province and at least eight provinces have schools of music, art and ballet. Special achievements of Cuba's educational system are the networks of urban schools located in every province and the country's successful agricultural and sporting, or recreational institutes. Over 1 million adults were taught to read and write in the great Literacy Campaign of 1961.

Adult education now totals more than 400 000 students, and this figure is expected to be doubled by the end of the decade. Well over 100 000 children now attend the nursery schools throughout the country. Special programmes are constantly improving and up-dating the education service, which takes only third place on the list of budget expenditure together with public health, in the years to the end of this decade.

Visitors to Cuba often remark on the smart universal school uniform of khaki or blue, white shirt or blouse, and red necker-chief. School children are frequently taught outside, in the open air, in courtyards or town squares. There are many schools located in the countryside and near citrus or other agricultural installations and plantations. Occasional assistance in these rural schemes by students provides useful knowledge, a chance to get out into the open, and much appreciated help for the farm workers. A secondary school in the country is known as an ESBEC, and a pre-university country institute, an IPUEC. There are also agricultural colleges located across the countryside. A special polytechnic for teaching tourism skills reflects the growth in the tourist trade.

Cuba's educational system has given the world of culture a number of celebrated authors through the past decades. Names like Dora Alonso, Onelio Jorge Cardoso, Mario Rodríguez Alemán, José Antonio Portuondo, Samuel Feijóo, Salvador Bueno, Miguel Barnet, Manuel Pereira, and the writers, Norberto Fuentes, Alejo Carpentier, Fernando Ortiz, and José Lezama Lima are all internationally acclaimed. Authors from abroad, like Ernest Hemingway, Graham Greene and Françiose Sagan have all been influenced by the particular sophistication of Cuba's social and educational make-up.

Cuba is also a land of poets. Author Nicholás Guillén has made a name in the field of poetry since the 1930s. Other poets include José Zacarias Tallet, Félix Pita Rodríguez, Eliseo Diego and Jesús Orta Ruiz (Indio Nabori).

Medical care

A free, modern medical service for all takes precedence in Cuba's budget. Intensive health care and dental programmes, undertaken in Cuba since the triumph of the Revolution, make this country one of the most medically advanced nations. Cuba has one of the highest health indices in the world. New health schemes are currently

Hermanos Ameijeiras hospital in the capital, is one of the most advanced units in the western hemisphere.

underway in almost every field of medical science.

Cubans benefit from free dental, hospital and medical care, and there is one qualified physician for every 480 inhabitants – far in advance of many westernised nations. The Hermanos Ameijeiras Hospital in Havana is one of the most sophisticated in the Americas, and there is a hospital, or polyclinic within easy reach of every individual in the country. Modern research, technology and equipment, combined with some of the nation's most experienced specialists, has created such an advanced medical environment that the world's leading health experts come to study in the country.

After eradicating most diseases endemic in the tropics, Cuba is concentrating on care for the young and the elderly. Nine new hospitals are being built, and 34 existing hospitals are undergoing expansion, completing one of the finest health-care systems in the world. By the

year 2000 Cuba expects to have 65 000 physicians in its medical service.

Visitors and tourists also benefit from the high standard of healthcare, and the free service is extended to everyone in the country. The provision of trained medical staff at all hotels, villa areas, chalet developments and tourist resorts, is a priority of the Institute of Tourism in Cuba. Polyclinics and hospitals are strategically placed nationwide, and there is a good pharmacy in every town. General, maternity and children's hospitals are located in every major centre.

Housing and accommodation

Cuba is the most populous island in the Antilles, with more than 85 inhabitants to the square kilometre. For this reason the government have been concentrating on alleviating the threatened congestion in some municipalities. Housing programmes have produced new, open-plan townships and communities like the city of Alamar, several miles to the east of Havana City.

Many modern townships have been built over recent years by the microbrigades –

groups of professional and semi-skilled workers, who either temporarily take leave from their regular occupations, or work in their spare time to assist in building programmes. Passing the construction sites, one might see a technician laying bricks, a nurse operating a cement mixer, or a university professor painting window frames. Everyone joins in the effort to improve housing, as does the government, which has placed the importance of the new programme high on its list of priorities.

It is not just the suburbs of the cities which benefit from the work of micro-brigades. In rural areas, new school accommodation is being built and agricultural villages are receiving similar attention. Here new housing accommodates farm labourers and the elderly or retired. The homes provided by the government, for retired workers can now remain in the family indefinitely.

New tenants of some state-owned apartments are able to purchase them by instalments. Rent in Cuba is generally no more than 10 per cent of the tenant's sum salary.

A recent modification of the housing laws provides for house owners, with large properties, to let rooms or sections of their accommodation, so easing potential overcrowding in city areas. Large tracts of sub-standard housing are now being cleared in most cities, and new, spacious

Visitors from around the world have admired the housing and facilities freely available to the retired and aged

High rise housing need not necessarily be plain, unimaginative structures, as this Vedado, Havana, block demonstrates

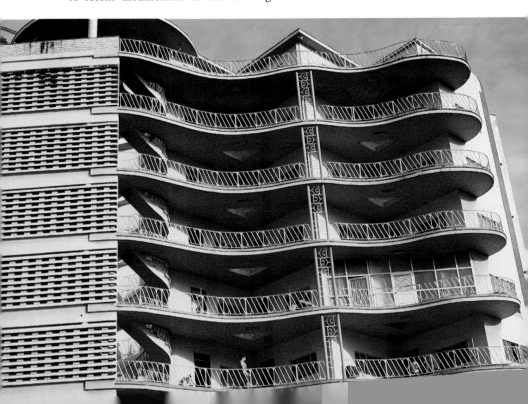

properties are replacing the dilapidated legacy of pre-revolution Cuba. Tourist accommodation is also receiving special attention as new developments are created and extra staff housing is being constructed. Large sums are being channeled into improving existing tourist facilities and building new tourist resorts and hotels.

Cuba can boast some of the most spectacular architecture in the western hemisphere. The baroque designs in court-yarded villas embellished with deep, cool archways, brilliantly coloured glass windows (*vitrales*, *lucetas* and *mediopuntos*), balconies, patios and wrought ironwork, are some of the most delightful examples in the world. Each corner turned in Cuba's villages, towns and cities, can produce breathtaking vistas of colonial elegance or later traditional elements. Trinidadians particularly, are proud of their living heritage and will often invite the visitor to browse inside their own homes.

Agriculture

The face of the Cuban countryside has changed dramatically over the past quarter of a century. Where once there was impenetrable scrub, there are now some of the world's finest citrus groves. Where there was once rocky mountainside, there now are coffee and cocoa plantations, and mangrove swamp has been replaced with new afforestation programmes. Even remote areas like the Caujeri Valley in the Sagua-Baracoa Mountains have been put to the plough and contribute to the economy.

Sugar is still the agricultural mainstay – the country is the world's largest cane sugar exporter. Harvesting on the vast canefields, for the 161 centrales or sugar producing factories, is now more than 60 per cent mechanised. Sugar and its by-products, alcohol, rum, bagasse, molasses, etc. are the basis of the economy, followed by seafoods and fish. Vegetables, honey, tobacco, citrus fruits and juices, coffee and cocoa are also important agricultural exports. Just about every Cuban, at some

time, has worked on the land, generally in the new citrus programmes, or in some area of food processing.

Cuba's small-scale farmers produce around 650 000 tonnes of root and other vegetables annually. Development programmes include the expansion of the seven sugar shipping terminals, modernising vegetable processing plants, creating new refineries, constructing more advanced food-produce packaging plants, and improving the country's fishing terminals. There are thirty-four major fishing ports around the coast.

Poultry and pig farming is widespread, and egg production is increasing with assistance from the Food Industry Research Institute. Hog raising contributes, in export terms, an important range of products in great demand by nearby Latin American nations. Dairy farming in Cuba has received international recognition with the genetic production of the famous F1 strain of cattle at the modern chain of 38 dairy farms in Picadura Valley. Zebu and Holstein strains provide supportive cattle stock and the keeping of goats, oxen and donkeys is popular in rural regions. There

Ramon Castro, Fidel's brother, interviewed here by the author, is a world-renowned agronomist and developer of the famous F1 strain of cattle.

are two dozen dairy enterprises across the country, and beef production is on the increase, with the creation of new pastures in previously inaccessible areas.

Other important agricultural products include rice, sisal and wood, all of which are also exported, along with henequen products. Locally farmed produce such as potatoes, malanga, boniato and platano are often mixed with the cultivation of tomato, pimento, melon, peppers and fruit such as mango, avocado, pineapple and guava. Rice is grown extensively in Pinar del Rio, Matanzas, Ciego do Avila, Camagüey and Granma – little is produced in Sancti Spiritus and Havana Provinces. Coffee production is mainly confined to the provinces of Granma, Santiago de Cuba and Holguín – but a small percentage emanates from Ciego de Avila, Sancti Spiritus, Santa Clara, Matanzas, Havana and Pinar del Rio Provinces.

Industry

Industrial production commands a prime position in Cuba's development plan, and technical advances have had a far-reaching effect on the nation's lifestyle. Much of the country's industry is centred around the agricultural sector. New plants for processing foods, packing factories, distilleries and flour mills, are changing the industrial skyline, as are the recently constructed prefabricated-concrete units, canning, animal and poultry feed factories, new breweries, wire and radio plants.

All agricultural sectors are benefiting from new technology, including the fishing industry, and the important production of sugar by-products and fertilisers. Both agricultural equipment and fishing boats

From car assembly to paper mills, from chemical works to thermo-electric schemes, a thriving network of industry spreads across the country.

are produced in Cuba, as are vehicles, including those used in the construction industry – Girón and Tainos trucks and KTP1 cane-cutting machinery.

The production of minerals for domestic use and export – nickel, copper, chrome, silver, iron and manganese, is expanding due to improvements in the development of machinery. Quarrying is also expected to grow in importance as the export figures for asphalt, kaolin, feldspar, marble and industrial lime soar.

The tobacco industry is only partly mechanised as there is a great demand for the traditional hand-rolled cigars. The tobacco growing industry has also made use of technological advances in the field, where research into growing and drying techniques have improved crop production. Visitors are able to tour both tobacco and rum factories by prior arrangement.

Most important industrial developments which have improved the Cuban economy are of oil and thermo-electricity production. Oil production in four provinces is currently running at fourteen per cent of domestic consumption. There are refineries on both the south and the north coasts where the oil is being extracted. A huge new thermo-electric station is being completed on the north coast. In the south of Cuba a thermal power programme will soon complement the hydro-electric schemes which produce power in many regions. The existing thermal power station near Cienfüegos is now benefiting from a closely-related hydro-electric scheme newly constructed in the Escambray Mountains.

In Camagüey a raw material recycling plant has been built and, in connection with this, the metallurgical and metal-mechanical industry is expanding. Cuba produces its own chemicals for both industrial use and medical application; textile and paper plants are also running at a capacity great enough for exportation. Cement and ferro-cement marine vessels are now also being exported.

The Soviet Union takes 65 per cent of Cuba's exports, 20 per cent goes to the rest of Europe, 10 per cent to Asia and exports are also sent to Africa, North America and the Middle East.

The story of sugar

'King Sugar', to give it its colloquial Antillian name, is still the backbone of Cuba's economy. The country is the largest exporter in the world. Not only does Cuba export over 70 per cent of its sugar production to the socialist bloc, but the island exports a host of by-products including torula yeast, molasses, alcohol, chipboard, dextrane and rum.

Today, even some building material and a proportion of the country's paper production is derived from sugar. Although current sugar production runs at just under 8 million tonnes per year and its by-products play an important role in export, it is hoped to reduce the nation's reliance on a single huge cash crop by expanding the cultivation of crops such as cocoa, coffee and other non-sugar exports.

How did Cuba come to be the sugar centre of the world? It was really due to

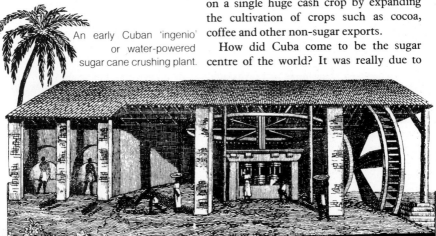

An early Cuban 'ingenio' or water-powered sugar cane crushing plant.

Christopher Columbus, as was the importation of a number of other crops. On his second journey to Cuba (1493), Columbus brought a quantity of cut sugar cane, really a variation of a grass crop, from the Canary Islands. It was not really cultivated until about 1548.

Sugar cane is said to flourish in the Cuban soil just by sticking a short length into the ground! This was certainly how the crop was introduced and, as settlers cleared more and more ground and expanded their cane fields the need for extra labour increased.

Sugar not only influenced the country's economy, but changed the whole face of the social system for hundreds of years. Indian labour became more scarce as the avaricious successors to the Spanish settlers strove to supply an increasing demand for sugar in the Old World. The solution was to supplement Indian slave labour with new blood from the west coast of Africa. Slavery had, by then, become rife throughout the West Indies, almost entirely due to the booming trade in sugar.

A refreshing, thick, sweet drink was all that was produced, in the early days, from the bamboo-like cane, and much of the crop went to feeding livestock. By the end of the seventeenth century larger sugar cane fields and primitive cane mills began to appear. It was not until the mid-eighteenth century that the trade in sugar began to boom and a rush for boatloads of black slaves began. The English occupation of Havana in 1762 encouraged sugar production. Thousands more slaves were drafted in from Africa. Used for transporting sugar, the ox-cart became the most common form of transport in the country.

The demand for Cuban rum (an important sugar by-product) increased with expanding trade links to Europe and the emergent states of North America. By 1825 the production of sugar on a nation-wide scale was in full spate. Black slaves brought language, rituals, beliefs, customs and colour into Cuba. A certain amount of integration took place but, since the earliest days of black slavery on the cane fields, the field workers had been in constant revolt. By the mid-nineteenth century there may have been as many as one million black slaves in the country. Their influence on every aspect of the Cuban way of life was becoming an increasing embarrassment to the Spanish farmers, landowners and government.

Uprisings by slaves against the Spanish had become so intense by 1868 that even landowners, led by Carlos Manuel de Céspedes, freed and armed slaves in the first major revolt against the government.

It was, therefore, because of the importance of sugar in Cuba that the Spanish-imported slaves eventually changed the entire history, attitudes and customs of the largest country in the Caribbean region.

Today, the 'millionaire brigade' (sugar cane labourers) are among the country's highest paid manual workers and, instead of the hacking, cutting, carrying, crushing and boiling work being done by hand, only about 40 per cent of cane is now hand-cut.

Harvesting on the immense Cuban sugar fields is a spectacle which should not be missed. Throughout the year the vast expanses of cane fields are hives of activity as there is always something that needs attention either during the nursery stage or during the 'zafra', or harvest.

Cane is still propagated by inserting a small segment into the soil with a little fertiliser and water. As far as the eye can see, the straight rows of new growth replace blackened scorched earth and remnants of a previous harvest. The cane grows to a height of up to three metres. When ready, it is cut, either by hand-wielded, wide-bladed machetes or by the giant blades of the mechanical harvester. Cane is trimmed of its leaves – which are used for fodder – and cut into lengths about as long as a forearm. From the field, the cane sections are taken for processing to the mill, usually located at a Centrale.

The vast fields, some as large as many of Cuba's neighbouring islands, the sugar

'Machetero' on horseback and the driver in his 'cosechadora', neither knew the hardships of King Sugar's early days.

mills, housing, shops, administration, railway station, processing plants, schools, hospital, clinic, workshops and post office – a small town – are called Centrales. There are about 161 Centrales in the country. Each is built on a basic model and operates as a complete cooperative unit. During the December to May harvest, tours are organised by resorts and hotels to visit the fields and Centrales. It is most educational to experience the vastness of this giant agricultural industry which forms the basis of so much which is often taken for granted – or granulated!

At the factory the cane is chopped and crushed, water washes out the remaining sugar, and lime is introduced to eliminate impurities. Heated juice is left to settle and is rotary-filtered; then it is steam-boiled in evaporators. The temperature is lowered gradually through a course of evaporators until crystallisation in the vacuum pan. In 'the basket' molasses and crystals are spun to separate molasses which are then used in the production of rum. Cattle feed and industrial alcohol are made from some of the molasses. Cuba has 155 sugar mills.

The juiceless, dried, cane fibre is used to fuel the factory boilers and for chipboard production. It is also used to make cardboard and paper, and even paper cups and straws with which to sip the most enjoyable of sugar's produce – rum.

The crystals of sugar, are delivered to ports for despatch abroad or used domestically in the production of a thousand syrups, candies, drinks, chemicals and confectioneries.

The major sugar factories, such as Antonio Guiteras and Jesus Hernández in Puerto Padre, Urbano Noris in Holguín, Venezuela and Ciro Redondo in Ciego de Avila and Uraguay Centrale in Sancti Spiritus Province, produce 170 – 200 000 tonnes during the zafra or harvest. Six new Centrales have been constructed since the triumph of the Revolution and, three more are due to come on stream – in Las Tunas (1986), Matanzas (1987) and in Camagüey Province in 1990.

The story of rum

'Yo-ho-ho, and a bottle of rum!' From Robert Louis Stevenson's book, Treasure Island, *inspired by the piracy history of the Isle of Youth.*

The distilling of rum (or ron in Cuba) is probably as old as the variety of sugar cane that it is derived from. Cuba, however, has specialised in perfecting the production of rum, and Havana Club is internationally respected as the world's finest.

Cuban rum started life during the buccaneering days of the pirates and the Spanish treasure galleons. The key to the plunder of Central America were the straits between Cuba and Florida which became a hunting ground for privateers until the port of Havana was safely established. The corsairs had obviously acquired a taste for Havana rum because they persisted in

Still preserved is the turn-of-the-century rum factory on the coast at Santa Cruz del Norte (above) and (opposite) the new sign to its multi-million dollar distillery.

harassing the Spanish fleets until, in 1714, a Royal Letter prohibited the manufacture of rum in Cuba.

This edict of King Charles was probably followed with tongue-in-cheek, until the English captured Havana in 1762 and actively encouraged an increase in rum production! In 1764 official distilleries were established near sugar cane plantations and trade in rum began to flourish. Cuba, restored in 1762 to Spain, began to establish its own liqueur identity among the inferior rums of other West Indian islands.

So great was the production, by 1825, that rural distilleries could not absorb the surplus molasses produced. Rum has to go through the stages of cane, molasses, fermentation, distillation, first maturation, filtering, elaboration and ageing. In 1840 it was decided to build large distilleries near the coast to facilitate the export trade. Modern plants were established at Havana, Matanzas and Cardenas by 1848.

When the search for a perfect, universal formula for Cuban rum began, Real Junta de Fomento offered a prize in gold and as a result the distinctive flavour of Havana Club was born. Almost 100 years ago the distilleries started to produce other liqueurs besides rum and now the famous Santa Cruz del Norte plant, near Havana, produces three rums – three-year-old, silver label, light rum; five-year-old gold label, old gold dry rum; and seven-year-old (Añejo) gold label, extra aged dry rum. It also produces 19 different, exotic liqueurs from such products as guava, (Guayaba) orange, (Amargo) mango, papaya, banana, cocoa, plum, pineapple, coconut, herbs such as mint, and coffee (Café Turquino).

The Santa Cruz distillery re-built in 1973, is Cuba's largest and the oldest in the Americas. It has a yearly production capacity of 30 million gallons of rum – soon to be increased by 70 000 litres – and 9 million gallons of liqueur. Mostly English-made oak barrels of 180 litres capacity, hold the rum for ageing in 12 storehouses for the first fermentation. Each storehouse contains 18 000 barrels, some of which are special, Scottish white oak barrels with a maximum capacity of 400 litres. Cuba's Havana Club distillery estimates its total storage of ageing rum at any one time at 200 000 barrels – about 50 million litres!

Apart from the Havana Club distillery there are those producing Caney, Santiago White Label, Matusalem or Marinero rum from the original Bacardi factory. This still stands, with the bat emblem and giant bottle motif, in Santiago de Cuba. In Matanzas Province, at Cardenas, a rum called Arecha is distilled. Although not a rum, La Guayabita del Pinar is a smooth brandy, Seca – dry, Liqueur – sweet. It is produced from the guayaba or guava in the westernmost province of Pinar del Rio.

Cuba's eight rum factories produce nine different types of the liqueur for export and ten different labels of rum for domestic consumption: at Havana (Santa Cruz), Matanzas (Yucayo), Villa Clara (Central), Camagüey (Puerto Principe), Granma (Pinilla), and two in Santiago de Cuba (Caney and Matusalem). Shortly new, model distilleries will be constructed at Santa Cruz, Villa Clara and near the Hatuey plant at Santiago de Cuba.

Distilleries may be visited, but tours have to be booked a long time in advance by Cubatur guides. The establishment at Santa Cruz del Norte is the most convenient, being only about 15 kilometres from Havana. Next to the new factory is the green and yellow, wooden building of the earlier distillery, built in 1919. On the opposite side is the new, computerised, 20 million dollar project which will increase Havana Club's total number of products to thirty-six – making it one of the most important distilleries in the Caribbean area.

The great variety of rums are used in the production of many cocktails in Cuban bars. Further details of these are given on page 82.

The story of tobacco

'There is no substitute for our tobacco anywhere in the world. It's easier to make good cognac than to achieve the quality of Cuban tobacco. It has to do with the soil, the microclimate and other natural factors, one of the privileges that nature gave to our island.'

FIDEL CASTRO RUZ

Cohiba, the Indian name for tobacco, was smoked only by the Shaman, or holy man, during ritualistic prophesying sessions in the chief's hut. Smoke was breathed directly into the nostrils via reeds. The early settlers adopted the habit by rolling the leaves into 'tabacs' and inhaling through the mouth. The popularity of smoking spread from Spain and from North America, via England throughout Europe, until tobacco became one of Cuba's major industries. At the end of the sixteenth century the plant even spread to the Philippines when the Spanish galleon, *San Clemente* took 200 ounces of seed to the East from Havana.

Unlimited, cheap, labour resources and a crop which was easy and fast to cultivate – tobacco plants grow to more than 1.8 metres in height in about six months –

A skill developed over centuries . . . creating a delight enjoyed before Columbus

produced a thriving export trade in a product which was unrivalled in quality anywhere in the world.

The industry developed a sophistication through the special routine of the cigar factories or tabaquerias which was directly related to the methods involved in cigar production.

By the mid-1800s the present-day layout of the cigar factory was organised. The bundles of leaves arrive in bales, packed in outer palm leaves, from the tobacco farms. Every bundle of five leaves, each up to 50 centimetres in length, is shaken out to loosen them. The leaves are then carefully dampened and left hanging to absorb moisture for two to three hours. The leaves are then binned to ensure even drying and at this stage look and feel like huge, tough, damp, golden lettuce leaves. From the drying room the leaves are sorted for colour, strength and suitability for either machine fabrication or hand rolling.

The tough stalks are stripped from the centre of the underside of the leaf, *despalillado*, which is then flattened out. Leaves are again classified and checked for flaws and then passed on, in bundles, to either the mechanised department or the area for hand rolling, after sorting, for use as binders or wrappers.

The cigar-making machine sits on a desk in front of the operator who feeds a mixture into a hopper at the top and places two binder leaves on a plate where they are cut. The two leaves are then positioned, overlapping, on a moving belt which feeds them into the rolling machine. This wraps the measured amount of filler and expels the completed cigar. From here the following process is similar to that of the hand-made cigar.

Hand-rolling is a deft and expert skill. Each whole 'binder' leaf is dextrously cut by hand, the filler leaves are selected, rolled in the binder, sliced at one end and placed in a wooden mould, as are those made by machine. These cigars are in the press for about half an hour. Ten cigars in each press block are then all turned

Typical of Pinar del Rio's landscape are these giant tobacco curing houses or 'vegas'.

individually as the presses create a pinch line on the primary binder. The cigars are again pressed for another 20 minutes, in wooden block presses which are often over 100 years old!

The waist-high presses are then opened, the moulds removed and the final wrapper rolled by hand onto each cigar. The end is then trimmed with the maker's semi-circular knife blade. A tiny circle of leaf is cut to bind the cigar's sharp end and adhered with a special paste. Finished, the cigars are then taken in bundles of fifty for the familiar cigar labels to be attached.

National cigars are wrapped, twenty-five at a time, in paper, and cigars for export are carefully sorted for colour and boxed in the highly decorative cigar boxes known world-wide. Each layer of cigars is then meticulously scrutinised again before a thin layer of cedar is placed above the cigars. The paper liner of the box is closed and the completed box sealed with the traditional guarantee of Cuban Havana cigars. Each separate procedure in the making of a cigar is swift, precise, and checked thoroughly for perfection, creating that most excellent of cigars – the 'puros habanos'.

Every cigar ring denotes its colour, quality and size. Those for domestic sale have orange rings for nationals; Red = Cazadores and, those of lower grades, Green = Crema, Brown = Breva and Blue = Petit Cetro.

It is often considered that, the darker the colour of the cigar, the stronger the flavour, but the colour of the cigar can only be determined from the shade of its wrapper. A dark wrapper is generally high in sugar content, and therefore sweeter. The main classifications of cigars, corresponding to colour and generally appreciated strength are, according to brand: *oscuro* (black and strong); *maduro* (brown-black and full bodied); *maduro colorado* (brown and aromatic); *colorado* (reddish-brown and more aromatic than its predecessor); *colorado clara* (light brown and milder); *claro* (tobacco-brown and mild); *clarisimo* (green and very mild).

A fully conditioned cigar, to be at its best, should be smoked 12 to 18 months after manufacture. The best flavour is considered to be six to ten months after production. Green cigars are often sold in glass containers to preserve their freshness and some superior cigars are sold in aluminium tubes for the same reason.

The sizes and shapes of cigars are important to the flavour. There is the Torpedo (fat, pot-bellied, closed at both ends); the Corona (rounded, closed head, straight sides); Perfecto (half pointed, closed head, cylindrical shape, tapering); the Panetela (thinner but similar to a Corona); Lonsdale (between a Panetela and Corona in size but similar in shape); the Calebras (flat but smaller than Lonsdale); and the Demi-Tasse (smaller than a Panetela).

Placing the ring on a finished cigar completes the process for each cigar. This could have taken a full ten hours from the time the cured tobacco leaf entered the factory. A special discipline is needed in the cultivation and curing of the leaf in the tobacco fields as in the factory. Careful nurturing, often protection from intense sunlight by gauze, muslin or cheesecloth for the milder tobaccos are customary. Delicate picking of the five different strengths of leaves on each plant during

the ripening season – November to February – and slow drying are today technical skills.

Most leaf is still dried in the tall palm-thatched, wooden houses, called 'vegas', after being left in the open air on wooden or bamboo racks called 'cuje'. The vegas always align east to west to get the benefit of the day's sun and, today, there are many new-style vegas with bright silver, corrugated iron roofs. Maize is generally cultivated in the empty fields after picking.

The best leaf, generally used in the making of wrappers for the highest quality cigars, comes from the Vuelta Abajo, Semi-vuelta and Viñales valley regions of Pinar del Rio Province, but tobacco is also grown in Vuelta Arriba, Remedios and some in practically every province in Cuba. This special leaf needs particular attention and the campesinos, or small-holding farmers who grow 70–80 per cent of the best leaf, and are often called 'veguero', can still be heard talking to the plants as they mature in the specially enriched soil.

One can almost say that the tobacco leaf hears the sound of human voices from plant to cigar. In the factory, on a high desk in the front of rows of cigar makers or tabaqueros, a reader of verse, poetry, philosophy, literature and political works, has had his place since the beginning of factory production in the early nineteenth century. It is the reader's position to entertain the tabaqueros as they work and also educate at the same time. Some say that a contributory factor towards the triumph of the Revolution was the freedom of the tobacco factory reader to educate and inform the workers of developments in the struggle, and how to undermine the dictatorship of the Batista regime. The reader has an eminent position in the cigar factory and is traditionally highly respected for his learning. Each worker listens attentively as he reads extracts from political essays, the newspapers or informative journals through their eight hour per-day shift. Most factory workers operate on a six-day week with one Saturday in every fortnight off.

The end product is as familiar through-

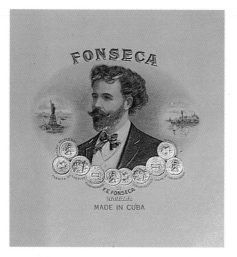

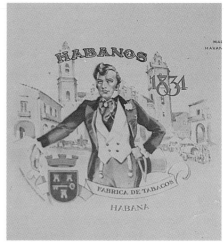

out the world as the Rolls Royce or champagne. The names of the famous labels are also legend; Punch, Romeo y Julieta, Montecristo, Bolívar, El Rey del Mundo, Churchill, Fonseca, Partágas and the elite of all, Davidoff and Cohiba, once a noted favourite with the Cuban premier. Lesser known brands, but still the world's most exquisite varieties, are Diplomáticos, Flor de Cano, Hoyo de Monterrey, Por Larrañaga, Qui D'Orsay, Quintero, Ramón Allones, Sancho Panza, San Luis Rey, Troya, Caney, Los Satus de Luxe, Juan López, José L. Piedra and Cifuentes y Rafael González.

The more important cigar factories are based in Havana. Their names are synonymous with the exotic names of the best cigars – Partágas, La Corona, H. Upmann, Romeo y Julieta and El Laguito. There are twenty-five main tobacco manufacturing centres and the product is grown in nine provinces although Pinar del Rio accounts for the majority. The local factory in this province is known as 'Serbio'.

Cigars are made in a variety of shapes and sizes, colours and tastes and Cuba also produces cigarette tobacco, tobacco for the pipe and for chewing. Around 45–50 000 tonnes of cigarettes and cigars (300 millions) are produced annually. Tobacco constitutes 10 per cent of Cuba's exports and 140 varieties of cigars comprise the largest proportion of this trade.

By far the largest, and probably the best known tobacco factory in Cuba is the H. Upmann establishment, just behind the old city in Havana. It is particularly well-known as it is one of the most popular for visiting tours. These can be arranged by Cubatur guides, or a group can be joined by request from Cubatur representatives at the major hotel receptions. A tour of a cigar factory in Havana is a treat not to be missed even if you do not smoke!

Four adages cannot be omitted when considering the importance of Cuba's tobacco and its cigars. Rudyard Kipling is reported to have quipped 'And a woman is only a woman, but a good cigar is a smoke'. Also on the values of choosing the right cigar, the French writer, Colette observed, 'When a wife can purchase her husband the right cigars, their relationship is blessed'. 'In the book of *Gigi*, Aunt Alice advises: 'Let me think how I will teach you to choose cigars . . . when a woman knows a man's preferences, cigars included, and when a man knows what pleases a woman, they are well armed for life together!' From Somerset Maughan: 'Men have laboured for years under the tropical sun and crossed the seven seas to bring this pleasure to your side'.

CHAPTER 4

The Natural Order

28th, October 1493
'The verdant greenery reaches almost down to the water . . . trees
all along the river, beautiful and green . . . with flowers and fruits
each according to their kind, and with countless little birds singing
very sweetly . . . That island is the most beautiful that eyes have
ever seen.'

CHRISTOPHER COLUMBUS' diary

Fauna

Cuba's varied landscape offers refuge for a fascinating variety of wildlife. From its mountain peaks to the depths of its lakes and its multitude of cays and inlets, the island is a natural paradise.

It is in the coastal marshes, mangrove swamps and maze of shoreline waterways, that the two species of Cuba's endemic crocodiles and several types of alligator can be found. In earlier days these were often kept as pets – just like one would keep a dog. Today, however, many thousands are enclosed in crocodile farming zones, particularly on the Zapata Peninsula – a source of hides and of meat. Other reptiles

The Cuban Land Crab and its relations are regular inhabitants of the mangrove swamps in some southern regions.

The rare Cuban Jutia, once an Indian delicacy, now protected by law

include the iguanas which live on many of the island's offshore cays. There are an interesting selection of tortoise in Cuba, unusual terrapins and attractive chameleons. Sadly, almost depleted, are the Manatee, or Sea-Cow, and its snub-nosed relative, the Manjuari. Their friendly nature, vast size, and tasty flesh once made these mammals a target for wholesale slaughter. Once they were the supposed source of mariners' legends of mermaids in the tropics, now they are carefully protected in jealously-guarded reserves.

Cuba is the home of the smallest amphibian, the minute Dwarf, or Banana

Many people keep baby turtles as pets

...on the other hand, few nowadays keep a crocodile or alligator as watchdog

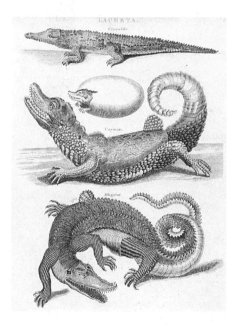

Frog and world's most tiny mammal, the extremely rare Almiqui (*Solenodon cubanas*). This is an insectivorous, shrew-like, 'living fossil', and is found only in the Baracoa region of the country. A long-clawed mammal, it is protected by law, as is the Hutia (Jutia), a large, edible, forest rodent rather like the Coypu, of which there are eight species. The size of a giant Mongoose, the Hutia was once as common as the Conejo Cimarron, a Cuban breed of rabbit. The Hutia's family consists of the Conga, the Aguti and a rarer breed, the *Capromis garridoi*, occasionally found on isolated cays in the south of the island. Other small land animals comprise small rodents, squirrels, rats, mice – including dormice – and a selection of the rarer species of seed-eating rodents.

Cuba has fourteen types of snake, none are poisonous, but the Cuban Boa can grow to the daunting size of four metres! The Lagartija Lizard is often seen because of its bright green colour, yellow neck and red wattle. There are more than sixty other reptiles inhabiting the rocky and desert regions of the south, the cool, dark, moun-

tain caves of the west and the jungle forests of Cuba's mountains. Most commonly seen, is probably the comical, Curly-Tailed Lizard, the house-dwelling, tiny Gecko or the beach favourite, the Sand Lizard. Cuba has forty-six lizard genera altogether.

Turtles abound in the cays and in the coastal waters around the island. A reserve has been set up for Loggerhead, Green, Leatherback, Hawksbill or Carey turtles – (Tortuga in Spanish) – on Los Cocos, a cay like Cayo Largo just off the south-west coast.

Frogs such as the tree and leaf varieties are more often heard than seen, especially the bull frogs in the evening, croaking their two-tone serenade. Toads are also quite prolific. Many toads come to grief on the roads around marshland, only to become carrion for the voracious Aura Vultures. Newts, some of them the blind, rare, albino, cave-dwelling species, include the Axolotl, one of nature's strangest creatures.

Among Cuba's largest animals are the feral cattle and horses which, since the days of Spanish settlers and buccaneers, roam the tiny islets and cays off the island's northern shores. Red Deer and a forest variety, (*Venado odocoileus-virginianus*), about a metre in height, were introduced quite recently. They provide the hunter with sport in the more mountainous regions and in thick wooded areas. The Wild Boar, although much more rare, can occasionally be found in more isolated locations (like the cays of Camagüey and La Belen or the Najusa Hills.)

The smallest bat in the world is Cuba's Butterfly or Moth Bat, some other quite

At least five varieties of turtle are found in Cuba's maritime waters.

rare varieties, live in forest, wood and in farming areas. Unique to the island, is the Cuban Flower Bat and its fruit-eating cousin, prolific in the Caribbean they are often a common nuisance!

Bird life

The *Polymita picta* snail is probably one of many hundreds of types of snail which have fallen prey to Cuba's most vivid and

Everyone's favourite, the dolphin display at Baracoa seaquarium is a regular attraction

prolific variety of birds. About 388 species of birds have been recorded throughout the country, but the island and its cays are resting places and holiday homes to many more.

Cuba has a surprising variety of birdlife from the smallest bird in the world, the Zun Zun, Zunzuncito or Bee Humming-bird, to the four-foot-tall, Pink Flamingo – locally known as *Cabellero d'Italia*. The most extraordinary is the Sijus – these natives are the only birds, other than the owl, capable of turning their heads through 360 degrees. Just recently the Ivory-Billed Woodpecker was found to be nesting in Cuba – it was previously thought to be extinct.

One of the Trogon family, the Cuban variety emulates the national flag with its red, white and blue colourings.

Cattle Ibis

Magnificent Frigatebird

Pelican

Most noticeable is the Aura Vulture, wheeling above its prey or catching the morning sun, with outstretched wings, perched on a telegraph pole along the roadside. In contrast to the great, black vultures are the host of minute, brilliantly irridescent Hummingbirds constantly hovering around the tropical blooms, especially those of the Hibiscus.

There are a few more colourful birds than the Cuban Trogon, or Tocororo (similar to the Copper-Tailed Trogon) – so called for its strange cry. This blue, black, red, white and dark green bird of the rain forests has been adopted as the national bird. It coincidentally reflects the red, white and blue colours of Cuba's flag. Also in the forests may be seen little green finches sporting yellow neckbands – *Tomeguin de Pinar*, The Royal Woodpecker, or *Carpintero Real*, the Cuban Green Parrot, *Cotorra*, and the Pygmy Owl. Among other protected birds are the Ferminia and, more difficult to spot, the strutting, hawk-like, fawn, chest-

In Cuba there is more than one bird species for every day of the year, the native parrot is a particularly colourful example.

nut, black and white, Cararia, which is very similar to the Senegalese Snakebird.

Common around human habitation are the familiar House Sparrows, the large, black Judio, the Toti and the wedge-tailed Chuchinguaco. Out along the country roadside the *Coco Blanco*, or Cattle Ibis, its cousin the *Coco Negro* and the Cuban Grassquit, Crane, or *Grulla*, and the blue-headed Quail Dove are common. In early morning, or after one of Cuba's short, sharp showers, Everglade Kites soar above carrion. In scrub areas and Marabou thicket the little Solitaire can be spotted,

Cuba's extensive coastline is a natural sanctuary for several flamingo species.

Spoonbill are frequent visitors to the island's northern coast.

The Cararai is a rare hawklike species seen on the savanna.

and Pigeon, Dove, Swallow and Swift are common near the cane fields at harvest.

Anywhere near water, the variety of game birds is staggering. From the Spoonbill and Blue Heron or *Garza*, to the Guinea Fowl, Common Quail and Pheasant, the countryside is alive with wildfowl. Out in the marshy regions the booming cry of the Diver, or *Codorniz*, is a common sound particularly near freshwater lakes. Also found in these areas are the resident and migratory birds – one especially unique species to the island's shores is the Cuban Tody. The Yaguaza, a cross between a goose and a duck, and its relative, the smaller Yaguazin, mix with Migratory, Bahamas, Mallard and Fulvous Tree Duck. Wilson's Snipe, the Avocet-like Cachipora, White-Crowned Pigeon and Mourning Dove, are regular game birds. Not so common, are the large-footed, snipe-like, Guateao, the Vireo, the Hobby, the bankside Yellow-headed Warbler, Cuban Gnat-catcher and jewel-like Kingfisher. American Coot are common along the margins of lakes and Columbus even records that near the sandy, northern bays, he heard a Nightingale!

The rare Black Tern, Cormorants, *Rabihorcado* or Frigate Bird, and the inevitable variety of gulls, or *Gaviota*, can be seen all along Cuba's coastline. Ponderous Pelicans, or *Pelicano*, display remarkable flying and diving skills and, in the more rocky bays, one can sometimes be treated to the stunning aerobatics of the Sea Osprey, or *Gincho*. In the salty, mangrove swamps it is possible to spot the rare Water Thrush.

More than 100 species of migratory birds descend on the island's lakes, rivers and coastal waters each year, attracting migratory humans in the form of ornithologists and wildfowl hunters.

Marine and fresh-water life

The prolific waters around this varied island also attract their fair share of visitors in the form of fishermen, scuba divers, marine biologists and underwater photographers. About 900 different species of fish have been recorded in the three seas around Cuba's shores, its 40 major rivers, numerous reservoirs and large lakes. Game

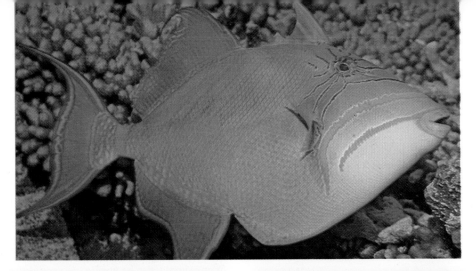

Both young and adult French Angelfish (above) are as prolific as the brilliant Queen Triggerfish (top).

fish include white, black and blue Marlin, Sail, Sword and Sawfish, Permit, Dorado, (Dolphin), Wahoo, Common Jack, and Barracuda. A variety of Shark, Bonito and Tuna are regular catches, as are a variety of Rays, Mackerel and Snappers.

Commercial fishing is represented by a 40-strong fishing fleet. Coastal fishing industries are localised, and Oyster, Lobster, Sponge, Squid and a unique, salt-water variety of Tilapia – as opposed to the more common African, freshwater species – are farmed. Trucha or Black and Largemouth Bass bring game fishermen to the country's lakes in droves. International championships in both salt and fresh-water game fishing make this sport an industry in itself.

The occasional Whale has been seen quite close to the Atlantic shores and Dolphin, Porpoise and Flying Fish follow

any coastal vessel. Leatherback, Hawksbill, Green, Loggerhead and Sea Turtles, plus a fascinating variety of terrapin are quite common, although these are best seen in the special reserves, zoos or breeding stations. Octopus and several harmless and spiteful varieties of Jellyfish are well known in these consistently warm waters. Some more unusual inhabitants mix with the more familiar crabs and Spiny Lobsters like Cascadura.

It is more in the clearer waters on the landward side of the thousands of coral reefs that the visitor, apart from the game fisherman, will find interest. Here, over the reefs and in the lagoons the colours are dazzling. The coral itself can be variegated in a hundred hues – Red Fire coral, blue, green, violet and black Fan coral, brown Sea Fingers and orange Pillar coral. Brain coral, *Diploria clivosa* and *labyrinthiformis* can be almost any colour as can the leaf-like *Acropora palata*. Staghorn coral, *Acropora cervicornis*, is usually a brilliant yellow and *Porites millepora alcicornis*, and Pillar Coral can often be bright red. In the deeper waters the rare Black Coral strikes up branches, sometimes as thick as a man's thumb, through the opalescent waters. More than 65 different species of coral are found around Cuba's shores. The seabed and sandy shores are often littered with coloured Starfish and 'Sand Dollars'.

A myriad species of tropical fish thrive in Cuba's crystal-clear waters.

These magnificent coral and shell specimens were recovered at the Santa Lucia beach for this photograph. Similar souvenirs can be obtained from most hotel tourist shops.

Whether scuba diving, or just snorkelling, a myriad of coloured fish can be seen in some areas darting through forests of Elkhorn Coral. Most humorous is the flat-based, funnel-mouthed Cow Fish, with its sorrowful eyes. A few fish should be regarded with caution, like the Stone-Fish or the spiky, orange-red and white striped Lion, or Dragon Fish. Also to be avoided are those spines of Jimenea – a round fish whose Latin name denotes its unpleasant effects – *Diodon hystrix*, and the Puffer, *Rascacio*, or *Scorpanea plumieri*. Occasional sea urchins and jellyfish, like the 'Man o War', should also be avoided as should the *Morena pinta* – Moray Eel, and the wolf-like Barracuda, which can often scavenge inside reefs. The brilliant, flashing crest of the Lancer Dragonette can also cause a painful sting.

Most tropical fish appear to be more brilliantly coloured the smaller they are. The orange and white striped Clown Fish attend their pet Sea Anemone – immune to its deadly sting; magenta Cardinal Fish or Gobi, almost strut through the waters as hosts of fire-tipped *Angelote reina* – Queen Angelfish and yellowish angelfish in zebra-stripes, waft like clouds through coral

fronds. Parrot, Peacock, Butterfly, Zebras, Chromis, Tangs, Basslets and Porgies, drift through the ocean waters on unseen currents past shoals of Squirrelfish, Damselfish, the three-spinned Pez Perro, the yellow and black Cherna, Jocu and Dog, Red and Cuiera Snappers. Gorgonia, in shades of lilac and purple form forests with multicoloured sponges through which giant Grouper Fish, Sergeant Major and Grunt fish glide. Sea Wrasse lurk in the sea grasses near the shore where Goatfish, the spotted Trunkfish and three-spot Damsel Fish dart out of weed. Trigger and Parrot fish nibble at coral polyps and Flamefish flash in front of the diver's mask.

Look for the disturbingly large, but completely harmless Manta Ray, slowly winging its way over reefs and rippled seabottom sand. Watch out, though, for its cousin, the Stingback Ray's thorny tail, and the sometimes inquisitive Sea Bass or silver and black-striped Spadefish. Some flat fish make very good spearing game in the clear shallow waters. Lizard Fish and Sea Cucumber ripple through the sandy seabed below clouds of Casiopea Jellyfish and Squid.

Cuba's streams, rivers and lakes offer a different underwater world. Famed fish abound like the plentiful Black Bass, (*Trucha in a Cuba*), the Largemouth Bass, the inland bay Snook and Tarpon, the Tilapia, and a large variety of the coastal Bonefish. Cuba has one of the best Bass fishing waters in the world and many records for this game fish have been taken here. International championships are held regularly in the lakes and rivers, coastal and offshore waters.

At least four kinds of turtle and a host of terrapin inhabit both salt and fresh waters and favourite with every visitor are the real Dolphins and the Porpoise which follow coastal boats.

Many of the wonders of the seabed can be enjoyed by those who prefer to stay on the surface. Often, on a boat trip, attended by the inevitable Flying Fish, diver's guides

will oblige by searching for some of the fabulous shells which abound in the warm waters. The most famous of all are the Strombus family – the conches (pronounced – 'conk'). Strombus Gigas are the large, bright, pink-lined, ceramic-like *caracol*, or shell. Other conch include the beautiful, orange-lined, chocolate-lipped, Queen Conch and *Strombus pujilis*. The *Triton* group are well-known for their trumpet-like shape. A typical example in Cuban waters is *Charonis tritonis nobilis*. The spiky *Murex brevifrons* is a collector's item, like the *Melongena melongena*, the *Livona pica* and *Liguus* shells which resemble twirled ice cream cones.

Shellfish, although prolific in some of Cuba's waters, have suffered a certain

This Flamefish variety of Cardinal Fish darts between the spines of a common Sea Urchin.

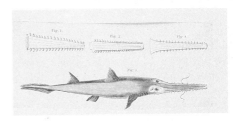

Sawfish

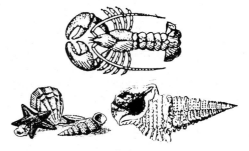

61

Pillar Coral can be found growing to more than three metres in height on some reefs.

amount of decimation. It is for this reason that crab and lobster do not appear on menus as frequently as one would expect. Some unusual crustaceans include Cascadura, Chip-Chip, Sea Eggs. *Ostra*, or Oysters and Conch are the basis of several local dishes and Mussels, Eel and Crayfish are a favourite food in some areas. A local delicacy are the Giant Mussels found in coastal mangrove swamps.

Lobster, Prawn, Langouste, Scampi, Homard and Crayfish are plentiful crustaceans but many are especially bred for the export market. Shellfish should be very fresh when eaten in the hot climate of Cuba. The aforementioned conch can sometimes be seen on menus although it is illegal to take them in some areas. The Clam also is a favourite, particularly with visitors from North America.

Shoreline fishing has a history which goes back to the first inhabitants of the island. The Taino Indians were particularly adept at catching turtles and other large sea creatures by a most unusual method. They would use the 'guaican' or Sucker Fish (*Remora*) which, when attached to a line, fastened itself onto the passing prey so drawing the game into the shore.

Nowadays the shore fishermen use woven fish traps similar to those used in ancient times. These woven cane, cone-shaped baskets are called 'nasas' and the small wire nets used to trap lobster and shrimp are known as 'jaulas'. Shallow-water fishing, especially in marshes and lake-flats, is a popular week-end hobby and pastime in Cuba, notably swamp fishing with spear guns in Ciego de Avila Province.

In the tourist shops a variety of shells, corals and stuffed fish can be purchased, but it is forbidden to take any shells, except the dead ones. Many beautiful shells are sold here as souvenirs. There are also certain areas designated as Marine Parks and conservation districts. Fishing, spear fishing and damaging marine life in these areas is an offence. Coral may not be taken from the sea under any circumstances – Cuba is most preservation conscious.

Insect life

There are over 10 000 species of invertebrates to be found in Cuba. Insect life is dominated by the vast number of flamboyant moths and butterflies. There are the giant moths, *Erebus odorata* and *Cocytius antaeus*, and the wonderfully intricate designs on the wings of varieties like the *Pholus viciis*. Three huge swallowtailed butterflies, in traditional colouring, but with truly eccentric tails, are the

Gundlach Swallowtail – *Parides gundlachianus, Papilo andrageus* and *Papilo thoas.* The common, large yellow *Phoebis seunae* is overshadowed by its brilliant red and yellow brother, the Red-Splashed Sulphur,

Orange-Barred Sulphur

The Monarch

or the *Phoebis avellaneda*. The *Mariposa Cristal* is an ever-present devotee of the buddleia flowers. Another colourful contender is the delicately painted *Danaus gilippus* with its teak and cedar-brown wings spotted with identical white dots. Typically tropical is the Zebra-Striped Butterfly, the *Helichonius Chartitonis*, as stunning in its size and black and yellow design as it is in its erratic, bat-like, dancing flight and curious swarming habit.

There are more than 180 species of day-flying butterflies in Cuba, and 28 are exclusive to the island. Other commonly seen extroverts-of-the-air include the large Orange Sulphur, the Cuba Guayacan Sulphur, the Cloudless Sulphur and Barred Sulphur. Some familiar names include the Red Admiral, Giant Brimstone and Scarlet Emperor. More unusual, though no less prolific, are the Mosaic and the Cuban Buff Zebra butterflies.

In Cuba the female of the smallest scorpion in the world grows to only 1.91 mm. This species is a record, unique to the island. Dragonflies of every hue, size and type can be seen near fresh water. At dusk, the air trills to the sound of Cicada, or in Cuba, *Cigarra*, the innumerable *Coqui* Frogs croak their two-tone serenade and Fireflies light the Cuban night.

Gulf Fritillary

One of Cuba's smallest inhabitants is the unique *Polymita* genus of snail, particularly the Picta variety, found only in north-east Camagüey, near the border with Las Tunas Province. It is said to have magical powers by medicine men of the ancient Afro-Cuban secret societies. These pretty, striped molluscs have now been adopted by the national tourist shop chain as a symbol mascot.

Trees

The woods of Cuba are known world-wide, having once provided the raw materials of much of Spain's early maritime fleets, hardwoods for their lavish palaces and for the country's excellent carved furniture. The island's many useful woods include sixty species of endemic palm. The stately Royal Palm, or *Palma Real*, is the National Tree. This is endemic to the Cuban forest and a prized species of palm which often grows to 30 metres. The fan-shaped *Licuala* and Traveller's Palm, the Date Palm, the bulbous Barrigona, the Cabbage Palm (from which 'millionaire's salad; palmito' or palm heart is derived) and the Coco Palm are most familiar. Mahogany, or *Caoba*, Ebony, Teak, Oak, Candlewood and Flame Tree are all in demand as precious woods on the international market. The Tulip Tree, Pine, Banyan,

The Royal Palm

Banana and Plantain

Bamboo, newly-planted Firs and the shiny-trunked *Almasico* and *Jocuma* are favourite local trees for fencing and building, screening and roofing.

Well known throughout the country is the 'living fossil' – the cycad Cork Palm (*Palma de Corcho*). Highways are lined with a variety of beautiful spreading branches including those of the Tamarind, the Carobi, the Oak Ocuje, *Lignum vitae* and the Turtle Bone tree. The deadly sap, leaves and fruit of the *Manchineel* should be avoided as should the Oleander. Indian Almond, Mangrove, Casuarina and *Uvachaletta*, or Sea Grape trim the island's shores whilst Wild Fig, pines and the tiny, white bloom of the Marabou thicket cling to rocky outcrops and roadside banks. Any available arable space, even beneath the spreading boughs of the Cedar or the Silk Cotton tree, is used to cultivate flowering or fruit-producing bushes and shrubs. The Sunflower is a typical and particular favourite here for its flower and useful seed. Most unusual, is the Baobab, or 'upside-down' tree, often said to have its roots in the air!

Several tree names are strangely tropical

65

but everyone knows the Giant Mahogany, *Swietenia Mahogani*. About 20 metres tall, when fully grown, the tree can grow for over 100 years and its wood is highly valued by the skilled Cuban craftsmen. The bark of Mahogany is often used to treat rheumatism, tetanus, pneumonia and other ailments. Other precious Cuban woods include *Acana, Ayte, Arabu, Cuaba* and *Cuaba Allua. Guayo Negro, Incencio Negro, Jicue, Majas, Najasi* and *Paola Albo*. Some words in a tree name may denote the nature of the wood like the curiously-named *Hueso Tortuga* – Turtle Bone; *Guama Candelon* – Candle Tree; *Maranon del Pinar* – Thicket Pine; the blue wood of *Majagua Azul*, and the *Vijaguara de Fuego* – Flamewood Tree. Known names are *Teka*, or Teak, and Liana, the climbing vine.

Ferns and other exotic flora abound, even the tiny, pink pin-cushion-flowered, Ground Frond, which immediately shrinks away at the touch! Many varieties of Bamboo can be seen, particularly near water, and the prolific *Yagruma*, the tree which competed against the *Palma Real*, way back in history, for the honour of becoming the National Tree. The deciduous statuesque *Yagruma* displays its individuality as its large dark green leaves, like the proverbial cloud are lined on the underside with silver. The Cola-Nut Tree hails from Africa and is the source of many medicines, as is the Eucalyptus Tree, another favourite for the garden.

There are many tropical forest reserves which can be visited throughout the country and tours can be arranged to plantations and jungle areas. Large tracts are now being cleared for re-afforestation and, from some highways, great swathes of hillside seem to be carpeted with tiny saplings which, one day, will grow to twenty metres and probably outlive the passers-by to survive for almost a century!

Fir forests are now being cultivated in the western region as a new experiment with conifers, but some of the precious wood plantations are over twenty years old. On many tours, the guide will point out particular areas of commercially important forest, or regions of botanical interest.

The mountain Olive Shrub and domesticated Fig Tree are a common sight edging hilly gardens. Cactus and Prickly Pear often fence the household plot in drier districts, such as the cattle plains of Camagüey, and the arid crags of the hot, southern provinces. So many trees, shrubs and flowering bushes are grown by the roadside in both towns and cities in the municipalities that the local homesteader prefers to grow plants which furnish the kitchen with their sweet-smelling twigs or the pot, with their aroma.

Herbs and spices

Herbs and spices are found in profusion, so much so that the inevitable sprig of local mint appears in the daily, rum-based mojito or punch. Herbs are used in just about every culinary creation and most homes make their own *salsa*, or piquant sauce from garden-grown spices. A tantalising variation of these highly seasoned concoctions include the firey Ajiguaguao, made from the red chilli, or aji.

Many of the sixty or so fruit and nut, pod and berry varieties which are edible on Cuba, have come from the western coast of Africa. Cacao however, came as *xocoatl*, with Cortez, from the Mayans and Aztecs of Central America. Many seeds, pods, roots and leaves, of herbs and spices grown for flavouring in Cuba, also originate in either South America or Africa.

Mint has a special place in the herb garden, *Hierbabuena* (in Cuba, yerbabuena = good grass), and has been cultivated and chronicled since 1535. Its medicinal value was quickly acknowledged by Spanish colonists. Later, the black community found even more uses for it, and now its common place is a mojito!

Tabasco sauces are also made in Cuba – the local variety in the far south is a challenge to the bravest of gourmets! Many

The Red Ginger is one of the most colourful of spice flowers.

herbs and spices are grown for, or used in, export food-processing.

A selection of well-known spices are often grown on collective plots. Cardomom, Capsicum, Pimento or Allspice, Nutmeg, Bay, Caraway, Coriander, Cinnamon and Cumin flavour stews, sweets and puddings. Pimento is a particularly important cash crop. The famous Copelia, award-winning ice cream, is flavoured with local Vanilla, Pistachio and a dozen different fruits. Herb gardens and even window-boxes are crammed with Parsley, Thyme, Sage, Rosemary, Tarragon, Oregano and Peppermint. More commercially grown are Ginger, Mustard, Black Pepper, Cayenne and Paprika. Many herbs and spices are also grown for export. Several of the rarer seeds, pods, leaves and roots, earlier used in medicines and for their magical properties, originated in Africa. Some of the more strange ingredients for early potions were Altheas, Black Lichen, crushed Cubebs, Dragon Tree sap, Cinchona bark, Fistula cane, Fumitory leaves, Red Sandalwood, Vetiver root and Papaya extract. Deer antler and Whale sperm were also among the unusual additives of ancient herbal recipes.

Still grown, and often seen in local use today, are Comfrey, Linden, Camomile, Pink Mallow and a host of plants and flowers sometimes recognised only as weeds. Foreign foliage is still evident in the secret herb gardens, many of which have been forgotten over the centuries. A few exotic plants are of Chinese origin, some emanate from Arabia, but many came from the dark coast of Calabar. Archaic voodoo and black magic rituals once lent significance to the attributes of Koriko, Owo, Camphor, Egbe and Yerbabuena (the old word for local mint). The root of the Siguaraya, the bark of Jocuma and Mahogany, the Tamarind, and a botanist's bible of flowers and leaves, went into the *ensaladas* and *alcoholaturos* of yesterday's herbalists.

More information can be gleaned from the Casa de las Infusiones, La Botica in Obispo Street, and the House of Brews. A great source of information is El Herbolario on Mercaderes Street, also in Old Havana.

Vegetables

To the gourmet's delight, in Cuba, most vegetables are crispy fresh when served. Very little of the food grown in Cuba is forced, as in Europe or North America, and the excellent soil needs little artificial fertiliser. One can almost describe Cuban vegetables as 'organically' grown.

Eating vegetables in Cuba gives the visitor the opportunity to sample some extraordinary and exotic produce, much of which lends its origin to importation from Africa during the slave trade. Examples of all unusual vegetables can be seen in the fields and gardens throughout the country.

No less the essence of the country than its fruit, are Cuba's many familiar and sometimes unusual forms of vegetables grown either on the large cooperatives or in tiny gardens or roadside allotments. Rice is grown on an expansive commercial scale as a staple diet and maize is a popular

Some of Cuba's fruit and vegetables

crop, often rotating with tobacco as a source of flour and fodder. Potato, carrot, beet, bean and cabbage fields, dominate the landscape in some areas, whilst other major sources of income are onions, scallions, radish, tomatoes, squash, marrows, pumpkin, or *calabaza*. Courgettes, melongene, eddoe, horse radish, okra and cucumber are firm favourites where water and soil conditions are right. Black beans, the type that, with rice, go to make up the Cuban speciality *Moros y Cristianos* 'Moors and Christians' (because they never mix!) are grown everywhere. The chard is a delicacy, as are cauliflowers, spinach, lettuce and celeriac. Celery itself, is seen only occasionally, but always seen are a few turnips, kohl rabi, peppers, aubergines and avocados or *aguacate*, on the local village plot. Manioc, sweet potato, *malanga* or cassava, (a major source of arrowroot), are grown extensively as sources of starch and the more common ingredients of Cuba's main meal. *Platano*, similar to the banana, but more usually grown as a savoury and a

An old print of the Havana vegetable market

vegetable, is seen in most gardens and growing by the wayside as a tropical forest tree.

Hotel chefs and restaurant cooks are only too pleased to discuss the variations of preparation of the more obscure vegetable types such as *taro*, yam, *chayote* and *gourge*. The favoured Juca tuber – often grown in forest areas, its shock of green foliage sprouting from a short, knobbly stem, is commonplace – a good indication of its popularity! Beetroot, sprouts, peas and green beans are a familiar sight, but *callaloo* and millet are less common; so are mushrooms – as they are often grown in caves, well out of the light and the sight of the passer-by! Mushrooms are however becoming an increasingly important crop. Cool, giant avacoado are a common sight on sale in street markets.

Tomato production increases as the demand for the Taoro canneries juice production expands through its thriving export market. Canning factories also produce a large quantity of mixed vegetables, diced turnips and carrot, for example. Ground peanuts, or *mani* are grown for the oil or as a delicacy and can be sometimes found with the universally popular potato crisps – *papita frita*, (sometimes called *saratoga*). Fried banana crisps, commonly seen at table, are known as *mariquita*.

Salads are a particular favourite with traditional Cuban dishes and are often served as a side dish. Everything is excitingly fresh and the country's piquant sauces add zest to Cuba's wide selection of vegetables. Ask for some of the more exotic, tropical varieties – most restaurants will be delighted to help.

Fruit

Cuba is a fruiterer's 'Garden of Eden', growing a wider variety of species than any other Caribbean island. This is the location of the largest citrus groves anywhere in the world. They produce mountains of oranges, or *naranja*, lemon, lime, and grapefruit. Mango and guava plantations spread as far as the eye can see. Much of the fruit is exported as juice by the national Taoro label of canneries. Taoro also bottle more than 500 tonnes of strawberries annually. Guava is either eaten raw, made into juice or a jelly, a paste, or the favourite, marmalade. The guava is also used as flavouring for a variety of ices, sweets and drinks but, from its tiny cousin, which grows only in the far west of the island, the choice, *guayabita* brandy is distilled.

The mango is a roadside companion, wherever one travels there is always a wild,

hillside variety nearby or the juicy fruit will tempt from a homestead's garden. Together with the papaya, or paw paw, (*fruta bomba* in the west), and banana (*platano*) the mango is a traditional garden tree for its shade, the beautiful birds and butterflies it attracts, and naturally, its incomparable fruit. A very sweet, miniature

Part of the expanding agricultural trend, the Cacao industry is becoming an important exporter. Before Columbus took samples back to Spain in 1502, the Indians were already imbibing the, now popular, drink.

Cuba is a veritable 'spice island'.

version grows in Cuba's southern provinces.

Fields of pineapple or *piña*, can be seen in more arid regions, across sweeping hillsides or in orderly rows stretching out to the horizon. This also is either eaten fresh, juiced, or canned, for local and export consumption, by the famed ZunZun enterprise. Cool, watery melons are carefully nurtured in backyards or in especially tended fields along with the refreshing, multi-seeded pomegranate, or *granada*. Wide selections of melons and citrus fruits are always available at the local free-markets – often the patient results of a local farmer's efforts, always deliciously fresh.

A multitude of exotic fruits, both strange and rare, all thrive in the island's amicable climate. Its rich soil and sunny environment brings the *nispero*, or *zapote* and *chamoney* to fruition, it ripens the exceptional breadfruit and star apple, the furry, *mamey colorado*, the *chirimoya*, the jakfruit and the custard apple. *Caimito* and *christophene* are almost as common as soursop, the mountain olive, known locally as plum, and the fig. Even more widespread are the much better-known nectarine, mandarin and tangerine, all cultivated on a wide scale in most provinces. Most unusual of all Cuba's fruits is probably the curious *marañon* (cashew apple) with its red-orange, cylindrical-shaped fruit terminating in a light brown seed which grows outside the fruit. The delicious, huge, prickly *guanabana*, or *anon*, is a rare delight, as is the passion fruit which is now grown as much for the variety of drinks and

Pineapples are an important cash crop.

flavouring uses as a raw fruit source. The unusual *canitel*, with its egg-like consistency, is known in other Caribbean islands as *akee*.

Grapes are now being grown in several selected areas of the south and west and wine will soon be the result of cautious cultivation. Nutmeg is a well-known source of flavouring and can be fermented into a form of brandy. Many exotic liqueurs are made from Cuba's varied fruits but the Sea

Grape, wild and common along the island's shoreline, is sadly useless, as is the tempting plumpness of the gourd (calabash), or *guida*. In some dry areas the delicately refreshing Prickly Pear can often be found growing wild.

Each of Cuba's multitude of tropical fruits is a discovery in itself and each deserves a tasting even if it does have the withered, prune-like appearance of the passion fruit, the dark, green-brown, tough-stalked solidity of the *chirimoya* or the brown skin and grainy texture of the *zapote* or *sapodilla*. The latex obtained from *sapodilla* is used in making *chicle* or chewing gum – an unusual gift discovered by early Indian inhabitants. If the fruit is a novelty as the lychee-like *poma rosa*, an unexpected delight such as the giant, green-black skin and pure white fruit of the *guanabana*, or it has the ever-tropical charm of the coconut, all Cuba's taste is there, in the warm, refreshing, smooth tanginess of its fruits.

Orchids are to be found in many parts of the country but Soroa botanical gardens claim a total of 700 varieties.

Flowers

Agricultural activity and land usage has not decimated the wild, natural beauty of this luxuriant, green country. Cuba is still covered by large forested and wooded outcrops which make up twenty per cent of the land surface. Where the original grandeur of the countryside may have bent

Parts of Cuba are particularly dry and arid, desert-like conditions are ideal for many species of cactus.

Frangipani

Petrea

to the demands of farmers and horti-culturalists, the authorities have been quick to preserve indigenous plants, flowers, trees and it unique fauna. Flowers bloom prolifically everywhere, and almost throughout the year. More than 8000 different varieties of flora abound, from the scarce orchids like the *Flor San Pedro*, to the hedgerow Hibiscus and abundant African Golden Trumpet.

The magical reds, blues, yellows and blacks of the rare *Ave del Pariso* Orchid are only matched by the pure white delicacy of Cuba's national flower, the *Mariposa*, or Butterfly Flower. A large bell-shape, the *Ipomoea*, similar to Morning Glory, is set off in its pink majesty by the stunning blaze of Blue Rosewood or Jacaranda. Congea climb the walls of colonial gardens with orange, magenta, mauve and crimson Bougainvillea showering an abundance of blooms over Poinsettia, Anthurium and Oleander. Colour is rife everywhere, among the myriad green hues of hillsides and river valleys, on the roadsides and along high-way embankments. Colonia and Azalea, Tulipano and the orange *Jubia d'Oro*, are often used to flank the thoroughfares and Jasmine, Indian Goldenrain or Gladioli spears, march down highway reservations. The vast groves of Lemon, Orange and Grapefruit add their own heady scent and colourful blossom to the overall scenery.

Trees afford great umbrellas of colour on street corners or on deserted mountain tracks. The huge, lily-like bloom of the

Yagruma, Flame Trees and African Tulip Trees provide shade from the heat of the noon sun. Frangipani also advertise their aroma with massive star-shaped flowers. The tiny-flowering Jerusalem Thorn often has competition in wild countryside with fencing posts, cut from the Pinon, or Coral Tree, which suddenly burst into bright pink efflorescence. Blossoming Hydrangea and Royal Poinciana are occasionally seen growing as wild as are the brightly flower-ing Cactus of more desert provinces. In the mountains, even the coffee flower matches the bursting colour of the Flamboyant trees. Gold Cup, Ohese and Crimson Cat's Tails are common among exotic grasses. Tropical sedges mingle with a variety of Dwarf Palm, a usual backdrop to the bright Rose of China or the Peacock Flower.

By the coast, the scenery is no less colourful with wild blossom. Water Flags mix sulphur yellow with the brown brush of the Bulrush and palm, or the Casuarina trees which shade delicately-flowering pondside reeds. Water Hyacinth and Lily pads with giant, brightly coloured blooms, are over-shadowed by *Uvachaletta*, the Button Tree, shoreline Wild Almond, and four varieties of Mangrove bough. In lake-side regions there are a multitude of delicate ferns and the tiny, pink-blossomed, shrinking, 'Shy Girl' plant. Drooping over these, in water meadows, the Coral Plant or *Lagrimas de Cupido* (Cupid's Tears), are commonly spots of brilliant scarlet in flat, green meadows.

CHAPTER 5

Travelling Tips

'Once again I feel below my heels the ribs of Rocinante. I'm on my way again, with my shield on my arm.'

ERNESTO 'Che' GUEVARA in a farewell letter to his parents

General information

Currency

The Cuban monetary unit is the peso (CUP), divided into 100 centavos. Centavos are minted in one, two, five, ten, twenty and fifty pieces. Prices are indicated only in Cuban pesos and its symbol resembles that of the dollar sign. Cuban currency is not valid in duty-free or tourist shops and many resort activities are priced in foreign currency.

Most foreign currency is accepted and all official and internationally recognised traveller's cheques, Access, Eurocard, Visa and Mastercard can be used. The payee's name or the date should *not* be entered on cheques.

A currency on a parallel with the US dollar has been created by the National Bank of Cuba in conjunction with the National Institute of Tourism. It consists of token coins in denominations of five, ten, twenty-five and fifty cents. Exchange certificates of 1, 5, 10, 20 and 50 pesos are

73

also available. The tourist coinage is often retained as a souvenir because of its attractive design, but it may be exchanged for its equivalent in US dollars on leaving Cuba. The foreign currency most acceptable, is the US dollar.

When money is changed into local currency – only at airport, bank, hotel or accredited exchange bureau, a white slip is issued. The slip is a record of purchases and should be retained and produced when required. On leaving the country and reconverting local money to foreign currency this slip must be presented.

About twenty convertible currencies, traveller's cheques and most credit cards are accepted on the island and Exchange Certificates bridge the gap between the peso and dollar. Convertible currency may be used in any of the authorised 403 tourist establishments in Cuba.

It is prohibited to make currency transactions with Cuban nationals. It is also prohibited to import or export Cuban currency, but any foreign currency may be imported. A declaration should be made, on entering Cuba, of the amount of foreign currency brought in – this also applies to personal belongings such as cameras, jewellery, radios, or sporting equipment.

The authorities must be notified of any loss of money, or of traveller's cheques, and Cubatur representatives, or travel guides will assist in the correct procedures for recovering the loss, or obtaining emergency funds. Cubatur should immediately be notified of any other loss, such as a passport loss, as should the relevant Embassy officials. Crime in Cuba is virtually unheard of, but the usual precautions should be taken with money and valuables.

Much of the visitor's main outgoings, meals, tours, etc will have been paid for in advance when making the travel arrangements, but incidentals like light refreshments, souvenirs, etc should be purchased in local or, in the resort areas, in foreign currency.

Shopping

Tourist – INTUR shops, or *Tienda*, are to be found in most of the larger hotels and resort areas around Cuba. They are not just souvenir shops but often act as a general store for most visitors' requirements from medication and personal necessities, to food and drink, books and records. There are three *Diplotienda* superstores in Cuba – two in the Miramar district of Havana, like 'La Maison' with an annex which specialises in gadgets, cameras and electrical equipment. Another is in Santiago de Cuba. These superstores stock everything from clothes to cosmetics, from children's toys to cigars.

Typical souvenirs are political posters, pictures, records, carvings, shell and horn ornaments, dolls in local costume,

This couple admires one of Cuba's more exotic souvenirs.

guayabera shirts, pokerwork items, coconut-shell work, leatherwork, bamboo and raffia work, clay and earthenware pottery, paintings and prints, the colourful Cuban stamps, straw or palm-work fans and hats, taxidermy in the shape of small alligators and turtles, mounted butterflies, jewellery, rum and cigars. In Havana the most popular shop for mementoes is the Palace of Arts and Crafts at 64 Cuba Street, Old Havana. The Lina Bazaar and Antique Bazaar are also good browsing spots as are the many galleries.

Most shops in the cities and towns open at 12.30 in the afternoon and close at 7.30 in the evening, but the *Diplotiendas* are open from 9.30 in the morning until 6 pm. In the hotels the *Tiendas* usually open at 8.30 in the morning and close at 10 pm From 5 pm and 10 pm on Saturday nights the plaza in Cathedral Square, Havana, becomes a marketplace for a variety of goods.

Local shopping precincts are similar to those of most towns and cities worldwide but the variety of goods available may not particularly appeal to the foreigner's tastes. The local system of coupons and rationing of selected items may seem unfamiliar but it ensures that every Cuban gets ample quotas of food, clothing and luxuries. Freeshops, found in country and town, usually selling agricultural produce, are becoming popular. In local markets one can also find the famous 'Regil' brand of coffee in small packs – excellent as souvenirs.

Time and important dates

Cuba is aligned to Eastern Standard Time in winter and Daylight Saving Time in summer. The country is five hours behind Greenwich Mean Time. National Holidays include New Year's Day, Liberation Day or the Anniversay of the Triumph of the Revolution – January 1; Labour Day or

International Worker's Day – May 1; Anniversary of the Moncada Attack or National Rebellion Day celebrated on July 25, 26, 27; and the Anniversary of the 1868 Revolution – October 10. Other important dates in the Cuban calendar are the Day of Victory – January 2; Birthday of José Marti – January 28; Beginning of 1895 Revolution – February 24; Anniversary of attack on the Presidential Palace – March 13; Bay of Pigs Victory – April 19; Martyrs of the Revolution Day – July 30; Anniversary of the death of Ernesto 'Che' Guevara – October 8; Day of Mourning for the 8 medical students shot during independence struggle November 27; and *Granma* yacht landing Anniversary – December 2.

For three weekends in July, leading up to the holidays of July 25, 26 and 27, carnival time animates the cities and towns across Cuba. The Havana and Santiago de Cuba celebrations, held at the end of 'zafra', or sugar harvest, are among the most spectacular carnivals in the world and Cubatur, or the Cultural Houses, will advise on details of events, etc. In January and February carnivals take place in the beach resort of Varadero and fiestas are widespread throughout the year in the country's regional and rural areas. A typical town fiesta is the *Parrandas of Remedios* in Villa Clara Province. The fiesta, held in July, combines carnival with unique local rituals. Offices in Cuba close on National Holidays and the rest of the year the office hours are from 8 in the morning until 5 pm.

Measures

The metric system operates in Cuba, although the occasional American or old Spanish units of weights and measures may be encountered. The UN system of Standard International Units is being adopted. Some old units of length which may be met are the *pulgada* = 1 inch (2.54 cm) and the *cordel* = 22.26 yards (20.35 metres). In area the square cordel may be found, the *hectarea* = 2.4 acres = 1 hectare or the *caballeria* (an ancient measure of ground whose land could, in old Spanish times, support a mounted soldier and his family) equal to 324 square cordels. Unfamiliar measures of capacity include *botella, galon, garrafon, bocoy* and *lata*. In weight the *onza* – about one ounce, the *libra* – about one pound, the *arroba, quintal, saco* (a coffee measurement) and the *tonelados* may be encountered.

Power

In domestic use the electricity supply is 110 volts (60 Hz. AC); general use is 110 volts (60 cycles) and some electric shaver outlets can be 220 – 240 volts. Two-pin plugs of the flat-pin type are in use and screw cap light fittings are used. Some hotels like the Havana Libre Hotel use the continental two-pin round plug sockets. A small transformer can be useful for hair-dryers, razors, etc.

Equipment

It is advisable for foreigners travelling in Cuba to bring a small Spanish dictionary – and carry it with you! Stationery requirements, a small note pad, envelopes, etc are useful, and pack a few extra ballpoint pens – although most hotel shops stock a good selection of writing necessities. Only at the top hotels can typewriters be hired and visitors with tape recorders should bring ample tapes.

At least one replacement battery should be brought for all battery-operated appliances – remember, many cameras require the power from a battery, as do flash units. The humidity can often affect the performance of batteries, and cleaning cloths for camera lenses are essential. Take great care with film also because of the climate and, both entering the country and leaving Cuba, carry all exposed and unexposed film in hand luggage, and request that it should be examined at any airport – this means world-wide – by hand and not by being put through the X-Ray machines. Recording tape should also be carried in hand luggage. The conventional 35 mm film is generally available in duty-free and tourist shops in the main hotels, but it is wise to bring sufficient for your visit – and some more! Also bring enough flash bulbs, and do not forget filters – a skylight filter is a wise addition, as is any other photographic equipment, such as tripod etc.

Useful hints

Sunbathers or not, bring ample suntan lotion as some of the smaller resort shops can run low on supplies. Also check that you have the best screening factor for **your** skin as the sun's rays in Cuba, together with the reflection from the water, can be deceptive and can lead to severe burns. Remember, suntan lotion with a filter factor of 5 means you can stay out in the sun 5 times longer than normal. Sun glasses are necessary, as are your favourite cosmetics which may not be available in Cuba. Before leaving for Cuba it is advisable, if insect repellant is required, to find one with at least 80% *diethyl-toluamide* or DEET, these are the most effective.

Bring a few of the little wire, freezer pack seals, as the Cubatur polythene bags, found in most hotel bathrooms, are useful receptacles for small jars, bottles or tubes of toothpaste, etc with leaky tops! It is a good idea to bring your own favourite shampoo, toothpaste or soap and sufficient razor blades for the wet shaver. A small nail brush is very useful, and don't forget a bottle opener! Medications should be packed as should any special requirements for children. The following checklist may also be useful:

Documents Traveller's cheques, currency, passport, visas, tickets, insurance policies, cheque book, cheque card, credit cards, driving licence, maps and schedules, booking and addresses, labels, letters of introduction, vaccination certificates, dictionary or phrase book. As the flight from Europe takes around 9 hours, a book for reading on the aircraft is a handy extra.

Equipment Photographic equipment, binoculars, tape recorder, travelling iron, small torch and Swiss Army-style pocket-knife.

Clothes Beachwear, jacket, slacks, shirts, blouses, sandals, shorts, underwear, socks, footwear, ties, T-shirts, nightwear, dresses, jewellery, handkerchiefs, small umbrella and something warm if returning to a cold climate! A plastic mackintosh can be useful during sudden squalls between June and October.

Accessories Sunglasses, clothes brush, clock, shaver, razor and blades, nail brush, adaptor, toothbrush, toothpaste, soap, scissors, first aid items, brush, comb, needle and thread, bottle or tin opener, holdall (an extra, small folding grip can be useful), towels, lotions (remember, pressurised containers should not be taken in the aircraft), hair dryer, shoe-shine kit, nail-file,

In addition to snapping the sights, why not have your own picture taken by one of Havana's street photographers?

make-up, keys, magnifying glass for maps.
Personal Diary, medicines, children's requirements, female essentials, tissues, wallet, handbag, pens and pencils, address book, name and address of next of kin, watch, hats, handkerchiefs, creams, keys, etc; dry-cleaning fluid, shoe whitener, smoking requirements, any sporting gear like rod, raquet or gun (with valid permit). If you might travel on boats, sea sickness pills are recommended.

Photography

Photographs may be taken anywhere in Cuba except at railheads, airports, in military zones, inside museums and in other specifically prohibited areas. Remember to carry exposed film in hand luggage on exit from Cuba. Whilst in Cuba, try to keep all film in a cool place. It is courteous to ask first when taking a photograph of an individual or a group. Military personnel should not be photographed in uniform. On tours the guide will advise on points of interest and photogenic areas. Most film can be processed in Havana.

Water

The water in Cuba is perfectly safe to drink but ensure the tap is for filtered water. Many travellers however, prefer to keep to the bottled water which is usually in plentiful supply. Fruit from the trees, or raw vegetables should always be washed before eating.

Other useful information

There are no taxes in Cuba, either for goods purchased in the tourist shops, in hotels, or at the airports.

Gambling is expressly forbidden in Cuba and tipping is frowned upon although little gestures are politely received.

All countries, except the US, have diplomatic representation in Havana. The Swiss Embassy houses the US Interests Section. Cubatur will provide all the information necessary on the address and telephone number of individuals' diplomatic embassies or consulates.

Visas

Citizens of Italy, France, Switzerland, Finland and most East European countries need a valid passport and visa. Most travellers from other countries can obtain a simple tourist card from the relevant Cuban consulate or through travel agents or tour operators. Business visitors need full visas for entry into Cuba. A passport is always needed.

Health on holiday

No special regulations apply to travellers, unless arriving from an area where Cholera or Yellow Fever is prevelant. In Cuba, Yellow Fever, Malaria, Diphtheria and Poliomyelitis have been eradicated and the country has one of the highest health indices in the world. The health service runs a preventive curative scheme.

All medical services are free. First aid and emergency care is free to visitors and no charge is made for a doctor's first visit. Medicine is costed at the local rate. Dental treatment is also free. Most medicines are available in Cuba and nowhere is far from the *Cruz Roja* – Red Cross – or a polyclinic.

It is advisable to take the usual precautions when travelling. The accepted medicines for gastroenteritis, aspirin, insecticide, sun cream, elastic plaster, antiseptic cream and children's medicines are the wise items to pack. Mosquito repellent is essential in some areas. Women should pack personal requirements. Special individual medicines should not be forgotten.

Climate and dress

Throughout the two seasons Cuba's subtropical climate maintains a pleasant average temperature of 25°C (77°F). However, during the summer months – May to September – temperatures can reach 32°C (90°F) and even more in the south-east. During the summer, the weather can become quite humid with the occasional tropical rain giving an average of 1400 mm (55 inches) precipitation. The hurricane season occurs around October. The island is located at the source of the Gulf Stream and is wafted, throughout most months, by the balmy North-East Trade Winds.

La Seca is the dry season, from November to early May. Temperatures during this period can decrease to around 21°C (70°F). Sea temperatures rarely fall below 24°C (75°F), although the north coast, washed by the temperate waters of the Atlantic Ocean's Gulf Stream, can be cooler at times. Cuba experiences an average eight hours of sunshine per day and, on the Atlantic coast, has an average 8.5 days with rain per month. This is considerably less on the hotter, southern coast. Some torrential rain from cyclones, and the tail of hurricanes, can cause extensive flooding towards the latter part of summer and early autumn.

Dress is casual during the day and cotton clothes are the most comfortable, but a travelling iron is an invaluable asset as laundry facilities are not always available. Easily washable clothes are most convenient. Open-neck shirts or blouses are more satisfactory for casual wear. In the cities, and for special occasions, it is accepted practice to dress for dinner or for visiting nightclubs. Beach clothes and a large beach towel are essential. It should be remembered that revealing clothes worn in the streets, apart from resort areas, can attract disapproval and those who wish to be more revealing should be most cautious about their choice of location! Beach shoes are particularly useful protection when walking on hot sand, or paving, or when climbing or walking on the coral reefs. Canvas shoes or sportswear are ideal, as are sandals for the town. A locally-made palm-leaf or straw hat will give shade from the sun's powerful rays.

Sunglasses should not be forgotten. A travel umbrella, or plastic mackintosh is often useful during the summer shower period and a jacket or ladies wrap may be required on cool evenings. For both men and women jeans, or light slacks, are almost the national dress and shorts, or a wrap, are useful alternatives. The *Guayabera*, a light, colourful, cotton shirt/jacket is the traditional men's costume. With embroidery, tucks and buttons, it has also been adopted by Cuban women and is acceptable wear for any occasion. *Guayabera* are available everywhere and are an inexpensive, practical purchase. The origin of the *Guayabera* is said to be eighteenth-century and the garment supposedly evolved from the lightweight, loose shirts, peddled by an Andalusian tailor in the ancient village of Yayabo, Sancti Spiritus Province. The name, *Guayabera* allegedly derives from that of the Yayabo River. Also the name *guayabas* is given to the guavas found locally and kept as a snack in the four pockets of the long, peasant worker's shirt. It became a symbol of patriotism during the Independence War and, worn together with the woven straw or plaited palm-leaf broad-rimmed hat, can truly be called the Cuban national costume.

Food and dining out

In Cuba almost all food is fresh. This, and the emphasis on dairy produce, chicken and ham, are immediately noticeable when eating out in the towns. In resort areas or tourist hotels the introduction of various foreign cuisines has transformed the traditional Cuban menu, but local cuisine remains the prime attraction. There are 7 categories of bars and restaurants.

In outlying districts, or in country villages, generally only fresh local food is available apart from the occasional tinned produce. The further south in the country one journeys the more *criollo* or creole-style, the food becomes, as the taste is influenced by the African preference. Local

swordfish steak in batter. *Bacan* is minced pork and bananas, boiled in banana leaves. *Garbanzo*, another delicacy, is bean soup, rice, fried plantain, yucca and roast pork. *Sopa marinero* is Cuba's bouillabaisse and a corner shop favourite is *Churros*, deep-fried dough rings.

Try tasting some of the many exotic, fresh Cuban vegetables and delicious home-made cheeses. Many local dishes have a creole flavour, although the food is not generally as spicy or as hot as one would first expect. In some cases, when an extra tang is required, ask for *salsa picante* or piquant sauce, but treat it reverently! Side salads are common; *Ensalada mixta* speaks for itself, but try *Ensalada de chayote* or *Ensalada de pepinos y col* – cabbage and cucumber salad. Most meals start with either fresh fruit – pineapple or papaya

dishes include the mixture of black beans, local rice and spices called *Moros y Cristianos* – Moors and Christians – a creation that can almost be called the national dish. Sea foods and fish are always excellent, also lobster, or crab, in season. Black bean soup is a speciality, as is *Ajiaco*, a thick vegetable soup made with juca, turnip, carrot, malanga and herbs. *Arroz con pollo*, or chicken and rice, is a favourite, like *cerdo asado con frijoles negros* – roast pork on a bed of black beans. *Piccadillo* is made from beef, onion, chilli, black pepper, spices and tomato. *Sofrito* is made from onion, rice, pepper and garlic, and *Bistec de palomilla empanado* is a fillet of shoulder steak cooked in a pie crust.

Unusual foods include frog's legs, crocodile steak, shark, quail and conch. Other delights are *Bistec de Caguama* – turtle steak on a bed of rice and red beans; *Bistec Uruguayo* – a delicious pocket of steak, stuffed with ham and cheese, in a crispy pastry jacket like a poor man's carpet-bag steak; or *Filete de emporador rebozado* –

(*fruta bomba* in Havana), fresh fruit juice – *naranja*, or orange; *guayaba*, or guava; and *jugo toronjas*, or grapefruit juice. An especially favourite aperitif is *Coctel de ostiones* – small, raw oysters in salty tomato juice with piquant spices – not everyone's favourite, but a real national Cuban delicacy.

Cubans are renowned for their imagination when it comes to sweets and puddings. *Tatianoff* is a particularly tasty chocolate cake with lashings of cream. The coconut is a base for many sweet dishes such as *Coco Quemado*, a coconut pudding; *Coco Rallado y queso* is grated coconut with cheese in syrup; or there is caramalised plantain covered in grated coconut. Egg custard, créme caramel, are known as '*flan*'. Guava jelly and piquant cream cheese in a bun is called '*pastelito de guayaba*'. *Brazo gitano* is a custard-filled roll. *Cucurucho* is a mixture of coconut fruits and cocoa pressed into a cone shape by wrapping tight in banana leaves – a rare treat! Most famous, and available everywhere in Cuba, is the prize-winning ice-cream called *helado Coppelia*. Internationally regarded, the delicacy comes in a myriad of flavours from pistachio and almond to pineapple or passion fruit. Real nuts and chunks of the fruit are used in the ice-cream which can be bought in the streets anywhere at *Coppelia*, or *Coppelita* (little Coppelia) stalls, or from ice-cream vans in the countryside. Fresh fruit is one of the inevitable indulgences after one of Cuba's famous sweets.

Breakfasts are not so imaginative, but in the resorts and at hotels, the traditional bacon and eggs, scrambled eggs or omelettes (*tortillas*) can be served with toast (*tostada*) and marmalade (*mermelada*), generally guava paste. Ham or beefburgers have become popular in Cuba at any meal and, as there are not many hamburger bars in the cities or resorts, and pizza is competing as a fast food, with pizzerias everywhere. There are self-service buffets in most hotels. *Pio Pio*, fried chicken, and *Pio Cuac*, fried duckling, have become firm favourites in the fast food business and at cafés, the thick sandwich – *bocadillo* – often makes a full meal! Snacks, sometimes available at street corner shops, are known as *tamales*.

It is impossible, when on the subject of food, or indeed any Cuban topic to omit the local life-blood – coffee or café. Cubans drink vast quantities of the thick, strong, very sweet refreshing brew. Cuban coffee is of excellent quality and comparable to that of Jamaica's Blue Mountain variety or the Columbian blends. On every corner, on almost every main street in the country, there are cafeterias selling non-stop coffee in tiny cuplettes. It is usually a dark, boiling, syrupy liquid which has a

The Floridita Restaurant

pep-up effect on Cuba's *Mucho calor* or scorching-hot days. Every meal ends with Cuban coffee, but American coffee, tea, or coffee with milk (*cafe con leche*), can be ordered in most large hotels and at most tourist resorts. Ideally the Cuban coffee should be supplemented, after a meal, with an aromatic Cuban cigar.

Cubans enjoy their food and are no strangers to making a meal of dining out! At weekends and in the evenings the whole family will make an excursion of eating out at restaurants or at favoured hotels. Evening meals generally start quite late and, although service is good in most restaurants, a meal can easily last two to three hours. Food is consumed in a leisurely fashion with long smoking breaks between courses. Cuban people love to be seen dining out and will often queue for hours waiting for a free table at a favourite restaurant.

It is always advisable to book in advance at popular restaurants, or ask the hotel reception, or Cubatur guide to arrange seating. Visitors are often surprised at how inexpensive meals are, even at the top restaurants in the country. Tipping is not expected, but a kind word or compliment to the server or chef, is appreciated. Bills in restaurants and hotels are paid in foreign currency.

Many package tours will have included meals in the price of the visit and, if excursions are booked into the itinerary, eating arrangements will have been organised by the travel agent, or Cubatur representative, en route. Extras at table, or aperitifs, are not generally included in package tour costings. Meal plans often include three meals per day, but this is for the individual to check. A Spanish-English dictionary can be very useful at table, as ordering can be difficult, and entire meal orders are usually taken in advance. Menus are often printed only in Spanish.

Many leading restaurants are not purely places where one can enjoy good food, drink and company. A pianist, guitarist and groups of troubadors are often on hand to render traditional and modern accompaniments to your meal. Decorations are often priceless antiques, as at Havana's

Restaurants are constructed in a variety of styles including this classic rustic complex designed along Indian lines.

1830 restaurant with its china treasures, or the 1646 eating place, bedecked with cannon, muskets, swords and suits of armour. Often the surroundings can distract from the culinary attractions with massive, carved, beamed ceilings, opulent paintings and rare statues. Visiting Cuba's varied restaurants can be an excercise in antique-spotting as much as an indulgence in some of the Caribbean's most delicious cookery.

Drinks

The country of Cuba is a veritable cocktail of tastes. Its bounteous gifts of fruits, and its copious supply of sugar makes the island a leader in rum-based beverages. During the 1920s, 30s, and 40s, Havana was the centre of cocktail ingenuity. An essential ingredient of many of the island's famous cocktails is cola – now locally produced – *Tropicola*. The names given to the barmen's myriad inventions, were as eloquent and as colourful as their many ingredients. Synonymous with Cuba, Havana and Hemingway, are the *mojito* and *daiquiri*.

The aromatic *mojito* is created with a teaspoonful of sugar poured over cracked ice, stirred with a quarter ounce of lime

juice. A sprig of Cuban mint is added and gently crushed onto the ice and the mixture blended with two ounces of Light Dry Havana Club rum. The glass should be topped up with soda water, two drops of Angostura bitters added and the mixture stirred with two short drinking straws. The frosted *daiquiri* has the same basic ingredients, but with a quarter of an ounce more lime and extra, crushed, ice. All the ingredients are blended without the mint

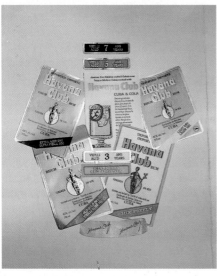

or Angostura, then poured into a cocktail glass, where the drink should stand like a miniature ice mountain.

Today's Cuban drink is the *Cuba libre* – its most famous tipple. Add the juice of half a lemon to two or three ice cubes, a slice of lemon peel and two ounces of Light, Dry Havana Club rum. Top up the glass with Tropicola and stir well. A Rum Collins' ingredients are, one and a half ounces of Light Dry Havana Club rum with a tablespoon of sugar, a half ounce of lemon juice, topped up with soda water and a slice of lemon. More exotic is the Tropical Paradise – one teaspoonful of sugar, an egg white, a half ounce of orange juice and the same of lemon juice, a half ounce of Light Dry Havana Club and two drops of grenadine, shaken in a cocktail shaker, poured into a glass frosted with fine sugar. For a surprise, ask for the ever-popular *Mulata* or *Cubanito*!

A total of nine varieties of rum are produced for export and ten types are made for the domestic market. Liquor, other than rum, is quite expensive, but, at most large hotels and resorts, the selection is international. The Cuban barmen are always delighted to demonstrate that they have not lost their touch since those days earlier in the century, when they earned the tag of being the greatest barmen in the world! Most bars carry a variety of fruit juices, soda and soft drinks plus the universal coconut milk – always kept frozen.

Wine is available in most hotel and resort restaurants. Cuba is now producing a very small quantity of domestic wine but most is imported from the USSR, Bulgaria, Spain, Portugal and Algeria. The quality of imported wines is generally excellent. Good Russian vodka is also imported – an interesting basis for many cocktails.

Several beers are imported and can be tried at many good restaurants. The standard is higher than most of the domestic beers, which range in strength from 8° – 18°. Beer is called *cerveza* in Cuba, rum is known as *ron* and wine as *vino*. There are breweries in most major towns and a new, 24 reactor plant has opened in Camagüey, which is to produce a new beer called *Tinimas*. A variety of labels are produced in Cuba, the most common variety has no label, is universal, a light colour and not very strong. Labels include *Polar*, a favourite, and often the first Cuban beer a visitor will taste as it is the brand served on Cubana, the national airline. Other brews include *Hatuey* – in several strengths, *Tropical Negra* and *Lobo*

Mixing any drink from the daiquiri to a rainbow cocktail comes as second nature to the barman whose country created the art.

– a very dark, malty beer, *Cristal* beer, *La Modelo* and *Manacas* beers.

Most restaurants, bars and some cafeterias serve beer in bottles but, in more rural districts, and in some towns further from the capital, beer can be bought from roadside dispensers in paper cups as in the seafront park, Havana, and the *Malecon* in Cienfuegos. A typical favourite among Cuban men is a mixture of the light, *ligero* (lager-like) beer and canned or bottled tomato juice.

Also sold at high street corner shops and roadside stalls, is *guarapo* – freshly pressed sugar cane juice, which is very sweet, but most refreshing when served ice-cold. Other drinks vended on the streets include tea or *chia*, and *piña fria*, an iced drink made with pineapple essence and often sold at bus stations from a wheeled handcart, like orange, lemon and lime crushes. Ice-cream, or *helado* is often dispensed in the same way.

Probably Cuba's most famous drink, apart from the sugar cane derived rum, is coffee, now grown quite extensively, particularly in the southern mountains. Cuban coffee, in the tiny cuplettes, is always available from bars or roadside stalls. It is often sipped with ice water. Cacao is also grown and, as a supplement to the celebrated rum, there is always the refreshing milk of the inevitable coconut. Mix this with Cuba's excellent rum to produce the popular *Sahoco*.

Both the Baobab and the Tamarind are used locally in the preparation of a lemonade-like drink. The dark orange, sticky pith of the Tamarind pod, when soaked for days in water and sugar, makes a delightful and efficacious preparation. Similarly, the hard seedpod of the Baobab, before ripening, can provide an interesting sherbet-like dip by the addition of water, or a tartaric-flavoured drink with water and sugar. Both of these recipes and many of the island's now common plants and trees, nuts and fruit, emanate from Africa.

Further information on unusual natural drinks can be obtained at La Casa del

Agua, La Casa de los Infusiones – House of Brews – both in Old Havana.

Entertainments

Cuba will never relinquish its hold on the title 'the liveliest island in the Caribbean'. Havana still boasts the most lavish and exciting show under the stars and the

the Rumba Saturday, a special afternoon of folkloric dance. A small, popular club is the Bandoneon Tango Corner and, just outside Havana, at the East Beaches, there are the cabarets of the Atlantic Hotel, Guaicanamar, Guanabo Club, Habana Club, Pinomar and the Rincon Azul. At Varadero, in Matanzas there are four discotheques and the famous 'Cubanita' show at the International Hotel. Also on the beach resort strip are the cabarets of the Caballito

flamboyance of the Cuban peoples is matched only by the exuberance of the island's resorts, clubs and spectacles.

Many of the large hotels incorporate their own shows like that of the Copa Room in Havana's Riviera, The Parisien Cabaret at the palatial 1920s Nacional Hotel, the Caribe's two shows at the Havana Libre Hotel and the Salon Rojo cabaret at Havana's Capri Hotel.

There are nine theatres and 166 cinemas in the capital. Also held in the capital are

de Coral, in the amphitheatre, the Cueva del Pirata, Eclipse and El Legendario Tavern.

In Pinar del Rio, the Rumayor has a cabaret show and two discotheques and in Viñales Valley there are two other discos. Cabaret nights are held at most hotels in almost every resort. Special entertainment visits to farms, Afro-Cuban nights and barbecues are regular features at most beach resorts, many of which offer visits to Havana's highspots.

Possibly the most famous show on earth is Havana's Tropicana. It is not known as 'Paradise under the Stars' for nothing! For around five dollars cabaret-goers are embraced in a wonderworld of light and colour, sound and movement. Meals are served and a drink is often inclusive. The whole show is generally held in the open air. Tier upon tier of performers seem to reach to the stars all around the tables and the auditorium seats 1500. The Panorámico Restaurant seats 160. Set in nearly 10 acres, the Tropicana nightclub and its magnificent surroundings is one of the world's greatest spectacles.

In the island's second city, Santiago de Cuba, there are two main theatres and two leading cinemas. Santiago also has several nightclubs and cabarets. These include the San Pedro del Mar, Las Americas and El Rancho.

Sporting events, baseball matches and

Whether an impromptu 'guajira' from a trova group or the dazzling spectacle of Havana's Tropicana – 'paradise under the stars' – Cuba is likely to burst into song at the drop of a straw hat!

national or local rodeos are among the typical Cuban entertainments. Boxing matches and soccer attract large crowds, but the highlights of any town or city are the carnaváls.

Carnaval

Towards the end of July, at the time of the great sugar harvest, or zafra, Cuba explodes into animated celebration. This is the time of *Carnaval*, (spelled the Spanish way). Every town and village prepares months in advance for the annual event which occurs the three weekends up to the culmination of holidays on 25, 26 and 27 July. Fantastic costumes, decorations and floats are prepared, traditional and modern music is rehearsed for the advent of local dances, parades and fiestas.

Cuba glories in the presentation of Latin America's most spectacular carnivals. These take place in the two main cities of Havana and Santiago de Cuba. No expense is spared in order that the performers (and spectators!) are dressed in the most flamboyant costumes and each group, society, club and even street, designs and festoons the most gaudy and imaginative of floats.

Many thousands of hours of patience goes into creating the most spectacular costumes.

Some bizarre costumes and images are used at Carnaval

Children and adults, even the very old, learn, practise and teach the dances which have been handed down from the days of early slavery during Spanish colonialism. Both music and dance at these celebrations can be traced as far as the native African coasts of Guinea and Calabar. Many have merged with ancient religious festivals and magical rites.

From the enchanted hour that carnaval begins, cities become a melée as people dressed in vividly elaborate costumes throng the streets, horns and trumpets,

Santiago de Cuba has a museum tracing the history of Carnaval

stringed instruments and drums burst forth in a cacophony of frenzied, sensual and ecstatic rhythm. On street corners pork and goat barbecues, beer, sweetmeats and candies are distributed and decorations, firecrackers, whistles and flutes are on sale.

The most exuberant and erotic, and certainly the oldest carnival is the 18th century version held for five days and nights in Santiago de Cuba. It is probably the most original, traditional and most exotic celebration known. Its roots are lost in time and in the depths of West African forests, in primitive magical cultures which have somehow adopted saints and signs, rites and symbols from the ancient Spanish church. The swirl of dancers gradually becomes a pattern. They develop shape and form distinguishable in the rainbow of colours, and the beat of drum and pipe or fife establishes an ancient, monotonous beat. At last the form becomes clear – it is the conga, the rumba, the mambo and every dance and Cuban musical sound rolled into one. The throng forms a pulsating line which winds and twists its way through the raucous streets until it seems as though the whole world is caught up in the haunting rythmn and mesmerising beat.

This is carnaval. A chance to see the people at their most colourful and effervescent. The visitor can have no more fascinating memories of the expressiveness and gaiety of the Cubans as they celebrate the culmination of a year's work well done.

Details are available from Trova Houses, Culture Houses and Tourist Boards in both Havana and Santiago de Cuba, and from Cubatur representatives.

The media

There are two national television channels, *Tele Rebelde* and *Canal 6*, and many radio stations, which can be received, apart from a radio channel broadcast from Jamaica. Visitors will notice that lack of advertising in the media. *Canal del Sol*, (the Sun Channel), promotes attractions for the

tourist on the television network. Tourist activities and events are also announced over *Radio Taino*.

All hotel reception lounges boast a television set for passing viewing and many have a set in each room. Films, serials, (some British, US or Canadian) are shown, together with cabaret, shows, news and light entertainment, plus showings of the dramatic arts, news and current affairs. Almost every home in Cuba has either radio or television.

Newspapers are available in hotels and on the streets. *Granma*, the official Communist Party newspaper, is published daily in Spanish but also has a weekly review in English, French, Portugese and Spanish. *Juventud Rebelde* is an organ of the Young

Communist League, published daily and available every afternoon. The worker's newspaper, *Trabajadores*, is published daily, *Tribuna de la Habana* is published for the population of Havana, and *Sierra Maestra* for Santiago de Cuba.

Periodicals include *Cuban Sunshine* – tourism news published by the National Institute of Tourism; *Cuba International, Revolucion y Cultura* and *Casa de las Americas; Bohemia* and *Moncada*, are the popular journals; there is also *Prisma*, a Latin American focus; *Mujeres*, an informative women's magazine as well as a number of children's magazines available like *Misha* which emanate from the USSR. Several others are published in Cuba. Visitors will be interested to learn that the curious scent of the local newspapers is due to the fact that the newsprint is actually derived from the sugar cane itself.

Cuba's international periodicals include *Revista Cuba International* and the most universally distributed, *Granma Resumen Semanal*. National newspapers, published for special subjects are *El Caiman Barbudo, Unión, La Nueva Gaceta, Cine Cubano, Conjunto* and *Cartalera*.

El Deporte and *Semanario LPV* are both sporting journals and the two tourist business journals are *Revista Sol de Cuba* and *Cuba: noticias turísticas*. Two information agencies PRELA and AIN provide the press with news, views and features.

Communications

Of special interest to visitors and philatelists is the ancient, mask-shaped post box in the Cathedral Square in Havana. Mail posted here receives a special overmark which commemorates the earliest mail service of the island. Cuba's stamps are among the most colourful, varied and sought after in the world. Long distance mail can take several weeks to arrive.

There is direct dialling access by telephone to Cuba and, from some hotels, international calls can be made. All local calls can be direct-dialled. Telegrams and telex calls can be made in the normal way through most hotel's facilities.

Transport

Most roads in Cuba are in excellent repair and well signposted. Traffic drives on the right and cars can be rented, with or without a driver, on production of a current driving licence. The resort areas also offer for hire small jeep-style vehicles, motor cycles and bicycles. Most cities and towns are easily accessible from urban centres as the Central Highway runs almost the entire length of the island, and petrol is reasonably priced. Service stations are located at regular intervals.

Havanautos have a large fleet of *Fiats* available for rent by contacting the hotel reception. Taxis can be hired from most hotels or flagged down on the street. Although taxis are few and far between in the cities, rates are quite reasonable. Transtur cars, whose fleet now totals 160 cars, may also be commissioned for day tours or special visits to places of interest or resorts. Some towns, such as Cardenas and Bayamo, run a string of traditional, old, horse-drawn carriages as taxis on local trips. Visitors will be interested to note the number of pre-1960, American and English vehicles still plying the roads in very

Antique horsedrawn carriages are used as taxis in many towns.

Some city taxis and many private vehicles sport the sleek lines of immaculately preserved Buicks, Cadillacs or Pontiacs.

serviceable condition.

City buses (*guaguas* or *wah-wahs*), are frequent and pay-as-you-enter. Inside city limits the fare is five centavos. Buses tend to be crowded during rush hours and on weekends when city-dwellers make an exodus to the nearby beaches. Modern express coaches travel inter-province throughout Cuba but seats should be booked well in advance. Hotels often provide courtesy transfer and excursion transport.

The first stretch of the new subway in Havana City is due for completion by 1993. It will connect Sports City to the Central Park and the complete system should be finished by the year 2000.

The five thousand miles of rail track in public service links most major towns. The trains are comfortable, inexpensive, and offer an efficient service together with light snacks on lengthy journeys. Seating must be booked in advance.

The new, blue, Pegaso, Transtur coaches seat 54 people comfortably. They make long and short-haul tours. Some are equipped with washroom and bar and have tinted windows.

Air transport links 18 world cities by *Cubana de Aviacion*, and the national airline services 14 major domestic airports. Havana – José Marti, Santiago de Cuba – Antonio Maceo, Camagüey – Ignacio Agramonte, Holguín – Frank Pais, Cienfuegos – Jaime Gonzalez, Isle of Youth – Rafael Cabrera, Manzanillo – Sierra Maestra and Varadero's Maurice Bishop are all international airports. There are also airports at Bayamo, Victoria de Las Tunas, Moa, Baracoa, Nicaro, Ciego de Avila and Cayo Largo.

Boat services link most of the important outlying islands including the Isle of Youth. The capital's harbour, Santiago de Cuba, the Hemingway Marina and Varadero, all have tour ships. An itinerary of 7 – 10 day cruises in the Caribbean may be available through Cubatur. These are designed to visit Cozumel, in Mexico, Grand Cayman and Jamaica, as well as Havana and Santiago de Cuba.

Cuba has nine international airports. This is Cayo Largo Airport.

CHAPTER 6

Where and How

*'The line rose slowly and steadily and then the surface of the ocean
bulged ahead of the boat and the fish came out. He came out
unendingly and water poured from his sides. He was bright in the
sun and his head and back were dark purple and in the sun the
stripes on his side showed wide and a light lavender. His sword was
as long as a baseball bat and tapered like a rapier and he rose to his
full length from the water and then re-entered it, smoothly, like a
diver and the old man saw the great scythe-blade of his tail go
under and the line commenced to race out.'*

'The Old Man and the Sea' by ERNEST HEMINGWAY

Hotels

Nationwide, most of the 275, star-rated
hotels have air conditioning, bath or
shower, radio and television, and are fully
serviced. In some rural areas more spartan
conditions are not uncommon. The occasional country chalet or outlying ranch-
style villa may lack hot water on tap, but
this is being remedied. Extra comforts can
usually be arranged through reception, or
carpeta, such as special provisions for
baby's food or children's sleeping accommodation, extra towels, bedclothes, etc.

Most hotels have a duty-free shop and national tourist *tienda*, currency conversion desk, post box and communication switchboard. The larger hotels and motels boast Olympic-size pool, several restaurants, bars, cabaret, gymnasium, steam bath, cafeteria and conference facilities. Some have the

added attraction of a nightclub or use one nearby. Cuba has a number of charming, thatched chalet-style units, personalised guest hotels and some self-catering apartments.

Many major hotels away from the capital, are constructed to a uniform design. Visitors may find that the compulsory use of the elevators, instead of the stairway, can be an inconvenience at times. Helpful attention by the service staff, however, compensates for any slight problems which may occur as the accommodation regulations adapt to the requisites of the tourist.

Accommodation is generally pre-booked and the concierge can advise on any additional requirements. Tipping is frowned upon, a token gesture or friendly word suffices. Most hotels offer Cubatur services through the lobby, and these should be able to deal with translation, information and visits or tour requests. Guides and local information leaflets, newspapers and journals are often found at the reception desk.

There are currently about 45 international-style hotels, 19 tourist villa sites and eight country resort locations which are recommended officially for booking by foreigners. Economy hotels range from fifteen to twenty dollars per night and three meals can be had for about the same price. By the end of the decade another twenty hotels are planned for construction to ultra-modern standards and these will provide a total of almost a 22 000 room capacity per day throughout the country.

Credit cards are accepted at the hotels provided they are not drawn on a US account and are internationally recognised. Baby sitters can be arranged almost anywhere and the larger establishments have their own beauty parlours. The hotel lounge generally is serviced and has a television or video which often, in tourist hotels, shows internationally current films. Sports facilities and equipment are provided at most hotels. Tuition in most sporting activities is often available, including diving training at coastal resort hotels.

Camping, chalet and budget trips

Inexpensive travel in Cuba is easily arranged through agents of Cubatur. It is possible to travel the length and breadth of the country, stopping at selected sites, by any means of transport. Self-drive car, or driver-hired vehicle, motorcycle, bicycle, bus, train, domestic airline, coastal sailing or motor boat, or even horses, can be utilised or hired to travel the island from many centres located near tourist resorts. Cubatur also offer a wide selection of carefully planned tours for budget travelling. These can include the hire of transport of any nature. Public transport is quite inexpensive in Cuba, as is petrol.

Accommodation is most competitive in price and quality of hospitality in comparison with any other Caribbean island. There is a choice of budget living quarters from camping sites, hunting lodges, beach

and country chalet accommodation, special ranch-style cabins, rustic village apartments and even Indian-style village stilt-huts! In the more remote areas running hot water is often lacking, but this is being remedied where it is considered necessary. Most have the provisions for self-catering and all provide washing and cooking facilities. Shops sell most essentials, and act as booking offices for any desired onward leg or change of transport and the rental of any extras required.

There are a number of permanent campsites on beaches, by rivers or in mountain resorts. Most have every modern convenience including electricity. One hundred of these, with tenting accommodation, *Campismo Popular*, lease sleeping bags, air mattresses, camp beds, etc, organise cooking arrangements and washing facilities, and arrange inter-camp transport from and to resorts or town centres. Tours can also be made from site to site or out to points of local interest.

For the younger, fitter, and more adventursome camper there are many more remote and isolated locations where conditions are more basic. There are the young people's campsites in Havana Province at Jibacoa beach, Girón and Puerto Escondido, near Matanzas; in Pinar del Rio, the Jardin Aspiro site; at Cienfuegos, the El Ingles Beach camp; in

Overnight visits to Havana and the Tropicana nightclub: Day visits to Santiago de Cuba, Nuevitas, Camagüey, overnight to the city of Cienfuegos and visits to Trinidad. Day visits to Holguín and Las Tunas cities. Day trips also include a country beach picnic, safari to Bonito Beach, boat safari, fishing safari, trip to Los Cocos Beach, a visit to the black sands of Marea del Portillo or Mirador de Mayabe, and, in the evening, a sunset booze cruise!

Trips of special interest include a visit to a cigar factory, a rum factory, or to a sugar mill. Visits are also offered to the main hospital or school, to historic sites, or to places of natural or botanical interest. Gourmets can join excursions to Italian, Chinese, French, seafood, or local restaurants. Barbecues can be arranged after fishing or shellfish-gathering trips.

Other visits include Naranjo Beach, a dolphin show, oysterbeds, Gibara Beach and a sea-marine reserve visit to coral reefs.

Among the other facilities offered by a typical top-class hotel are, car rental, horse-riding, mopeds, bikes, tandems and beach motor scooters. Water sport equipment for hire ranges from powerboats, minisails, paddleboats, windsurfers, rowboats, sailboats, hobbycats, to water skis, flippers, masks, snorkels, scuba equipment and surf-jets or aquascooters. Charters are available at some resorts and harbours.

Varadero the Rio Canímar; in Camagüey, the Cangilones de Rio Maximo, and, near Santiago de Cuba, La Sigua campsite, to name but a few.

Other facilities include the hire of water sports equipment, games and sporting equipment, horses or alternative touring transport. Dances, discos and barbecues are generally held in camping sites at weekends. Any extra arrangements can always be attended to by the local Cubatur office in each municipality, or by the site management.

Excursions and activities

Every hotel has facilities to arrange excursions and activities for its guests and even for independent travellers requesting special trips, visits, or participation in organised activities. Typical of the larger beach resorts are the following tours, visits and stayovers from one of the more famous north-east coast hotels:

94

Lessons are given by trained instructors in Cuban dancing, aerobics, gymnastics, beach and pool exercises, Spanish language, water sports and scuba diving. Foreign/English language film shows are regularly shown and many resorts arrange fashion shows and competitions. Games include horseshoe, volleyball, baseball and football. Indoors, darts, snooker, billiards, table-tennis, pin-ball and other games are provided for. Some resorts also cater for the avid golfer.

There are many bridle-paths and interesting country walks from resort areas and tough, mountainous climbs for the more energetic. These excursions should be carefully pre-arranged with experienced local guides or with Cubatur representatives, as should mountaineering or hiking trips.

Horse-riding, trekking and botanical, ornithological, or zoological trips can also be catered for at many of the country or coastal resorts, as can white-water and river exploration trips.

Hunting in Cuba attracts avid devotees from Europe and North America because of its varied game life. As well as wild boar and forest deer hunting, the island's specialities include pigeon, dove, duck and waterfowl shooting. Pheasant and guinea fowl can also be hunted in some areas. Hunting

trips can be organised in almost every province, and guides, beaters and guns can be hired at most hotels near hunting sites.

Not all activity holidays need to be physically orientated. Because of the varied nature of Cuba's history and its spectacular architectural heritage, most visitors to the country are eager to take tours to outlying towns and villages. Havana itself is a treasure house of museums, art galleries, culture houses and monuments, as is the country's second city, Santiago de Cuba. Many visits to Cuba are based purely on historical, artistic, photographic, archaeological or sporting activities.

Professional conferences or seminars are often organised in conjunction with tourist leisure activities. Clubs, societies, institutes, Trade Unions and associations often organise these tours from their home bases. Cubatur can assist in any arrangements through Tourist Boards or directly by contacting the head office in Havana. Havanatur offices can make special preparations for visitors and can organise group visits and long or short distance transport in Cuba. Excursions to Mexico, Disneyland and other Caribbean islands are available.

Specialist holidays

Sun, sand and sea are the most obvious attractions of Cuba's varied island. Once in Cuba the visitor suddenly becomes aware of the multitude of alternatives to soaking up the sun on the tropical beaches.

Sea

There are a host of activities for the sportsman and many of these are connected with the sea because of the island nature of the country. The beach enthusiast will be able to select from windsurfing, para-sailing, jet skiing, surfing, sailing, water skiing, speedboating, para-kiting, dinghy racing, canoeing, snorkelling and, of course, swimming.

Specialities include inshore fishing,

spear and harpoon fishing and deep sea game fishing. Scuba diving is also a favourite with many resorts where dive boats, instructors, guides and the most modern equipment are available. The fascinating coral reefs and wrecks which encircle the island have become an international attraction for divers world-wide.

Game fishing, in the waters of the Atlantic, Mexican Gulf or Caribbean, is a long-established sport for which the island is renowned. Ernest Hemingway put game fishing in Cuba on the map. From the huge marina which bears his name, or from any of a thousand quays, charter boats can whisk you out to try your skill against Bonito, Tuna, Blue and White Marlin, Kingfish, Sailfish or Barracuda.

Land

Inland fishing in the freshwater lakes, which are scattered across Cuba, has attracted visiting enthusiasts from every country in the world. The most popular fishing is for Tarpon, Snook and Bonefish in coastal bays, and Black, or Largemouth Bass, in the island's extensive lake system. Anglers have been known to take a fish every minute and the Largemouth Bass

record stands at just under 4.5 kilos! Carp and Tilapia abound in Cuba's lakes and rivers, and fishing trips are organised from local hotels through reception or Cubatur representatives.

Tennis and badminton, squash and athletic enthusiasts are catered for in most larger hotels, and in some selected areas, like Varadero, the golfer can participate in tournaments and locally arranged competitions. Other sporting activities are available, or can be arranged, and many hotels have an Olympic-size swimming pool and games room.

For the rock-climbing, caving and pot-holing experts, the limestone regions are ideal grounds for expeditions both above and below ground.

Underground

Cuba has the most outstanding cave system in Latin America. Almost every province attracts speleology enthusiasts, but the most extensive area of caves is in the Majaguas-Cantera range. Here only 25 kilometres of caves have been mapped so far. The 12 caves in the Pica-Pica Valley of Pinar del Rio have more than 65 kilometres of subterranean passages and galleries. The island's limestone is an ideal geological strata for exploration by both the tourist and the scientist. Popular bases for expeditions are the campsite at Hoyo de Montana Ranch and the Pinar del Rio Hotel. Sites include the Gran Amistad Cave, the caves of Amadea, Pío Domingo's Cave, Borrás and Atollajosa systems.

The country's largest cavern is Los Pájaros in the Majaguas-Cantera system in the Sierra de San Carlos, Pinar del Rio Province, it measures 300 × 100 × 148

metres. The longest cave, at Rancho Mundito is 26 000 metres long and the highest is the Furnia de Pipe in Santiago de Cuba Province – 145 metres high. It is always 'on the cards' that a visiting speleologist may discover caverns that will change these records!

Holidays with children

Many hotels and resorts cater for the younger travellers or children who arrive with adults. Families are in their element in Cuba, which is like a 'Treasure Island' to children.

Where else would they find golden, sandy beaches with waving palms, boat trips to the sites of sunken treasure ships, tales of buccaneers and privateers and even a genuine pirate's cave at the famous Varadero beach? Cuba's outdoor life is ideal for children's games, which are

Holiday resorts are geared up to accommodate and entertain the youngsters from creche to teenage disco.

arranged at most holiday areas either in the countryside or on the coast. The beaches are also 'made for children' as, in many resorts the sandy sea floor slopes gradually, making swimming, even for the tiniest tot, perfectly safe – a great place to learn!

All children in Cuba get priority treatment. Cuban people have a great regard for youngsters and everything is done to make them comfortable, and entertain and educate them. At some resorts, the playground and facilities for children's games take pride of place with a little section of the beach watched over by child attendants and, as is usual in every hotel or resort, a nurse is on call at all times. It is wise not to forget extra baby's requirements, food containers, clothes and favourite children's toys.

Adventure is the by-word for children visiting Cuba. Each day produces a new discovery, apart from the opportunity to meet youngsters from another country there is – horse riding, caving, climbing, sailing, beach games, gymnastics, rafting, tennis, canoeing, snorkelling, windsurfing, motorboating and dance lessons. Every day is a new expedition for children, when the Cubatur information desk arranges such activities and includes indoor evening pastimes such as table soccer, table tennis, indoor quoites, films and slide shows, billiards, videos, records, dance and snooker.

A host of athletic experiences are just part of the enjoyment in store for the youngster. Guides are always able to provide details of forthcoming activities and will arrange for anything from creche and baby-sitters to tours and outings, games and competitions for youngsters and the young at heart. For children, Cuba is truly an island of adventure.

Freshwater fishing

Where are the best freshwater fishing resorts in Cuba? Known world-wide for its prolific inland waters, the island has about a dozen famous fishing areas. There are Grande Lake and the lake of Cuyaguateje,

in Pinar del Rio Province, western Cuba; a lake area south-west of Havana City and another to the east; Alacranes; Treasure Lake in Matanzas and Hanabanilla in the Escambray Mountains near Cienfuegos; the Zaza dam and Jibaro lake near Spiritus Sancti; two areas in the centre and north of Camagüey Province; near Nuevitas, and Virama, in Granma Province, south-west of Santiago de Cuba.

River fishing is excellent the length and breadth of the country. Most freshwater fishing is for the Largemouth Bass as it reaches great proportions in Cuba and is such good sport. *Trucha* is the local name for the Largemouth Bass and they have been taken weighing nine kilogrammes on the Grande Lake in Pinar del Rio. It is this three square-kilometre lake, and the artificial lake of Cuyaguateje, the river of the same name, surrounding canals and lake bays with its satellite lakes, which have produced the most spectacular results. In three days' fishing recently, 15 anglers caught a total of 1478 Bass weighing up to 7 kilogrammes on the Cuyaguateje lake system.

Maspoton Fishing Club and nearby Juventud Reservoir also have their share of trophy fish. In Havana Province fishing is good on the north-west coastal lake of Mariel and at Ariguanabo, in the Valle del Peru, to the city's south-east and Bacuranao-Campo Florido and Jibacoa

'Milk Lake', one of Cuba's main game sports centres, near Morón, Ciego de Avila

municipalities. Treasure Lake, in the south, is an excellent source of Bass and has a replica Indian village resort where fishermen can stay on its beautiful shores.

Lake Hanabanilla has one of the best names in fishing circles, if it is mountain scenery and excellent fishing that the fisherman requires. Set in the Escambray Mountains Range its trophy weight Largemouth Bass can exceed 4 kilogrammes. In the centre of the country the Hanabanilla Hotel is situated on the banks of the lake. It offers all facilities, modern equipment and boats. As in Hanabanilla, Zaza Lake, the largest artificial lake in Cuba, has a fully equipped, lakeside hotel. The lake has more Largemouth Bass than any other lake in the country.

In Ciego de Avila Province, to the east of Sancti Spiritus, there are two famous lakes near the town of Morón. Just 11 kilometres from Morón Hotel, a 136-room, modern establishment, the lakes of Redonda and Laguna de la Leche (Milk Lake), offer excellent fishing, including Black Bass, Trucha Snook, Tilapia, Tarpon and Bonefish on the lakes. Visit the gamekeeper's cabin where he keeps chickens and hogs, both of which he appears to feed on coconut husks! 66 year-old Balmaseda welcomes tourists to his 200-acre kingdom.

In the larger province of Camagüey, and

Largemouth Bass is a popular catch in Cuba's teeming lake waters.

The Blue Marlin

near the city itself, are two important fishing lakes, Presa La Manana de Santa Ana and Presa Munoz near Florida, Camagüey Province. North of Camagüey City is Presa Maximo. *Presa* is Cuban for dam. On the far north coast of the province, Nuevitas Bay is another favourite fishing spot. There are hotels near all fishing areas in Camagüey Province.

Fishing on the Virama and Leonero lakes in Granma Province is a comparatively new activity and has supplemented the many hunters flocking to the area. Here, as at all fishing locations, equipment and facilities can be rented.

An inexpensive licence should be bought in order to fish in Cuba. Services include transfers, fishing guides, translators, boats, packed lunches on the lakes, eight hours fishing in most areas, cleaning and freezing of catch and other optional tours.

All arrangements can be booked before arriving in the country or by contacting the Cubatur guide or hotel reception. Fishermen are best advised to bring their own equipment and to protect themselves against bites, not from the fish or crocodiles, but from the midges and insects!

Deepsea and offshore fishing

Where are the best bases for deepsea fishing in Cuba? All three seas – the Gulf of Mexico, the Atlantic Ocean and the Caribbean – are famous game fishing waters. Cuba proffers the choice and leaves the fisherman with a bewildering selection.

There are twenty-three recognised offshore areas recommended for deepsea

Marlin Fishing Tournament, started in 1950 by 'Papa' himself. There are also a combination of several beaked fish competitions held in the springtime off Havana. Fidel Castro himself, won the first organised Tournament. The city's east beaches provide good fishing at Jibacoa.

Further east along the north coast the waters off Varadero's Punta de Hicacos offer similar fishing in the great Gulf Stream that runs between Key West in Florida and Cuba. From this point, for 500 kilometres along the north coast, the islands and deep offshore waters provide some of the best Marlin fishing in the world. The cays off Santa Clara Province are well known grounds, like Cayo Guillermo. Records include a 500 kilogramme Blue Marlin, a 40 kilogramme Sawfish, a 38 kilogramme Barracuda and a 500 kilogramme Swordfish. Wahoo have reached 65 kilogrammes, Common Dolphin-Dorado, (not the mammal), 39 kilogrammes, Tarpon 130 kilogrammes and a 50 kilogramme Sailfish has been taken in these waters. Cayo Coco, Cayo Romano and Sabinal all offer excellent fishing off Camagüeys north coast.

fishing excursions along the island's south coast. Three particularly good areas are listed in the south-east, and eighteen fishing bases are given along Cuba's northern seaboard.

Each centre has its own standard of facilities and equipment, boats and opportunities, like the choice of alternative activities. In some areas the fishing trips are restricted to seafaris and coastal fishing tours for smaller, warm water fish. These generally include, Red Snapper, Cherna, Banana Fish, Yellow Jacks, Red Grouper, Barracuda, Sea Bass, Grouper, Bonefish, Tarpon and a variety of colourful fish found around the hundreds of coral reefs.

It is the deepsea game fishing for beaked fish which has made Cuba one of the most attractive areas on the fishing atlas. Swordfish, Sawfish, Bonito, Yellowfin (Tuna), Sailfish, White, Black and Blue Marlin, Blackfin and Skipjack, Albacore, Dolphin – Dorado, Wahoo and a variety of Shark are the island's most favoured game fish.

Internationally renowned as one of the best deepsea fishing marinas in the Americas, the Hemingway Marina, just a few minutes west of Havana City, offers docking for up to 100 yachts, hires game fishing boats and gear and has every conceivable facility. It is from here that the national and international tournaments are held, including, the annual Hemingway

As far along the north coast as Guardalavaca and Baracoa, or west to the Archipelago de los Colorados, in the Gulf of Mexico, the waters in spring abound with game fish.

On the south coast there are provisions for deepsea fishing from the westernmost tip of the Peninsula de Guanahacabibes, around the Bay of Batabano, the Isle of Youth (*Isla de la Juventud*) to the Archipelago de los Canarreos and Cayo Largo or Cayo Avalos. Off Girón and Playa Ancon, near Trinidad, the waters provide excellent opportunities for record-catching attempts.

Becoming famous in game fishing circles is the Archipelago Jardines de la Reina, in the Gulf of Ana Maria, towards the southeast and between the fishing bases of Tunas de Zaza and Manzanillo. These myriad islands and cays provide waters where a number of fishing records have been set, particularly for Horse-Eyed Jack, Great Barracuda and Bonefish. Floating hotels in the cays offer all the facilities required for the most experienced deepsea rod-and-line fisherman. *Jardines de la Reina* boatel accommodates 12 guests as does the *Lost Paradise*. Night and day fishing excursions are also organised. Four good fishing sites have been established in this isolated group of islands.

From Santiago de Cuba, the country's second city, set in the centre of the southeast coastline and facing both Jamaica and Haiti, three game fishing resorts are accessible from the surrounding quays. Pilon is probably best known.

Most fishing boats are equipped with galley, guides, tackle, etc. Cleaning and freezing facilities are available and trophy fish can be shipped or Custom clearance obtained. Contact hotel reception, Cubatur or INTUR representatives for details on fishing in Cuba's deep-water grounds.

Diving

Considered by enthusiasts to offer some of the best diving in the Caribbean, Cuba has become a leader in accommodating visiting

Many beaches are provided with the most up-to-date scuba or snorkelling equipment.

professional and amateur divers alike. The waters are so safe that no special skills are required for goggling or snorkelling enthusiasts. Lessons in other diving techniques are given at most resorts.

Of the country's one hundred and twenty most popular beaches about 30 specialise in scuba diving and almost all are ideal spots for snorkel diving. The island's three seas, the Atlantic, the Gulf of Mexico and the Caribbean are unrivalled in their variety of sea life. More than 5750 kilometres of coastline provide the diver with a fascinating variety of waters. This section gives a representative tour of the established dive sites around that coastline.

Temperatures range from 24° – 28°C (75° – 82°F). From the gently shelving, sandy beaches to the 7000-metre deep Fosa of Battle or Cayman Trench, the island is a veritable treasure chest of diving locations.

Not every wreck is a Spanish treasure galleon, but this massive anchor looks promising!

Events such as Photosub, Cinesub and the World Underwater Film Festival have been held in Cuba. Among the 1600 cays, islets and kilometres of reefs only a small percentage have so far been developed as diving attractions. Permanent scuba event locations are promoting more varied resorts. Over the past few years a determined effort by the authorities has spearheaded a move to develop the awareness of Cuba's underwater heritage and marine life. Pre-revolutionary plundering has decimated some unique reef areas and indiscriminate pollution has been eradicated in the interests of nature and sealife.

Cuba has more than 70 species of coral and 900 species of fish. All may be photographed, but coral must not be taken. Today the endangered areas have recovered. Preservation moves have rescued hitherto jeopardised stretches of coral reef and large areas have been designated marine reserves and seaquariums.

Of special interest to the visiting diver are those sites which are easily accessible from a hotel base. Most famous is the beach at Varadero, some two hours' drive from Havana City. Along the 20 kilometres of sandy strand the peninsula has seven major hotels which provide facilities for the scuba diver. Eight more hotels are soon to be added to the list which will make the resort the largest in the Caribbean and possibly the most active in diving circles. Each hotel, the Internacional, Kawama, Oasis, Bellamar, Ledo and the twin hotels of Siboney and Atabey, offer dive equipment for hire although, for snorkelling, it is wise to bring one's own. Lessons are also given at most hotel pools. A CMAS, or World Underwater Federation instructor, is generally on call on most dives.

At Varadero the dive sites are as spectacular as anywhere around the island. Dives at a site called Neptune's Haven are among the most popular. On the eastern side of the long, narrow, northern resort, in the clear Atlantic waters, a series of marine caves have been found. Many of the caverns here, to a depth of twenty metres, are freshwater, and a tunnel leads through an underwater ravine to more seawater caves extending far out underneath the sea. Stalactites, giant Black Coral, a red variety of the cylindrical and conical *Montastraea cavarnosa* coral, and spectacularly large, deepwater fish are features of this dive spot. Underwater cliffs and deep drop-offs, strange rock formations and wrecks dating from the World War II era and earlier, are all attractions for the diver in Varadero. A total of 23 dive sites are marked and underwater guides are available from the resorts' major hotels. A particular speciality of Varadero's water, apart from its prolific Black Coral, is the coral sponge known as Sweetheart's Bouquet, a rare treasure, to be photographed but not removed!

Nearer to the capital city the seven beaches of Havana, the *Playas del Este* or Blue Circuit beaches, offer a wide choice of

studied by Cuban archaeologists and divers. Modern equipment and dive boats are available for hire here and there are eight marked dive sites. Accommodation at Jibacoa is either at the Villa Loma bungalows, the rustic cabins of El Abra, or the modern El Tropico Hotel.

Two other beaches in the east Havana resorts have facilities for divers, but boats can be taken out for dives off any of the seven. A boat trip can also be made to Matanzas Province to dive off the Carbonera coast. Santa Maria beach offers dive facilities at the 188-room Marazul Hotel, and the Villa Bacuranao, at the beach of the same name, has dive equipment, boats and guides.

West of Havana, a modern development, the Hemingway Marina, stocks first-class equipment and rents out dive boats with guides. There are twelve dive sites marked

dive locations. A coral reef extends all along the shore about 200 metres out and visibility can be more than two metres. An undersea cliff drops 12 metres and there are about 30 different varieties of coral to be found on the reef. Here, Jibacoa is the best beach to dive from. Two sunken pirate ships lying in the bay are being

off the marina coast. Santana Seabed is the trace of an ancient river, Santa Fe Point, a centuries-old wreck; the bed of the Mosquito river reveals the remains of a seaquake; Viriato is famous for Brain, Floral and Elkhorn Coral, as is the Hollywood Star dive site and the remains of a sunken shrimp boat. A Spanish galleon, the *Santisima Trinidad*, sunk by pirates, lies just a few kilometres from the shore and other wrecks are still being located for the enthusiastic divers who make special trips out to the Marina for its particularly unusual marine life. Every facility is available at the Hemingway Marina with excellent bungalow accommodation and the alternative of deepsea game fishing expeditions. The private houses of the Barlovento residential area also offer accommodation to visiting divers.

In the great southern bay of the Gulf of Batabano, the oyster-shaped *Isle de la Juventud*, Isle of Youth, has 16 marked dive sites and regular excursions are made to other sites at Cape Frances, dubbed 'The Blue Paradise', and Pedernales. The Colony Hotel specialises in diving vacations and hires out top equipment. Located in the Caribbean, on the island shelf, and in the Canarreos Archipelago, the Island of Youth is now a scuba-diving centre of international standard and renown. A 90° drop-off, lined with coral of 50 different species, Gorgonians and Yellow Trumpet Sponges, provides an underwater paradise.

Dive sites on the Pirate's Coast include Tarpon Cave, the Hidden Passage, Mystery Grotto, Blue Grotto, the Tunnel of Love, Parrot Fish Valley, the Wall of Black Coral, the Huge Grotto, the Black Grotto, the Pirate's Anchor dive, Coral Valley, the White Valley, the Striped Paradise, with lines of a wide variety of coral, the Jump Off, the Road to Eternity – known for its profusion of *Acropora cervicornis* coral and the spectacular Hill of Coral. These marked dives are all off the south-westernmost point of the island and describe, just by their names, the great variety of sites to be found in these waters. Other dives can be arranged to wrecks, including that of the *Jibacoa*. Lessons are available and night dives can also be made on request.

After the wonders of the dives from the Isle of Youth it is difficult to imagine their equal. On Cayo Largo, however, the same iridescent waters reveal a multitude of magical wonders of the deep. Two specialised diving cruise ships ply the waters between the Cay and the Island of Youth. Manned by French-Cuban crews and reaching the deeper dives out to sea, the ships can accommodate ten divers at a time. Cayo Largo has its own diving arrangements based at the 59-room Isla del Sur Hotel and more are to be added with the completion of the new Cayo Largo Hotels. The tiny island resort is a sanctuary for Green, Loggerhead, Leatherback and Hawksbill Turtle and its reefs are a haven for a myriad tropical fish. Prize winning underwater films have been made of the coral and marine life off the sandy shores of Cayo Largo and its neighbouring coral islands.

Back on the mainland, the island's marine topography is a striking change from its southern islands or its northern shores. In the Zapata Swamp in Matanzas Province a natural pool, Cuevas de Copey, is 70 metres deep. It is reached from Girón. Casilda, near Trinidad, is a port which served the old Spanish city in its heyday. Today, the attraction for divers are the deep dives to wrecks lying on the hundred treacherous coral reefs offshore in the blue Caribbean waters. Diving expeditions can be arranged from the Hotel Ancon or Costa Sur Hotel near the harbour.

Further along the south-west coast off Camagüey in the Archipelago of the Jardines de la Reina (the Queen's Gardens), a totally different environment beckons the dive enthusiast in the form of floating motel, boatel and hotel. Its coral islands string out in a line 120 kilometres long between 100 and 20 kilometres off Cuba's coast. The *Last Paradise* floating boatel provides for diving excursions in the archipelago. This *Jardines de la Reina Hotel* accommodates twelve guests. Completely unspoilt and largely unexplored, the hundreds of other islands offer a unique opportunity for divers to discover new sites to list against the famous Tarpon Cave and its 'hedge' of Black Coral.

No dive beaches have really been developed along Cuba's southern shores near Santiago de Cuba, but Guama and Baconao are probably the best bases, not forgetting the three wrecks at Mar Verde.

Back on the north coast of Cuba two very

important diving locations provide excellent scope for the amateur and professional. At Guardalavaca, nearby Pesquero Nuevo beach and Naranjo Bay, the opportunities for spectacular dives are legion. Dive sites off the reef, between 300 and 400 metres offshore, describe the variety of marine interest: Fishing Terrace for Giant Sponges, Gorgonians and Star Coral; Diver's Paradise for black and multi-coloured coral; The Jump for Swordfish, Barracudas, Wrasse and Black Margates; Coral Kingdom for Leaf, Butterprint, Brain, Star and Club Finger Coral; Sponge Rock for the variety of sponges including a tubular, violet-coloured sponge; Grouper Canyon for Seafans and Red and Black Groupers. Accommodation and all equipment can be found at the 222-room Guardalavaca Hotel.

Just a short distance along the coast is the resort of Santa Lucia. Its shelving beach has a drop-off forming the second longest coral reef in Latin America. Seven fissures break the reef, which often protrudes from the sea at low tide. The reef stretches 36 kilometres and can be 2 – 3 kilometres wide. Its excellent diving scope is renowned in the Caribbean and eleven dive sites are marked and buoyed. Laundress Rock has two coral-coated ledges; Dune Centre has coloured sponges, tunnels and fissures; Sponge Paradise is marked by Buoy three; Coral Tower also has valley and tunnels; Buoy five, The Hole is, in fact, three undersea peaks; Gorgonian Garden is a sandy plain covered with marine life. Bonita Stairway features a coral cavity; Coral Stairway, Buoy eight, is a terrace of coral and Gorgonian lined rock; the Hidden Canyon dive includes a circular mound covered in sponges and a cave; Ocean Window reveals Black Coral and four peaks, whilst the dive at Buoy eleven is the site of the 1898 wreck of the *Mortero*, sunk in the Nuevitas Canal.

Parrotfish, Chromis, Basslets, Angelfish, Squirrel Fish, Cardinals, Dog, Red and Cube Snappers, Dogfish, Rays, Porgies, Clownfish, Grunts and Zebrafish, all are prolific in the crystal-clear waters. Accommodation at Santa Lucia is either at Mayanabo Club, a 225-room, 12-suite beach hotel which rents diving equipment, or at the top villas of Tarraraco and Bahamas. Dive excursions can be arranged through Cubatur representatives or at the Mayanabo reception.

Hunting

Where are the best hunting resorts in Cuba? There are eight main hunting areas in the country: They are in Pinar del Rio Province, the Isle of Youth (*Isla de la Juventud*), in Havana Province, Matanzas, Villa Clara, Sancti Spiritus, Ciego de Avila and Granma Provinces. It really depends on the base location as to where hunting is most enjoyed. From Havana, most hunting resorts in the west part of Cuba are easily

Why not a combined fishing and hunting trip?

Yaguasa make fine sport from a motor-boat

is very good hunting for White-Crowned Pigeons (late July – late October).

In Havana Province there are few hunting facilities but further east, in the Cardenas/Varadero region there are opportunities for Mourning Dove, Wilson's Snipe, Coot, Yaguasin and White-Crowned Pigeon hunting. The three areas are at Laguna Rabo de Nube, Pelayito and the Camarioca/Varadero/Cardenas triangle. An abundance of Pheasant and Quail are to be found in the Cubanacan region of Villa Clara.

In Sancti Spiritus Province the Hunting Club of Jibaro specialises in Mourning and White-Winged Dove, Yaguasin, Coot and Wilson's Snipe and at the Zaza reservoir there is hunting for Mourning and White-Winged Doves (September – February).

Most famous of the central hunting regions are the areas around Moron/Moron Hotel, and Ciego de Avila/Ciego de Avila Hotel. At Moron, near *Laguna de la Leche* (Milk Lake), hunting is arranged for migratory ducks and Mourning Doves. At Agachales de Falla there is hunting for migratory ducks and coot and at La Redonda Lake, Roseate Flamingo, Ibis, Jacana and Gallinules can be seen from the 24 hides. Hunt in the cooperative's fields for Mourning and White-Winged Dove, Masked, Ruddy and Wood Duck, plus Spoonbills, Pintails, Widgeon and Teals which can be also taken here. At La Turbina, hunt for White-Crowned Pigeon and at Plan Semilla Barague, for Mourning and White-Winged Dove (October – March).

In the vast lakeland of Virama and Leonero Lakes, in the south-west, one can hunt on horseback, by boat, or from the 28 hides. From Bayamo it is possible to rent one of the many hunting cabins (with adjacent restaurant) at Caneyes Virama. Here, in Granma Province, is one of the most prolific hunting grounds in the country. There are six beating areas in the swamps and woodlands, where a host of game can be taken, also *Yaguasin Cubana*; Bahama Duck; Ibis (white and black);

reached. Those in the central region, from Morón or Sancti Spiritus City, and, in the east, the hunting regions can be best visited from Bayamo or the nation's second city, Santiago de Cuba.

In the west is the hunting club of Maspotón which has 34-guest accommodation, restaurant, bar, pool, shop and games room. The surrounding, 189-square kilometre plain, with its lakes, Maspotón, Buenavista and Pica Pica, mangrove swamps and ponds, are a favourite hunting region for ducks and dove. In the Municipality of Los Palacios, and 62 kilometres from the town of Pinar del Rio, there are 14 fully equipped, two-bedroom *cabanas* and six singles. The club also provides horse riding and car trips and offers a variety of other activities as well as hunting. Maspotón has 62 blinds for hunting Wood, Pintail, Fulvous, Tree, Yaguasin, and Shoveler Ducks or Blue-Winged Teal; six stations for Mourning and White-Winged Dove hunting; five for Snipe hunting; four for Pheasant and three for Guineafowl hunting. Some of the area spreads over rice fields where Coot can be taken. The club supplies all equipment on a hire basis (October – March).

On the Isle of Youth, in the south-east, the hunting club is near the Colony Hotel. At Punta del Este and Punta Frances there are reserves where, in wooded areas, there migratory Duck; Guanabaes; *Bescasinas; Paloma Rabiche; Gallareta; Torcaza Cabeciblanca;* Codorniz, or quail; *torcaza cuellimora; Paloma Aliblanca* and *Gallina de Guinea,* or guineafowl, there are *Conejo Cimarron,* or rabbit; Huita Conga; Aguti, or Brown Huita; Crocodile and Alligator. Wild boar are also an attraction in some areas and on some of the offshore cays surrounding Cuba.

Most hunting areas have comfortable, fully-equipped cabins and hire out camouflage suits, raincoats, guns, etc. Shells can be purchased and the picking of game is provided for, freezing of game and the supply of a guide and translator is available where and when required. Relaxed hunting laws make the country one of the most pleasant for foreign visitors, but remember to take mosquito and insect repellent on all hunting trips.

A corresponding hunting permit issued by INTUR is required which indicates game to be hunted and the seasons. Arrangements should be made previously for those wishing to take their own guns. Escorts are officials of the Tourist Hunting Service and all arrangements can be made through hotel receptions, Cubatur guides, or even prior to arrival in Cuba. Hunter's guns and a maximum of 50 shells are allowed to be brought into Cuba.

Cuba's hunting grounds provide equipment, transport and guides, plus adequate accommodation facilities for the many thousands of sportsmen who return year after year – like the million game birds!

One of the most unusual night hunts is that organised at Miguel Salude Lake, in the western province of Pinar del Rio. The sport is a frog hunt, a regular excursion from the Pinar del Rio or Vueltabajo Hotels which includes the preparation for eating of the frogs caught!

CHAPTER 7

The Cuban Experience

'Ye tropic forests of unfading green,
  where the palm tapers, and the orange glows,
Where the light bamboo weaves her feathery screen,
  And her tall shade the matchless ceyba throws.

Ye cloudless ethers of unchanging blue,
  Save, as its rich varieties give way,
To the clear sapphire of your midnight hue,
The burnished azure of your perfect day.'

Early 19th Century poem on Cuba
by the Earl of Carlisle

Each of the fifteen divisions in Cuba offers a fascinating variety of natural beauty spots and sites of particular interest. Every province has its own peculiar topography, which provides the visitor with a range of country resorts, and each has a seaboard where marine life and underwater formations can be viewed. The island's present geological make-up reveals the many influences which have gone into its creation.

From coral limestone, eroded by wind and water, to the jagged serpentine mountain ranges, thrust up by seismic activity, both land and seabed provide a wealth of unique attractions. Travelling from west to east, through the length of Cuba's twelve hundred kilometres, each region has something of special interest for the naturalist

and the casual traveller alike. Whether mountain climber or rambler, speleologist or botanist, marine scientist or snorkeller, fisherman, hunter, scuba diver, photographer or just a seeker after tropical sun-drenched beauty, the island of Cuba more than fulfils the visitor's desires.

The island's great empty beaches and forested mountain ranges provide unlimited scope for recreation, sport and a variety of hobbies. Cuba's countryside and shoreline are havens for wildlife of many kinds and paradise for bird and marine life.

Cuba's famous beaches

The island's coastline is estimated to be almost 6000 kilometres long with 1200 cays and islets, reefs and *playas* or beaches. So numerous are Cuba's bays and coves that it is impossible to detail its thousand beaches.

Officially there are 290 beaches catalogued, about 120 are extremely popular, and 50 have permanent tourist facilities. There are no private beaches on the island, but some tend to cater to the local tastes and others to those of visiting tourists. There are still many secluded beaches with tranquil waters yet to be discovered by the

With sky and sea competing for the clearest blue, and white sands brushed by bright green palm fronds, the only choice is – which beach?

adventurous traveller. The following pages take the visitor on a tour around Cuba's more popular beach resorts.

Atlantic coast

The bay on which Christopher Columbus first set foot – Cayo Bariay – on the north coast, is surrounded by six beaches. A short drive from Holguín, **Cayo Bariay** itself is an attraction for sightseeing.

Just a little further east, **Guardalavaca** is one of the north coast's most popular beaches. The provincial capital, Holguín, is just under an hour's drive away, through interesting, hilly countryside, sugar plant-ations and steep, small, conical mountain peaks (pitons). The name Guardalavaca – 'guard the cows' – is said to come from the days of the Spanish treasure fleets and

Varadero beach appears to go on for ever

All types of craft can be rented on Cuba's idyllic beaches.

pirates. It is suggested that, as this coastline represents the last 'jumping off' point for sailing ships passing between Cuba and Florida and heading for Europe, Guardalavaca acted as a last pick-up for fresh cattle meat and water. Frequent raids by pirates prompted the Spanish to stockade the pastureland around the beach area.

Horned cattle still graze with horses on the carefully tended greenswards along the 3 kilometre, brilliant white, sandy beach. The area, which includes the nineteenth century rocky bay attraction of **Estero de la Piedra**, has been developed as a sophisticated resort, and its 225-roomed Guardalavaca Hotel offers all modern amenities, recreations and tourist facilities. Scuba diving, snorkelling and game fishing are excellent, activities on the water, sailing or boat trips, are always available, and land-based activities – horse riding, cycling beachcombing, and tennis are ever-popular.

Cabarets are organised for evening entertainment and a dance floor encourages nightlife participation. A restaurant with 164 seats, a terrace room for parties of up to 130 people, games room, television lounge, cafeteria, shops and bars, provide for every requirement. The Olympic-size pool or gently sloping beach, shaded by Sea Grape trees, offer opportunities for all watersports. Tuition is available in most activities on or off the white coral sand or in the kingfisher-blue sea.

A lengthy list of tours includes trips to a sugar farm, a tobacco factory, seafaris, the Yaguajay Hills for hikers, the 700–metre long **Estero Ciego** beach, 220–metre long **Blanca beach**, **Cayo Naranjo** aquarium, archaeological exhibits at Banes (where there is the Cave of the Cuatrocientas Rosas – 400 roses), tours to the 400 metres of sand at **Yuraguanal beach**, or the world-famous fine sands of **Puerto Rico beach**, to natural lookouts, coral reefs, tours of Holguín and Santiago de Cuba or overnight visits to Havana.

A group of about 45 cabins is available for hire near the main hotel building. These are self-catering, can be pre-booked and sleep four in basic conditions. **Don Lino beach** or Club Carousel, is a tiny beach with stone and wood, 105 double chalets, restaurants and bar. On the other side of the Bay of Nipe, from Banes, are several local beaches within easy travelling distance of Mayari on the north-east coast of Holguín Province. Between Mayari and Cayo Mambi the beaches offer basic facilities for bathing and watersports. On the Bay of Nipe, itself, is Cayo Saetía and Juan Vincente beach, near the modern holiday Motel Bitiri.

West, along the north coast into Las Tunas Province, six beaches have become particularly popular with Cuban locals: **Playa Llanita**; the beaches at **La Herradura, Caletona** and **Genovesa**; and **Playa Las Bocas**, a similar distance from Holguín city to Guardalavaca and, much further west, the beach of **Juan Antonio**. It is not, however, until you cross into the Province of Camagüey that the more developed beaches are found. West of the low Sierrecita Hills, and north of a nine-square kilometre lagoon, is one of Cuba's most magnificent beaches.

Santa Lucia beach, Cuba's third longest beach, 18 kilometres of magnificent, powdery-white sand, is located in the far north-eastern corner of Camagüey Province. Easily accessible from both the Port of Nuevitas and the city of Camagüey, it lies on the Atlantic side of Nuevitas Bay. The beach is protected by one of the longest reefs in the Caribbean – 36 kilometres of red, white and black coral – a diver's paradise. The shallow waters and gently sloping beach are ideal for all watersports and equipment for all sporting activities, on land or water, are provided at the tastefully modern Mayanabo Club. Deep lagoons near here are ieal for snorkelling enthusiasts.

The 225-room, 12-suite hotel, named after a local Indian Chief, has a 180-seat restaurant, bars, cafeteria and a boutique. Try the excellent black bean soup and steaks at the Azul Cielo restaurant. Daytime activities are organised from the reception area and, at night, there are cabarets and dancing. Lessons are given by specialists in most watersports and the area is famous for its marine life, birdlife – including a flamingo colony, fauna and flora. The three villas of Tararaco, Santa Lucia Cottages and Bahamas offer alternative rustic accommodation and the option of two restaurants. Every requirement is provided on Santa Lucia beach, from polyclinic to children's camp.

Tours and excursions include visits to other beaches – **Bonita**, or those near Nuevas Grandes Bay, bus and minitrain trips, visits to the ballet, a ceramic workshop, local and international restaurants, trips to Havana, Camagüey or Santiago de Cuba and tobacco factory or sugar plantation excursions. This beach is a veritable magnet for scuba divers and snorkelling enthusiasts, but also offers horse riding and boating facilities.

Just across the narrow entrance to Nuevitas Bay is the attractive resort of Los Pinos, at Punta Los Pinos on **Cayo Sabinal**, home of a secluded fisherman and destination of a popular seafari from Santa Lucia. Look north-west from here at a hundred deserted cays and islets which form the **Camagüey Archipelago –** a million metres of desert island beaches, coral reefs and unexplored waters. These include (on what was once called 'The Island's of the King') **Cayos Guajaba, Cruz, Paredón Grande** and **Cayo Coco**. This last island resort now has a 1300-metre runway.

The north coast of the next province, Ciego de Avila, offers only three selected beaches near the northern city of Morón. They are more suited to local tastes but have facilities similar to their counterparts in other provinces. **La Tinaja beach** lies east of Milk Lake and **Guaney beach** a little further east from the beautiful **Isla de Turiguanó**. Out on the Punta de San

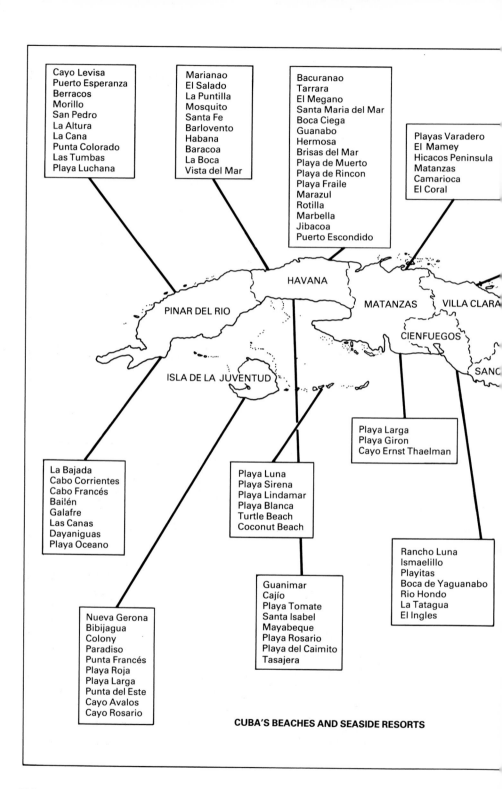

Cayo Levisa
Puerto Esperanza
Berracos
Morillo
San Pedro
La Altura
La Cana
Punta Colorado
Las Tumbas
Playa Luchana

Marianao
El Salado
La Puntilla
Mosquito
Santa Fe
Barlovento
Habana
Baracoa
La Boca
Vista del Mar

Bacuranao
Tarrara
El Megano
Santa Maria del Mar
Boca Ciega
Guanabo
Hermosa
Brisas del Mar
Playa de Muerto
Playa de Rincon
Playa Fraile
Marazul
Rotilla
Marbella
Jibacoa
Puerto Escondido

Playas Varadero
El Mamey
Hicacos Peninsula
Matanzas
Camarioca
El Coral

HAVANA

PINAR DEL RIO

MATANZAS

VILLA CLARA

CIENFUEGOS

SANC

ISLA DE LA JUVENTUD

La Bajada
Cabo Corrientes
Cabo Francés
Bailén
Galafre
Las Canas
Dayaniguas
Playa Oceano

Playa Luna
Playa Sirena
Playa Lindamar
Playa Blanca
Turtle Beach
Coconut Beach

Playa Larga
Playa Giron
Cayo Ernst Thaelman

Rancho Luna
Ismaelillo
Playitas
Boca de Yaguanabo
Rio Hondo
La Tatagua
El Ingles

Guanimar
Cajío
Playa Tomate
Santa Isabel
Mayabeque
Playa Rosario
Playa del Caimito
Tasajera

Nueva Gerona
Bibijagua
Colony
Paradiso
Punta Francés
Playa Roja
Playa Larga
Punta del Este
Cayo Avalos
Cayo Rosario

CUBA'S BEACHES AND SEASIDE RESORTS

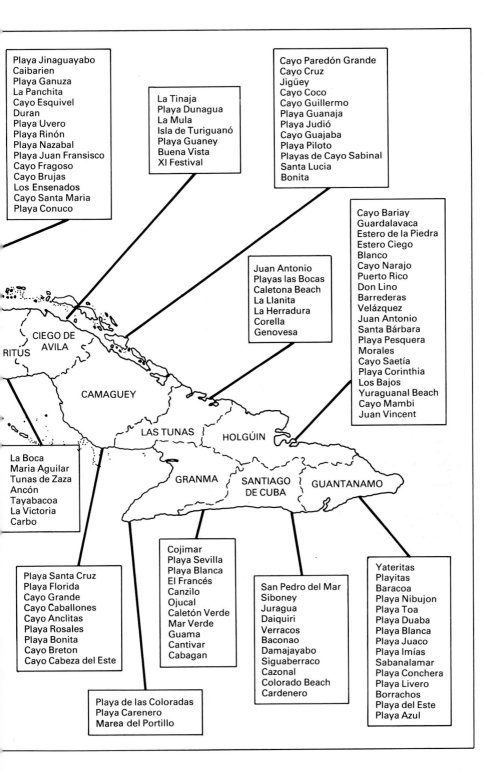

Playa Jinaguayabo
Caibarien
Playa Ganuza
La Panchita
Cayo Esquivel
Duran
Playa Uvero
Playa Rinón
Playa Nazabal
Playa Juan Fransisco
Cayo Fragoso
Cayo Brujas
Los Ensenados
Cayo Santa Maria
Playa Conuco

La Tinaja
Playa Dunagua
La Mula
Isla de Turiguanó
Playa Guaney
Buena Vista
XI Festival

Cayo Paredón Grande
Cayo Cruz
Jigüey
Cayo Coco
Cayo Guillermo
Playa Guanaja
Playa Judió
Cayo Guajaba
Playa Piloto
Playas de Cayo Sabinal
Santa Lucia
Bonita

Cayo Bariay
Guardalavaca
Estero de la Piedra
Estero Ciego
Blanco
Cayo Narajo
Puerto Rico
Don Lino
Barrederas
Velázquez
Juan Antonio
Santa Bárbara
Playa Pesquera
Morales
Cayo Saetía
Playa Corinthia
Los Bajos
Yuraguanal Beach
Cayo Mambi
Juan Vincent

Juan Antonio
Playas las Bocas
Caletona Beach
La Llanita
La Herradura
Corella
Genovesa

CIEGO DE AVILA

RITUS

CAMAGUEY

LAS TUNAS

HOLGÚIN

La Boca
Maria Aguilar
Tunas de Zaza
Ancón
Tayabacoa
La Victoria
Carbo

GRANMA

SANTIAGO
DE CUBA

GUANTANAMO

Playa Santa Cruz
Playa Florida
Cayo Grande
Cayo Caballones
Cayo Anclitas
Playa Rosales
Playa Bonita
Cayo Breton
Cayo Cabeza del Este

Cojimar
Playa Sevilla
Playa Blanca
El Francés
Canzilo
Ojucal
Caletón Verde
Mar Verde
Guama
Cantivar
Cabagan

San Pedro del Mar
Siboney
Juragua
Daiquiri
Verracos
Baconao
Damajayabo
Siguaberraco
Cazonal
Colorado Beach
Cardenero

Yateritas
Playitas
Baracoa
Playa Nibujon
Playa Toa
Playa Duaba
Playa Blanca
Playa Juaco
Playa Imías
Sabanalamar
Playa Conchera
Playa Livero
Borrachos
Playa del Este
Playa Azul

Playa de las Coloradas
Playa Carenero
Marea del Portillo

113

Juan, north of Morón, the **X1 Festival beach** is rather isolated but is excellently situated near a group of famous caves and the beauty spot of Lomas de Yeso. The town of Máximo Gómez, nearby, offers all facilities for the visitor and tours can be arranged around the magnificent **Buena Vista Bay**. Further out, in the archipelago, is the island nautical club resort of **Cayo Guillermo**.

On the short, northern coastline of Sancti Spiritus Province, **La Victoria** and **Carbo** beaches provide local facilities and are near two famous cave areas at **Punta Judas** and a selection of beautiful cays just offshore. This is a particularly good fishing spot as is the province's south coast.

The Province of Santa Clara's extensive coastline includes a selection of national beaches. Fishing is good along this coast and the province even has an island beach on the shores of Lake Minerva, an artificial reservoir just four kilometres from the provincial capital of Santa Clara. Both Cayo Esquivel and Playa Rinõn have excellent sandy shores among a host of smaller beaches.

Further west, the Province of Matanzas can claim to have one of the world's most famous beaches. **Varadero** is unique. Here, 20 kilometres of sparkling sand and invitingly transparent blue water, reefs, shipwrecks, first class hotels and top nightclubs, attract sun and sea worshippers from around the globe. After a long, straight drive, with Screwpine and Casuarina hemming the coastal foam, and great fields of Sisal plants to the right, the Varadero resort opens out on a long spit of land.

The **Hicacos Peninsula**, site of the tantalising beach, is just 130 kilometres east of Havana City. Located just northeast of the provincial capital, Matanzas, Varadero is a small town in itself with shops, polyclinics, children's parks, motor servicentres, a post office, sixteen restaurants of international cuisine and cafeterias, boating centres, transport hire, game fishing centres, a regular bus service,

ice cream and refreshment cabins and a host of bars.

Almost thirty villas, hotels, motels or cabin sites will soon be supplemented by eight new hotels adding 2000 more rooms to the existing 3000 rooms. This will make Varadero the largest resort in the Caribbean.

The resort area stretches out into the Atlantic Ocean and backs on to the Bay of Cardenas. As the peninsula narrows towards Punta de Hicacos, the built-up area is left behind and Pines, Mangrove and lagoons instead of houses, villas, shops and hotels, line the roadside.

A natural sea-cave forms the venue for one of the region's evening attractions. The Cueva del Pirata provides cabaret, dancing and a bar until the early hours in an atmosphere reminiscent of the buccaneering days of the Spanish Main and decorated 'a la Tussauds' – dungeon style! Occasionally along the roadside can be seen examples of the region's special giant cacti.

Real Indian caves further along the peninsula at Cueva de Ambrosio reveal signs of early inhabitants of pre-Columbian Cuba and the ocean shelf reveals to divers the spectacular action of the sea in this region. Scuba diving, fishing, snorkelling and boating are the most natural pastimes in Varadero apart from swimming, horse riding, tennis, golf, sunbathing and generally enjoying the delicious ambience. Cabarets are Varadero's speciality, particularly that at the Hotel International. The culmination of festive activities is the celebration of selecting the season's favourite tourists, crowned as 'Papa Sol' and 'Queen Mariposa'.

Sightseeing tours are arranged to all parts of the country as the resort has its own modernised airport, Maurice Bishop, named after the late Grenadian leader. Cayo Largo, a desert-island, coralline resort in the southern seas of Cuba, reached by air, is a favourite two to three-day trip but should be booked well in advance. Havana to Santiago de Cuba, Viñales to

Trinidad, all are on the tour list as well as sea voyages, country excursions and visits to sites of industry or interest. The Cubatur representative or hotel reception will provide all details on trips and excursions and almost any sporting equipment and transport can be rented at this, the most famous of Cuba's resorts.

After Matanzas Province and Varadero's giant beach and giant cacti, the Province of Havana embraces the Province of the City of Havana. Not a quarter-hour drive from the centre of the city are the **Playas del Este**. Generally known as seven, but actually fourteen in all, they are strung, like pearls, along more than 50 kilometres of azure coastline.

Havana's eastern beaches offer something for everyone. They are naturally popular with the capital city's residents at weekends and holidays. They are also popular with Cubans from the furthermost reaches of the island and with many visitors who don't feel the need to travel far from Havana. Every taste and every pocket is catered for. Inexpensive camping sites with the most elementary facilities, but entirely adequate, attract young visitors – particularly those who wish to tour light.

On the other hand, it is possible to rent a rather luxurious villa for a family holiday, equipped with all modern conveniences, either self-catering or with staff, with or without a selection of watersporting equipment, and with its own beach. No beach in Cuba, however, can be called entirely private, but a sandy frontage and limpid blue waters just beyond your veranda give all the impressions of a private, secluded beach.

Of the 11 listed beaches of Playas del Este, the first, **Bacuranao**, is the site of the historic British landing, prior to the taking of Havana, in 1762. The modern facilities include semi-camping areas with 51 rustic cabins (Villa Bacurano) all with air-conditioning and the usual cooking facilities. This can be a busy beach on Cuban holidays. Built around a tiny bay alongside a small river, the resort caters for

all tastes and has a cafeteria and restaurant plus basic requirements. Next to Bacuranao is **Tarara**, a similar, but less important area.

East Havana's third beach is **El Megano**, also equipped with camping facilities, 51 cabins and villas. It is somewhat over-shadowed by its larger neighbour, **Santa Maria del Mar**. Overlooking both Megano and Santa Maria beaches are the vast villa complexes of Santa Maria Loma, or Santa Maria Hill. Behind the long stretch of glistening, white sand, the beach and its service road are separated from the hillside accommodation by a long lagoon. The Santa Maria complex has every facility, offers a large cross-section of activities and is ideal for family, single, double or group holidays. Early in 1986 the 198-roomed Itabo Hotel and three apartment hotels were built on this popular beach.

After Santa Maria beach, just past the Motel on the seaward side of Via Blanca, which runs the length of Playas del Este, are **Boca Ciega** and **Guanabo** beaches. Very built-up, the area offers a wide, sweeping curve of a beach, backed by beach houses, villas, cabins, shops, two cinemas, cafeterias, bars – a complete village in fact.

Every facility is offered at the Guanabo resort but it can become quite crowded on the beach because of its proximity to Havana. The area does, however, cater for everyone from student to family holidays. A little further east is the cabin and camping beach area of **Hermosa**, with its added accommodation of 102 cabins at Villa Hermosa. This beach, and that of Valenciana, are separated from the main village of Guanabo by the winding outlet of Rio Guanabo.

The next significant beach, **Playa Brisas del Mar**, apart from **Playa del Muerto**, is the last resort before the town of Santa Cruz del Norte. **Brisas del Mar** is quite built-up and offers similar accommodation to previously described beaches but is connected to a smaller area called **Playa del Rincon**. Continuing along the

Via Blanca toward Santa Cruz, the road passes the cafeteria El Cayuelo, on the beach side. The small roadside monuments are to the coastguards killed in action against invaders. Pass the oilfields of Jesus Suarez Gayol Complex and the new thermo-electric power station with its striped, lighthouse-cooling tower. Just before the plant, look for the hillside pebble-sign, 'No Pasaran', constructed by villagers.

Santa Cruz del Norte town is on the seaward side. It has an interesting free market for vegetables. On the hillside, opposite the quayside Havana Club Rum factory, is the giant sugar 'Centrale' of Camilo Cienfuegos and, just before the left turn for **Jibacoa Beach**, is the **Playa Fraile**, a slightly rocky coastal stretch.

Jibacoa is a five-kilometre sweep of beaches comprising six shell-shaped sandy bays. Indeed, the Indian word, Jibacoa, means, 'place of shells'. One of the most famous beaches in Cuba and the most attractive of all the eastern beaches of Havana, Jibacoa has low-level accom-modation for young people in seventy cabins. Villa Loma consists of 11 houses, 38 rooms, accommodating from one to eight people. All are fully equipped with the most modern facilities and a restaurant, bar and pool complete the luxurious mini-resort.

A lookout and dive area makes Villa Loma an exclusive paradise both for the sunbathers and the energetic vacationers. Motor scooters, canoes, peddle boats, boardsails and row boats can be rented and dive facilities are excellent – where else can you dive on two pirate wrecks in one tiny bay? These wrecks are now being carefully studied by experts. Seafaris, 'El guateque' – fiesta, horse riding, deepsea fishing, farm parties and Afro-Caribbean dance nights are just some of the activities available at El Tropico, Villa Loma's neighbouring hotel and cabin complex. The hotel area can accommodate 174 vacationers and offers everything from a games room to an excellent restaurant and bar, trips to cabarets, and also specialises in diving excursions on its rich, colourful reefs.

El Abra is a small campsite on the winding road through Jibacoa, just set back from the beachside El Tropico. A number of cabins provide ample student-type accommodation and basic require-ments such as washing facilities and cooking areas. More cabins and campsites are planned for the Jibacoa region. A host of tours and visits to local sites can be arranged through Jibacoa's helpful Cuba-tur representatives or from the hotel El Tropico. Indian caves, bird watching, a sugar mill, a distillery, farm trips and mountain hiking are just a few of the daily excursions which can be planned. For a special beach treat, make enquiries about visiting **Puerto Escondido –** the secret port. Jibacoa is an experience which epit-omises the concept of a Caribbean beach holiday – a resort which encapsulates the benefits of Cuba's varied tourism resources.

There are about nine recognised beaches to the west of Havana. These do not have the reputation of Havana's eastern beaches, but are still easily accessible from the capital city. Most of these resorts cater for local requirements and are also popular with the residents of Havana City.

Further west, from Havana Province, is the huge, tail-like promontory of Pinar del Rio Province. The long, thin, mountainous region, extends into the Gulf of Mexico on the northern side, and has a 250 kilometre Caribbean coastline in the south. Ten popular beaches are located on the Mexican Gulf side. A favourite haunt of Ernest Hemingway on this coastline was Bahia Honda. Not only do these bays provide relaxation for the inhabitants of Pinar del Rio City, but offer seaside alternatives to those visitors touring the interesting mountain resorts and lake fishing in the far west. **Cayo Levisa** and **Puerto Esperanza** are the best known beaches.

Caribbean coast

On the southern side of the province the fishing is excellent and its Caribbean beaches offer a complete change of scenery. The great Gulf of Batabanó encircles the Isla de la Juventud (Island of Youth), and provides numerous bays and sandy, coralline beaches for relaxation or watersports.

Into Havana Province's south coast, the shore is more swampy, leading to the great marshlands of the Zapata Peninsula. The occasional beaches on this seaboard are generally frequented only by local inhabitants. In the centre of the sweeping bay is Surgidero de Batabanó, the location for the main ferry to the Isla de la Juventud, and a well-known fishing port.

This ferry crosses the most spectacular waters of the Gulf of Batabanó to the island, where a fascinating coastline surrounds the oyster-shaped province. Hotels are excellent and offer all the facilities of diving, hunting, fishing, and watersport excursions. An airport on the Isla de la Juventud makes for easy access to superlative water activities in some of the most beautiful waters in the whole of the Caribbean.

Horse riding is a favourite pastime particularly on the Caribbean cays.

Just a short boat trip, or even shorter light 'plane ride away, is the magical coral island of **Cayo Largo**. Set in a sea which would turn a jeweller green with envy, the emerald gem of an island is surrounded by a hundred cays, islets and its own necklace of brilliant white sand and coral reefs. The long, slim island boasts six of its own beaches, a modern hotel and a small islet as an operational wildlife sanctuary. **Cayo Avalos** and **Cayo Rosario** also have resort status but have not been developed as Cayo Largo.

Between **Playa Luna** and **Playa Sirena**, on the widest, south-west part of the cay, is a little airstrip. **Playa Lindamar** and **Playa Blanca** flank the 59-room Hotel Isla del Sur, which is being constantly up-dated and will soon double its accommodation. Later this decade, another 1000 rooms will be made available at the new Cayo Largo complexes. The Villa Capricho is also soon to be expanded. A large restaurant and two bars at Isla del Sur offer ample space for relaxation, with fantastic views, while the outer shores of **Coconut Beach** and **Turtle Beach** are havens of solitude surrounded by unusual

What better way to get a good suntan than boardsailing across limpid blue lagoons?

vegetation and prolific wildlife. Excellent facilities for boat excursions, diving trips, mainland tours, and watersports, are available at the hotel and most beaches. Cayo Largo's perfect climate and location make this retreat a paradise, set in an iridescent sea, abounding with fascinating marine life and coral formations.

From Cayo Largo and the Archipelago of Los Canarreos in the Gulf of Batabanó, the scenery changes along Cuba's south coast. Into the southern seaboard of Matanzas Province, past the **Cayo Ernst Thaelman**, to the shores which are dominated by the vast swamplands of the Zapata Peninsula, conditions are ideal for fishing. For seashore relaxation, the marsh only gives way to sand on the offshore cays, or in the funnel-shaped mouth of Bahia de Cochinos, or Bay of Pigs.

Just south of Treasure Lake, and the Indian village resort of Guama, the popular, local beach of **Playa Larga** lies at the top of the bay. This beach is hemmed in by the Zapata swamp which surrounds the bay, but which is broken on the easternmost curve of its funnel, by Giron beach. **Playa Larga** and **Playa Giron** have restaurants, cafeterias and cabin accommodation with facilities for the hire of watersports equipment. Both beaches are recommended as day outings, with visits to the museum commemorating the infamous invasion of April 17, 1961, celebrating the defeat of imperialist forces, and tours of the local sights. Overnight stays can be arranged at Guama, or Giron, through Cubatur representatives, or hotel receptions. The eastern swamp of Zapata is thick Mangrove and marsh right up to the coast after Playa Giron, and no beaches exist until one enters the Province of Cienfuegos.

The massive, 'pocket' bay, of Cienfuegos, is an historical port and was traditionally the haven of armadas and fleets. It is renowned for its deep harbour and narrow outlet into the Caribbean. Only on the eastern lip of this harbour entrance have the beaches been developed, and a series of excellent resorts here skirt the southern shores of the Escambray Mountains. From the Hotel Pascaballo, opposite the fortress of Jagua across the mouth of the bay, to Motel Yaguanabo, about 50 kilometres south, the curve of Cienfuegos Province is a string of individual beaches.

Those which have been converted into resorts, include the beach at Rancho Club, just a few kilometres from the hillside hotel of Pascaballo. As a base, the hotel provides all tourism requirements, with 188 rooms, a pool, restaurant, cafeteria, shop, and its own rent-a-boat taxi service to the city of Cienfuegos. The beach at the Rancho Club is, however, surpassed by that at **Rancho Luna**, just a short drive from the famous Hotel Rancho Luna. Apart from its 225 rooms, 8 suites, restaurants, rental facilities for all sorts of water and land transport and the Olympic-size swimming pool, the Rancho Luna Hotel has its own small cove, 500 metres of beach with Caribbean-clear water.

Further down the coast is the shelving beach of **Playitas**. Near the hilltop pioneer camp for youngsters is the beach of **La Tatagua** and, easily accessible from the Motel Yaguanabo, are the beaches of **El Ingles**, (the Englishman), and **Yaguanabo** beach itself. All the hotels in the region organise visits to the local sights and arrange their own entertainments during the day and in the evenings. Tours to the old Spanish town of Trinidad are most popular but there are regular visits to the city of Cienfuegos, its botanical gardens, industrial developments and to the mountain resorts of the Sierra Escambray.

South of Trinidad are two very popular hotels which complement the town's Las Cuevas Motel. Both near beaches – **La Boca and Ancon beach** – the hotels of Costa Sur and Hotel Ancon offer a great number of seaside attractions, tours and day outings to points of interest. They also have the advantage of being close to one of Cuba's main tourist attractions of Trinidad.

The southern shores of Sancti Spiritus Province can also claim to be among the best locations for deepwater fishing and reef exploration. Off the cove-scalloped coast are a host of tiny cays. A few kilometres out from the beach at **Tayabacoa** and **Tunas de Zaza**, south of Sancti Spiritus City, the coral formations are prolific with spectacular marine life. The nearby hotel offers ample accommodation and facilities for those either visiting the sights in the area or taking advantage of the beach's maritime activities. A great pattern of canals separates the area east of Tunas de Zaza, Sancti Spiritus from its neighbouring province of Ciego de Avila.

Although the capital city, Ciego de Avila, is near the province's tiny coastline, the canal system and marshlands preclude the possibility of any established beaches. Vacationers from the city generally travel

This is the best way to enjoy a 'sahoco'. Fresh milk from the young coconut mixed with light, white rum and sipped through a straw whilst cooling-off at Cayo Largo!

to the north coast for seaside relaxation. Deepwater fishing from the small port of Jucaro is, however, highly rated.

The long coastline of Camagüey Province is one vast marshy, mangrove-infested, unexplored maze of rivulets and lagoons. No beaches as such exist for more than two hundred kilometres of coast from Tunas de Zaza beach to the most easterly point of Camagüey's southern shores. For the whole length of the Ana Maria Gulf to the Gulf of Guacanayabo the deserted coast appears to offer nothing much for the tourist or beach-lover, but a great deal for the ornithologist and fisherman. At the point where the two gulfs meet, Santa Cruz del Sur, the beach of **Santa Cruz**, seems to be Camagüey's only southern attraction apart from a few tiny sandy enclaves but, out in the cobalt waters of the Caribbean, a surprise is in store.

Archipelago Jardines de Reina, the islands of the Queen's Gardens, is an apt name for a group of tiny, sun-drenched, islets strung out in line between 100 and 20 kilometres off Cuba's southern coast. A paradise for fishermen and divers alike, the main three islands, **Cayo Breton, Cayo Grande** and **Cayo Cabeza del Este**, are bases for all types of nautical activities. The *Last Paradise*, boatel serves as accommodation, bar, restaurant and dive boat, although many other launches and yachts ply the island waters. Each year the facilities on the islands are being up-dated and there are extensive tourism plans for future development. The 'Gardens' are still an, as yet, little-discovered paradise as the name of its famous, two-storey, seabourne hotel suggests.

The Gulf of Guacanayabo is headed by the huge delta of Cuba's longest river, the Rio Cauto. Much of this region of Granma Province is swampland except near the mouth of the smaller Yara river where the fishing port of Manzanillo breaks the coastline. Yacht excursions can be arranged from the harbour. Hotel Guacanayabo, built in 1979, has 112 rooms, Golfo restaurant, bar and pool. Further south, the small, but beautiful beach of **Las Coloradas** severs the monotony of mangrove swamps and lagoons.

Bayamo, the provincial capital of Granma, is probably the best base from which to visit this area. Las Coloradas has

become a place of pilgrimage. Not because of its attractive bay sheltered by Coconut, *Uvachaletta* or Sea Grape, and Almond trees, or because of its rustic, open-air restaurant or secluded bar – the thousands of tourists who come to this isolated beach are there for historical reasons.

Just a short distance down the coast, off the new service road and into the Mangrove swamps is a grand monument. It is built in the shape of a giant yacht with a podium as a flying bridge overlooking a large meeting square. This is the point where Fidel Castro landed with 82 revolutionaries to found the Cuba of today. Both national and foreign tourists flock here for the long walk down a re-paved causeway, through bright green Mangrove swamp and across a lagoon, to a lookout jetty, the actual site of the motor cruiser *Granma's* landfall. Here, there is little to see except the tangle of Mangrove roots and the area of devastation caused when Batista's plane, alerted by traitors, bombed the heroes. Only survivors of the attack on that second day of December in 1956 met on the site of the monument to accomplish the Cuban Revolution. The concrete structure is now a meeting point for visitors and houses a restaurant and gift shop.

This small bay, and the beach at Las Coloradas, is practically the most southerly point, apart from Cabo Cruz, in the whole island, lying almost on the latitude of 20° North. From Cabo Cruz in Granma, on the map, the coast of Santiago de Cuba Province appears to follow the latitude in an almost straight line. Along the roadside feathery Coco Palms point their swaying trunks towards the Equator. Granma Province's main attraction on this coastline is Playa **Marea del Portillo**. There are 74 rooms at the resort's hotel.

The south-facing shores of what was once called Oriente Province are indented with a thousand bays, beaches, coves and harbours. Most of the beaches in this region must be reached from the capital, Santiago de Cuba City. A coastal road links **Ocujal**, in the west, with **Baconao**,

Finding a deserted beach of your own is no problem in Cuba.

through the city, although the most popular beaches are located between Santiago de Cuba and the eastern sector of the province towards **Cardenero** beach. Midway between the city and Ocujal is the beautiful beach of **Guama** near the motel of the same name. The motel overlooks two bays and offers eight rooms and four cabins for accommodation. Excellent vistas from the restaurant and bar are benefits, plus facilities for sea trips and fishing expeditions.

The road from Guama to the city provides spectacular views of the Sierra Maestra and rocky coastline dotted with copper and iron mines. At **Sevilla beach** three hotels designed as pyramids, overlook a vast expanse of sandy beaches and, further towards the city many small bays have been developed for national vacationers. There is also **Caletón Blanco** with its famous black sand and crystal-clear waters, **Canzilo** and, just before the beach of **Mar Verde**, the masts of three Spanish ships, sunk in 1898, project from the waters of a rocky cove, offering exciting diving prospects. Camping on this coast is very popular with week-enders from Santiago de Cuba.

East of the city a vast new development has converted about 40 kilometres of coast into a continuous tourism resort. **San Pedro del Mar**, just outside the city is most popular at week-ends. From **Siboney**, however, just a few minutes from the city, seven beaches cater for every taste and every pocket. Small camping areas are dotted along the undulating coastline and each beach operates as an individual unit with hotel accommodation, villas, cabins or rustic bungalows. Siboney beach is more popular with local visitors from the city. Further east is a large camping area for youth, then **Juragua beach**, followed by the famous **Daiquiri beach** with its Indian cave paintings. Interesting sculptures of a horse and groups of birds along the roadside can distract the visitor's view from the magnificent scenery on the way to **Berracos beach.**

Just behind Balneario del sol beach, on the rocky hillside, is a most spectacular prehistoric park with a museum and life-size dinosaurs strategically constructed on the roadside. Playa Berracos has 40 rustic cabins for rent plus a restaurant, cafeteria, children's play area and charming beach. Ancient sea caves and Indian dwellings along the coast add to the interest on the drive to the furthest beaches. Two new motels here have opened up the Baconao area. From the more developed beaches tours can be made into the city and to the points of interest such as Gran Piedra. The zoo, aquarium, dolphinarium, with seating for 120 visitors, cactus farm, coral farm in the ocean, country excursions or boat outings represent a host of daily diversions.

Many visitors choose to stay in Santiago de Cuba and drive to the different beaches. Inter-beach travel is also organised by means of a little train-like conveyance giving the passengers ample opportunity to view the spectacular scenery. The coast of this province has been earmarked for extensive tourism development, culminating on the thirtieth anniversary of the birth of the triumph of the Revolution in 1989.

Between the Baconao beach on the border of Guantánamo Province and Punta de Maisí, the island's easternmost point, just two main beaches deserve a mention. **Yateritas** is popular with the inhabitants of the capital city, Guantánamo, and, much further along the coast, **Playitas** is a beach more favoured by the local tourists from Baracoa on the northern shore. From Santiago de Cuba it is possible to drive through the east Sierra Maestra to Guantánamo and onto the coastal road through to the Atlantic coastal resorts.

Being a long, narrow island, the country has its fair quota of beaches and the visitor to Cuba is never very far from a spectacular coastline. Variations in geological structure, the island's unique climate and its location between three seas, have provided Cuba with rocky coves, vast sandy strands, coral cays, cliffside, pebbled, picturesque

Soroa's mountain retreat is both exhilarating and serene – a natural paradise with secret pools surrounded by a blaze of botanical beauty.

beaches and deserted islands. It is, however, advisable to check locally the conditions of tide, etc in the more remote beach areas. When collecting dead shells and coral on the reefs it is as well to wear gloves and to use an implement to turn rocks or specimens.

In Cuba, there is a beach for everyone, whatever his interest, above or below the waters or just for relaxing in the tropical sun which drenches its shores.

Cuba's country resorts

The varied terrain, climate and altitudes of Cuba's interior are unsurpassed in the Caribbean. The long, thin nature of the island makes all its country attractions accessible from the Central Highway. Trekking into the countryside is favourite with both Cuban and visiting tourists.

Guamá offers lakeside accommodation where one can resort to nature's provisions in lush tropical surroundings. Fabled Treasure Lake is the site of an ancient Indian village – ask about its legend.

Resort facilities are being up-graded and expanded with national camping capacity now exceeding 70 000. The following descriptions outline the country's more popular rural resorts.

Pinar del Rio Province

The extreme west of Cuba has many sites of Indian origin and Cueva Furche has been opened for tourist visits, the province also has the exciting Valley of Viñales.

This valley was originally an enormous cave, spreading over what is now the valley floor. The roof collapsed and the valley now presents an area of unusual karst scenery with cone-shaped knolls. The soil formed since the cave collapsed is rich red earth and supports forest vegetation on the strange hills. Nature has created a uniquely beautiful valley said only to be equalled in Puerto Rico and in China.

This area of the Sierra Organos is honeycombed with limestone caves once inhabited by the primitive Guanahacabibes Indians. The most famous of these, the Indian Cave, bisects a small mountain thrusting up from the flat valley floor. Well-lit after electrification in 1952, the journey through this cave is fascinating. Great bulbous stalactites hang from the cavernous roof and, about 250 metres into the cave, a river blocks the walkway and a row boat, or occasionally a motorboat, continues the underground tour on the milky-green, 3 – 6 metre-deep river.

The cave roof varies in height from 60 to 135 metres and cave wall formations pointed out by the guide include The Snake, The Skull, The Tobacco Leaves, The Three Musketeers and The Old Man. Be prepared for the magical view as the boat emerges from the cavern and go to see the waterfall. Around the steep, pock-marked side of the mountain, near the cave entrance, is a small cafeteria.

At the famous look-out over Mayabe Valley in Holguín Province, Pancho the donkey has an insatiable thirst for the local beer!

metres, Leovigildo Gonzalez, once taught by the famous Mexican Diego Rivera, directed the massive Archaeological Mural depicting a typical scene in prehistoric times. Another rocky outcrop in the valley is the home of Nino the basket weaver, a favourite stop-over for day visitors. Further from the valley are the cave sites of Sumidero and the Santo Tomás cavern.

Looking down on the valley from the clifftop motel, La Ermita, the *vegas*, or tobacco curing houses, scattered across the neat green fields and the *bohios* or thatched dwellings, appear like little blocks of wood on an emerald patchwork. The hotel has 18 rooms arranged in a semi-circle around a pool, a restaurant, bar and magnificent scenic views.

The largest hotel in the valley is Los Jazmines. Also built on a steep lookout, the neo-Spanish, 14-room, three-storey hotel has a large cafeteria on the ground floor overlooking a large pool, and restaurant and bar on the second floor. The rooms, each with balcony and marvellous view, are on the top floor. Los Jazmines has a capacity for 30 people. Two shops, a games room and a relaxation area complete the self-contained complex. Its delightful decor with the extensive use of wood and *vitrales*, or coloured glass fanlights and wrought iron, complements the magic of this spectacular valley.

The town of Viñales makes a rewarding visit for its peacefulness, its tiny church, square, art gallery, museum and old, wooden fretwork-embellished houses. Many of the tiny bungalow-style houses sport verandas or iron columns. The town is situated at the centre of Viñales' famed 'fantastic valley' and attracts tourists and international archaeological and geological societies

La Güira National Park, also in the Los Organos mountains, is famed for its variety of wildlife and popular with ornithologists. The gateway – Hacienda Cortina – and the pre-revolutionary houses are relics of the previous landowner, Cortina, who specialised in the trade of Cuba's precious

Just opposite the Indian Cave is Hotel Rancho San Vicente. With excellent tourist facilities, the hotel has 47 rooms including 14 cabins, a restaurant, nightclub, cafeteria, pool, sulphur baths, souvenir shop and games room. Tours, organised from the hotel, can be made to tobacco farms, a seafari to Levisa Cay on the north coast and to a barbecue at a local farmer's private house. Trips are also organised to the garden resort of Soroa and to other caves in the valley.

Further along the valley floor is a gaping cave which has been converted into a dance hall; day and night busloads of visitors come to dance, listen to the music or relax with a cool drink, as swallows dart in and out of the cavern's labyrinth.

Winding through the lush valley floor, carpeted in either tobacco plants or maize, depending on the time of year, the road leads out to a giant mural painted on a cliff face. On this stone 'canvas' 120 × 180 woods. A variety of sporting activities are available in the park and accommodation can be arranged at the Cabañas de los Pinos, in one of the 23 stilted, rustic pine cabins, served by one of the two restaurants in the park.

In the Sierra del Rosario Mountains is the camping and rustic-style resort of La Caridad which can accommodate about 1300 campers. This remote resort is part of a system of large campsites in the region. Another, Cajalbana, caters for 500 people in its 200 metre-high eyrie resort near La Güira National Park, in the historic Los Portales Caves area, and accommodates 1300 guests. Near Los Portales River waterfalls is a fourth campsite catering for one thousand campers. In these areas the facilities are deliberately rustic and spartan to blend with the natural rocky environment. Another similar resort in the area is Rancho Mundito, a hilly, forest resort with modern facilities not far from the mineral water spa of San Diego de los Baños. It is a

Traditional rustic-style replicas of Indian long houses serve as restaurants, shops or holiday cabins in many country resorts.

very rural township surrounded by Malanga plantations and with the possibility of horseriding trips and treks to Soroa or other mountain resorts. Nearby the Pica Pica valley is a favourite destination for speleologists.

Soroa, this lush 'Garden of Eden' has been dubbed 'Cuba's Rainbow' because of its prolific and colourful vegetation. It is a hillside park area about 700 metres above sea level and first conceived as a haven for rare plants and trees by the Spaniard Don Ignacio Soroa in the late 1920s. A former coffee plantation, the 35 000 square metres of garden was laid out in memory of his daughter. Natural lookouts present vista after vista of the surrounding countryside and dells, glades and hidden valleys dividing the botanical garden. About 50 kinds of native Cuban trees grow in the park, plus hundreds of different flowers and 800 varieties or orchid, including 250 indigenous species. Giant ferns, ancient trees and ornamental plants surround the main accommodation area. The resort has a new motel with separate cabins surrounding an Olympic-size pool. About 50 cabins and a camping area provide for all

types of tours and three restaurants and a bar offer facilities for day trippers. A new restaurant on the very top of the hill, all flagstone and marble, with a Spanish-style terrace and Don Quixote mural, is the most luxurious in the region. See the palm-leaf hatmaker fashion sombreros and model birds. Pick mango and *poma rosa* from the roadside trees and visit the secluded waterfall (Salto del Rio Manantiales), a long walk but a refreshing dip after a hot climb! Don't forget the local drink, Guayabita del Pinar, made from a special variety of guava.

Havana Province

Just on the eastern edge of the Los Organos mountain range, is the nearest mountain beauty spot to the capital city. Las Terrazas clings to the hillside surrounded by a reforestation area of precious woods. The scenery around the small town is charming and is worth a day trip from Havana.

Matanzas Province

In the far south of Matanzas Province is the idyllic lakeside resort of Guamá. A classic achievement combining history with the sophistication of today's tourist requirements. The reconstructed Taino Indian village blends with stilted log cabins and thatched amenities. A large restaurant, conically thatched, with a small rustic viewing platform reached by a logwork ladder, offers a choice of views. The resort of 44 cabins is reached by motor launch from a quayside just next to the famous crocodile breeding farm with its 40 000 specimens. A twenty-minute boat ride across waters teeming with Largemouth Bass, brings the visitor to a lakeside, life-size model of the Indian village discovered on the site. Treasure Lake is so called because of a legend which tells of the Indians hiding their gold in the lake to prevent its capture by the Spanish *conquistadores*. The oval lake is 9000 kilometres square and fed by a maze of wildfowl-filled canals.

A number of Indian figures sculpted by Rita Longa, the Cuban artist, show various activities in the village life of the original inhabitants. Look for the scene of dogs hunting the rodent *Jutia* in the trees and the sculpture of an Indian hunting duck by the novel method of grasping their legs from under the water. Indians also used the *Remora*, or Sucker Fish which attaches itself to other fish, in order to capture both salt and freshwater fish and turtles.

The resort has one other link with its native origin – Guamá was the name of a famous chief of the area. Another traditional link is the display of local ceramic craftsmenship at La Boca – the ferry terminal. At the resort boats are supplied for the cabins and all requirements can be met from shops and a cafeteria. Tours of the crocodile farm and nearby beaches or the site of the Bay of Pigs invasion are available. Ask Cubatur representatives or hotel receptions. As the resort is situated near the Zapata Peninsula with its prolific birdlife there is also the opportunity for excursions into the vast swamplands.

Cienfuegos and Villa Clara Provinces

Cienfuegos has spectacular mountain scenery around Lake Hanabanilla in the Sierra Escambray. The huge Hanabanilla reservoir attracts visitors for all kinds of countryside activities from boating to horse riding. On the lakeside is the 128-room, Hanabanilla Hotel. Situated 370 metres above sea level, it commands a magnificent view of the surrounding mountains. Fishing here is the main occupation and also the main sport for visitors – try local fish at the excellent restaurant. Rio Negro, on the other side of the lake, makes a good excursion both for the boat trip and for *criollo* food. Hanabanilla Hotel has a swimming pool, bar, shops and games room, and can organise excursions to the regional sights of La Para, the peaks of the Escambray and the mountainside cave areas.

Two large camping areas are situated a

little further north of the lake and provide reasonably cheap accommodation.

Sancti Spiritus Province

In the same Escambray Mountains, is a large forest resort. The Mirador de Topes de Collantes' Pinos hotel is more than 800 metres above sea level among the great peaks. Other resort hotels include the Las Cuevas Motel and Zaza Hotel on Zaza lakeside. This region is a haven for wild birds, flowers and trees. For the wildlife enthusiast it is a prolific paradise teeming with deer, wild boar, flamingo, herons, passerines, parrots, parakeets, pigeons and wild duck.

Cliffs, canyons and caves surround the resort which is becoming one of Cuba's most popular hill stations. Many tours are available from the hotels in this region, the beautiful Spanish town of Trinidad is a short drive away, the tower of Iznaga and the beauty spots on the coast offer ideal short day-trips from the resort. Transport, including horses can be hired in the region.

Camagüey Province

At Los Cangilones del Rio Maximo, in Sierra de Cubitas, a campsite with a capacity of around 1000 is the only country resort area in the Province of Camagüey.

Las Tunas Province

A short drive away from the city of Victoria de Las Tunas, in the middle of the country, are the 48 cabins of the El Cornito resort. A restaurant and full modern amenities make this a good resort for an overnight stay for those travelling on the Central Highway, or longer if one wants to enjoy the local sights, fish or explore the region.

Holguín Province

This province contains the fascinating Mayabe Valley. Before reaching the valley itself, and the 21 bungalows of the Mirador de Mayabe Hotel, the José Marti Park makes an interesting diversion from the Central Highway. In the park, which has a boating lake, hunter's club and the Restaurant El Valle and a host of activities, a pool and artificial beach attract weekenders from the city.

Three hotels offer excellent accommodation to the east side of Holguín: Hotel Pernick, on the city outskirts, has 202 rooms; Motel El Bosque and, nearer the magnificent Valle de Mayabe and the Loma de Sao del Macio beauty spot, Hotel Mayabe. A local attraction at the Mayabe lookout, on a terrace overlooking the pool and valley, Pancho the donkey eats casabe savoury bread and then drinks a bottle of beer from the nearby bar – if you buy him one!

On the Bay of Nipe is the resort area of Mayari Abajo. From here the Sierra Cristal mountain park can be visited and one good hotel provides all the facilities needed for a country break – the Hotel Bitiri with 21 rooms and a fine restaurant. Out in the park itself is the Pinares de Mayari hotel, a group of rustic units with recreational facilities and all the requirements for trekking, pony riding and climbing trips. Ask any hotel reception or Cubatur representative about country visits and accommodation in the area.

Santiago de Cuba, Granma and Guantánamo Provinces

This, the most southerly province of Cuba, offers several listed country resorts which are all quite different. Right in the southeastern area of the province, on the seaward flank of the great Sierra Maestra mountains, The Gran Piedra, a giant rock perched high on the mountainside, is the site of the fourth highest peak resort in the country with a tourist centre, 22 cabins, restaurant, bar and all facilities. An orchid garden and botanical park on the hillside offer other distractions from the huge rock as does the 'Isabelica' plantation mansion. If you climb the 465 steps to the top of the rock it is a good idea to take some refreshment – and don't forget a camera, the view north through the mountains and south over the sea is stunning. This particular resort can be visited on a day-trip from the capital city and the peaceful environment at Gran Piedra is rewarding, as is the chance of seeing the sunset over the mountains, from the rock.

In the depths of a fold in the Sierra Maestra, some way north of Santiago de Cuba, is the secluded valley of Tayaba. The Motel Valle de Tayaba provides adequate accommodation and there are many country sights to visit in the region including Contramaestre town, Palma Soriano and El Cobre. In the north-east corner of the province, on the Mayari River is the isolated town of Mayari Arriba.

A remote resort, it is situated in the Sierra Cristal Range. These beautiful mountains can be explored from the camping site of Loma Blanca or the modern Motel Rancho Mexico. A most stirring sight, and one that captivated Columbus, is that of the great table mountain, El Yunque, 'the anvil'. Tours with guides can be arranged through hotel receptions or Cubatur representatives.

As you round a corner of the road from Santiago de Cuba to the province's eastern resorts a startling panorama presents itself.

The prehistoric park is unique in Latin America with its life-size dinosaurs in the 80 000 hectares of parkland.

National Parks

National Parks throughout Cuba and sites of interest are detailed below.

Province	National Parks/Sites of interest
Pinar del Rio	Guanahacabibes
	Los Organos
	Viñales Valley
	La Güira
	Soroa
Havana	Parque Lenin
	Escaleras de Jaruco
	Valle Yumuri
Matanzas	Valle Yumuri
	Guamá
	Zapata
	El Balcon
	La Arboleda
	Bellamar
	Ambrosio Caves
	Varadero beach
Cienfuegos	Topes de Collantes
	Escambray Mountains
	La Bija
	Valley of Yaguanabo
	Cienfuegos Caves
Villa Clara	Lake Hanabanilla
Sancti Spiritus	Torre de Iznaga
	Salto de Vega Grande
	Salto del Caburni
	Salto de Javira
	Mirador de Topes de Collantes
	Valle de San Luis
	Valle del Alunada
	Sumidero del Rio Jatibonico del Norte
Isla de la Juventud	Pirates coast
	Indian cave sites
Ciego de Avila	Laguna de Leche
	Loma de Cunagua
	Playita de Majagua
	Laguna Redonda
Camagüey	Sierra de Cubitas
	Santa Lucía Beach
	Indian cave
	Hoya de Bonet
	Los Paredones
	Cave of the Generals
	Los Canjilones
	Sierra de Najasa
	Sierra de Chorrillo
	Loma la Deseada
Holguín	Silla de Gibara
	Valle de Mayabe
	Loma de la Cruz
	Sierra de Nipe
	Sierra de Cristal
	Chuchillas de Moa
	Park José Marti
	Puente Natural del Rio Bitiri
Granma	Yara Valley
	Sierra Maestra
	Virama
Santiago de Cuba	Pico Turquino
	Pico Cuba
	Pico Suecia
	Valley of Tayaba
	El Cobre
	Gran Piedra
	Laguna Baconao
Guantánamo	Sierra Cristal
	Toa River
	El Yunque

CHAPTER 8

From Tip to Tail

*'. . . find your way to Cuba on the map: a long, green alligator,
with eyes of stone and water.'*

NICOLÁS GUILLÉN from his poem *Largolagarto Verde.*

Cuba's provinces, towns and cities

Cuba's division into provinces, cities and towns can be compared with those of any European country. Its fourteen provinces and special municipality are divided into smaller 'boroughs' for administrative purposes. Each division is rather like a 'county', with its local town or capital.

Each city and town has its own

Parts of the Sierra Maestra are still 'untouched' by modern day standards.

individuality from the early sixteenth-century colonial treasure-house of Spanish architecture that is Trinidad town, to the mid-nineteenth-century opulence of more recent Cienfuegos City. Brand new towns have been founded, such as Las Terrazas in Havana Province, built since 1969, and La Ya Ya, founded in 1972. A wealth of architectural splendours and unique building styles spanning five centuries await discovery. This section of the guide presents each province, district capital and important town, where to visit locally and where to stay and eat from Santiago de Cuba in the east to Pinar del Rio's tapering peninsula jutting into the Gulf of Mexico.

Santiago de Cuba Province

'With the blond Head of Fonseca
I shall go to Santiago.
With the red roses of Romeo y Julieta
I shall go to Santiago.

F. GARCIA LORCA, from a poem
about his father's cigars.

This extensive province stretches along the country's southern seaboard and encompasses a large portion of the Sierra Maestra mountains. Bananas, coffee, cocoa, tropical tubers and fruits are cultivated in this region.

The capital city of the province, Santiago de Cuba, is the country's second largest city and the province's population is second to the national capital's, at 940 000 approximately. The city has an international airport, one of Cuba's four universities and the nation's second busiest port. Major highways and several rail links, including the Central Highway, connect the city to the rest of Cuba. Santiago de Cuba is an important industrial city with many factories, an oil refinery, processing plants and power stations.

Thorn and scrub savanna edge the coastline which is almost one long, Caribbean coastal resort. Beach facilities are made available at regular points, within reasonable striking distance of Santiago de Cuba City. Fishing and watersports are some of the best in the land. Tourism development is to receive a big boost as Cuba's highlight of the South. There are many attractions in this province on both the beaches and in the beautiful mountain regions. El Cobre, El Escandel, the Gran

Piedra and the Valley of Tayaba, are all easily accessible from the city. In the far west of the province, the peaks of the highest mountains in the Sierra Maestra range, Pico Turquino, Pica Cuba and Pico Suecia, plus La Plata retreat, are all beauty spots.

The province has probably more historical connections than any other. With its heritage dating back to the Tainos Indians, before the Spanish arrivals. Santiago de Cuba is littered with sites from the revolutions and battle memorials from many wars so much so that Santiago has been dubbed 'Hero City'. The first charge of the Mambises; with machetes, was made in Baire, in 1868; the site of Carlos Manuel de Céspedes death in 1874 is at San Lorenzo; the hill where General Jośe Maceo Grajales died in 1895, is at Alto Songo; Antonio Guiteras' Barracks attack in 1933 occurred at San Luis; the Siboney farm was the site of the revolutionary gathering and launch of the Moncada attack in 1953 and Fidel Castro's rallying point in 1959, was at Palma Soriano. This region is the most tropical and Caribbean of all provinces. The city faces Haiti across the notorious Windward Passage concealing the Bartlett Deep and the Fosa of Batle – the deepest ocean trench in the Americas. The south's

Santiago de Cuba's legendary fortress commands stunning vistas along Cuba's southern shores. The distant Sierra Maestra provide a background to silver-white beaches running from the Caribbean Sea to the Atlantic Ocean.

It is difficult to imagine this massive Morro castle being taken by a small band of pirates under the famous Captain Morgan.

geographical and climatic contrasts are almost as striking as its political background.

Santiago de Cuba's tropical climate, lush countryside and attractive coastline make it one of Cuba's most interesting provinces apart from its history. Its speedy development is also making it one of the most prosperous.

Santiago de Cuba

The country's second city, was founded in 1514, by Diego de Velázquez as Cuba's capital. It was named after St. Jago hence Santiago. Its ideal location on the large, south-facing bay, protected by the impressive Sierra Maestra, plus the area's mineral wealth, contributed towards the city's prosperity. Its first mayor, Hernando Cortéz

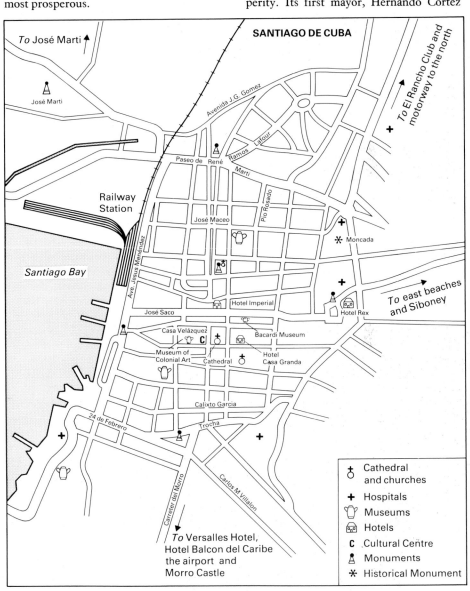

Complete in 1520, built by Hernando Cortéz
the conquistadore, and occupied by Diego de
Velázquez, Cuba's first Governor, this is the
country's oldest existing house.

led his *conquistadores* from here to the
greater riches of Aztec and Mayan Mexico.
The house which he built (1516 – 1520),
and which the first Governor, Velázquez,
moved into, still stands on Céspedes Square
as the Museum of Colonial Art, it is the
city's oldest building.

Copper and gold were mined here until
1554, when privateers raided the city.
Until this time Santiago was flourishing
and the Cathedral was begun as early as
1528. By 1640, the harrassment of the city
by pirates prompted the construction, over
two years, of the Morro Castle, overlooking
the majestic entrance to the bay. After
attacks by a succession of pirates, Captain
Henry Morgan, in 1662, sacked the city on
behalf of the British from a landfall at
Aguadores cove (near the river of the same
name, to the east of the city).

The church of Santa Lucia was begun in
1701 and the city thrived again for a short
period. By 1731, however, mining slaves

began protests over their conditions which
necessitated an increased influx of imported
labour – especially after the 1776 earthquake and the exodus from Haiti in 1791 of
almost 30 000 French settlers. In 1852
another earthquake hit Santiago. The city
had a chequered career until the 1868 –
1878 rebellion against the Spanish, led by
Carlos Manuel de Céspedes. The second
rising against the Spanish with José Martí
as the figurehead, involved such leaders as
the famous Maceo brothers. Santiago born,
they are buried in the city, as is Martí.

Spanish rule ended in 1898, but then
began a clandestine struggle for true
independence, which culminated in the
storming of the Moncada Garrison by
Fidel Castro and his followers on 26 July,
1953.

The southern city of Santiago was the
cradle of the Revolution. Granjita, the
little farm of **Siboney**, just ten minutes
from Santiago, was the gathering point for
Fidel's troops who were either massacred
in cold blood, killed in the attack or
imprisoned. The farm is now a most interesting museum. The **Moncada Barracks** are

This magnificent edifice in Céspedes Park dates from its consecration as Cuba's earliest Cathedral in 1528.

also now a museum and a school (every one of Batista's garrisons throughout the country was turned into an educational institution).

To walk the streets of Santiago de Cuba today, is to not only re-live history, but to experience one of the world's only cities where a thousand different bloods flow and mingle happily in the same vein. Spanish, African, Jamaican, British, French, Haitian and, way back in history, native Indian blood, have created a unique atmosphere. Because of the extreme tropical temperatures the music, arts and culture, tend to harp back to the other side of the Atlantic. The magic, cults and some religious activities, now preserved as part of the country's heritage, are directly reminiscent of identical practices on the west coast of Africa.

The evolution of Santiago's music can be heard at the **Casa de la Trova**, or Troubador's House. 'Culture Night' like a mini-carnival, happens every Saturday and Sunday. Here, on the famous **Heredia Street**, just off the main square, the ancient house reverberates to the olden song or Afro-Cuban rythmic folksongs. The history of the city's musical talent covers the walls in paintings and photographs and performances can continue into the light hours of the morning after.

On the same street is the **House of Cheeses**. Try an *El Cocal* – a local drink made with pepper leaves, vanilla, pine needles, soapberries and Indian root. The Cubatur office is on the corner and the **Museum of the Carnaval**, full of fantastic costumes and instruments, is not to be missed.

Carnaval in Santiago is the city's own special witching-time! During the last two weeks of June a transformation overcomes the city and its people. Some carnavál displays in the park can be as much as 20 metres high. Slaves from the Calabar coast of Africa brought the *carabalies*, a tribal dance form which was adapted and Cubanised during the 19th century. The carabalies dancers mingle with the folklore dancers of *Cutumba, Musigan, Tumba Francesa, Banda de los Perros, Muerte en Cueros, Changui, Sucu Sucu, Rumba, Congas de los Hoyos y Paso Franco* group and a thousand individual versions of a hundred dances, to form a whirling mass of colour and sound. This is Cuba's oldest carnival and probably the earliest performed in the Caribbean. The traditions of the old Oriente Province are all realised on floats rumbling over the cobbled streets, through seas of costumes and masks, from a multitude of cultures and societies. La Trocha street is a particularly good viewpoint. Replicas of the floats ca be viewed in the city's **Museo del Carnavál**.

The sights to see in this balconied, colonnaded, city, built on an amphitheatre of terraces, are not difficult to find. Santiago de Cuba is divided into various sectors. There are 14 museums in Santiago de Cuba. In the old city, from its centre at

The Moncada Garrison marks a turning point in the country's history when, on 26 July 1953, Fidel Castro's men stormed Batista's troops in this fort. All previous garrisons are now educational establishments.

Céspedes Park, and its attendant buildings of the **Cathedral, Velázques' House**, Town Hall, **Gallery of Oriental Art** and Casagrande Hotel, the Casa Heredia, Santa Lucia church, Theatre Oriente and the Museum of the Clandestine Movement, are just off the square. The Moncada Barracks are located north-east of the centre. The **Emilio Bacardi Museum** – a very worthwhile visit, to the east, opposite the docks, which are down below the main body of the city. Near the Emilio Bacardi Museum is the famous cobbled street called the '**Callejón Bofill**'.

The **Morro Castle** is probably the most visited, and certainly the most spectacular, monument from Spanish times in Santiago. Its companion defences were **La Estrella** and **La Socapa** on the opposite headland. The original name of Morro Castle was San Padre de la Roca Fortress. A maze of stairways, tiny dungeons, vast hallways and huge stone walls, are as impressive today as they must have been to the marauding pirates. A museum of piracy and Morro's history testify to its romantic

and ferocious past. A second museum, referred to locally as the '**Museum of the New Pirates**', is dedicated to exhibits and photographs documenting the invasion attempts which have been made in recent years, by CIA-inspired insurgents, since the early 1960s.

Near the **Museum of Clandestine Activities**, south of the city centre, is the **Excalinate Padre Pico**, the famous stone stairway with marvellous views across the bay and over the tiled roofs.

One area of Santiago which should not be overlooked is the new development to the north of the city. A great new industrial area includes three rum factories, a paper mill, shoe factory, textile plant, flour mill, three prefabricated building plants, two thermo-electricity complexes, an oil refinery and a brewery amongst others, making the city the fourth most important industrial region.

Hotels are all a little way out of the centre of the city, except the Rex Libertad, Venus and Imperial, which are popular with locals, as is the big Casagranda. Details are given at the end of this section. All the large tourist hotels have excellent facilities and amenities including pool, restaurant, carabet, bars, shops and tour services.

Restaurants and cafeterias in Santiago de Cuba are mainly located in the middle of the city. There are a dozen cafeterias and nine restaurants within the city limits, but the ones to look for are **Santiago 1900**, in a mansion which once belonged to the Bacardi family, the **El Baturro, El Criollo**, the Pizzerias El Gallito, Las Piramides, Fontana di Trevis and San Agustin. Visit the city's answer to Havana's Bodeguito del Medio, the **El Bodegon**, a truly bohemian experience. Evenings and weekend meals, at some of the more popular restaurants, should be pre-booked. Also try the ice-cream at Copelia Arboleda

EXCURSIONS FROM SANTIAGO DE CUBA

Beaches east of the city; Siboney; San

Along the road that the revolutionaries took on their march to the city, monuments like this give tribute to those that fell.

Siboney Farm is the site where Fidel Castro and his men grouped before advancing on Santiago city.

Pedro del Mar; Daiquiri; Verracos and; Colorado.

Beaches west of the city: Mar Verde; Canzilo; Caleton Blanco; Cojimar; El Frances; Cabagan; Cantivar; Sevilla and; Guama.

Inland: Gran Piedra; El Escandel; Sierra Cristal; Mayari Arriba; Tayaba Valley; the three peaks of the Sierra Maestra; La Plata and; El Cobre.

HOTELS IN SANTIAGO DE CUBA

Las Américas
Avenue de las Américas/General Cebreco
Tel: 8040/8466
Every modern amenity in this, centrally located, 68-roomed, hotel

El Balcón del Caribe
Morro Highway, 7 kilometres   Tel: 6561
All amenities in an hotel with 96 rooms and magnificent views

Casa Granda
On Céspedes Park
Central location with modernised facilities in period setting

Daiquirí Motel
Baconao Park Road
In beautiful park surroundings overlooking the Caribbean with 156 rustic cabins including all modern conveniences

Guama de Chivirico
62 kilometres south-west of Santiago de Cuba
Small, beachside motel with eight rooms

Leningrado Motel
San Juan Hill, Siboney Highway   Tel: 20923/29049
Rustic location for these double cabins in the city suburbs

El Rancho Motel
Central Highway   Tel: 33202/3
Thirty rooms of bungalow style, on the outskirts of the city

Versalles Motel
Altura de Versalles   Tel: 8050/54
Between the city and the airport, these 60 rooms have first class amenities and a beautiful location

RESTAURANTS IN SANTIAGO DE CUBA

El Bodegon
Plaza de Delores
Similar to the Bodeguita del Medio, in Havana, Cuban fare

La Isabelica
Aguilera and Calvario Streets
Popular gathering point for conversation and special brews

Leningrado Restaurant
San Juan Hill, Siboney Highway   Tel: 20923

Including the Salon Rojo, this is one of Santiago's largest and finest eating places

San Pedro del Mar Cabaret
Morro Highway, 7 kilometres
Next to El Balcon del Caribe Hotel, supper is served with the entertainment

Santiago 1900 Restaurant
San Basilio, between Pio Rosado and Hartman Streets
These gracious surroundings once hosted the Bacardi family and now the house specialises in a variety of Crillo favourites

Punta Gorda Restaurant
Facing Cayo Granma, this little eating house serves seafood dishes.

El Baturro
Restaurant/Bar, city centre

Baconao

Envisaged (by Fidel Castro in 1959) as the most spectacular resort in Cuba, this area is a major achievement. This is the most popular beach and park area, 52 kilometres long, in the province, and is intended to be one of the largest tourist developments in the Caribbean when it is completed in 1988. Here, the Balneario del Sol complex is an area of custom-built villas with its own beach and facilities. Visit Los Coloradas Restaurant on the cliff above the Bay of Dolphins.

Cayo Granma

This island in the centre of the bay of Santiago, was called Fisherman's Island or Smith's Cay – after an English slaver who lived there. A beautiful micro-society and mini-town, the island is best viewed from El Morro Castle, and reached by ferry which leaves hourly from Alameda harbour, in the city port.

El Cobre

As the town's name suggests, this area is one giant copper mine, in the mountains, due west of Santiago de Cuba. The quaint township and the vast, open-cast mine, however, are not the main attractions of El Cobre. Through the town and up on a high bluff overlooking the gaping maw of the mine, is one of the most spectacular churches in the country. Three great, glistening domes announce the vast structure from a distance.

The **Basilica of Copper**, dedicated to the patron saint of the island – *La Caridad de Cobre* – is a revel of Gothic architecture. In the gloom of its interior, behind the church's natural entrance, around the rear of the edifice, stand some of the most poignant shrines in Cuba. A thousand 'charities' or gifts, surround a cuppola shrine to the saint. A hundred candles illuminate stacks upon stacks of crutches and hoards of medallions, badges, watches, militaria, jewellery, ancient tiaras and chalices, all donated by the 'miraculously healed'. Relatives and invalids have placed all manner of artefacts here, over the centuries, as tokens of their thanks for curing pilgrims. Revolutionary war victims' friends and relations placed charities here, as did survivors of battles dating back centuries.

Gran Piedra

Far up in the heights of the Sierra Maestra range of mountains, overlooking the Windward Passage, between Cuba and Hispaniola, this peak can be seen for miles around. The reward of a spectacular view of the ocean and the wooded interior awaits the energetic visitor who must climb the 465 stone steps to its rounded summit.

As this is a popular tourist feature, restaurant and cafeterias provide refreshment, and accommodation consists of 22 cabins, a recreation room and all facilities for the visiting explorer.

The fascinating orchid garden includes a wealth of rare specimens and the **Ave del Paraiso**, one of the world's most sought after blooms.

Mayari Arriba

About 150 kilometres from Santiago de Cuba, this is the site where Manuel de Céspedes inaugurated his revolutionary government and Raúl Castro began the activities of the Second Eastern Front. The **museum** of its operations is the town's major attraction.

Siboney

Apart from this area, to the south-east of the city, being a popular beach, it is a place of pilgrimage for national and international visitors. It was from the small farm here that Fidel Castro, and about 70 revolutionaries, planned and executed the attack on Batista's garrison of Moncada, in the city. A small **museum** displays arms, decorations, clothing and documents, as relics of the 1953, 26 July Movement attack. A well in the grounds of the farm once hid the weapons used in the first attack which led, eventually, to the triumph of the Revolution.

Along the roadside towards Santiago, are twenty-six differently designed monuments to those who died during the uprising.

Guantánamo Province

'Unforgettable and beloved Guantánamo. I say this thinking of the struggles of Guantánamo's people throughout history, including our aborigines, led by Hatuey, the first Caribbean Indian who became an international fighter, and their most recent struggles waged to win complete independence and freedom for our country.'

RAÚL CASTRO
Second Secretary of the Central Committee of the Communist Party of Cuba and Minister of the Revolutionary Armed Forces (FAR)

In the far south-east of Cuba, this province has, until recent years, escaped the modernisation and development afforded to more accessible provinces. Its capital city is Guantánamo, on the southernmost delta of the river of the same name. The province's population is estimated to exceed 470 000 inhabitants, and there is a highway which runs around the coast,

Fishing is an important industry on this southern coastline.

skirting the mountainous region of the Baracoa Heights. The province has three airports at Punta de Maisí, Baracoa and in the capital.

The Guantánamo Basin is really the only cultivated region, and here sugar cane is grown. On the lower flanks of the mountains, much of which are carpeted in dense tropical vegetation, bananas, cocoa and coffee, are producing good results. Mining is done on the higher mountain slopes for minerals, and for the serpentine rock used in building and roadmaking. Natural sea salt is also collected.

The Toa and Yumurí rivers both run down to the northern coast, where there are many beach resorts and places of natural beauty. Other beauty spots in the province include the **Cuchillas**, or ridge of Toa and the **Yunque**, or anvil, of Baracoa, near the coast, and overlooking the Atlantic Ocean. Along the southern Caribbean shores, are many beaches and beach resorts which attract holidaymakers from the city and also from the next province, Santiago de Cuba. Fishing is particularly good off this coastline, which faces Haiti and has some of the deepest waters in the Greater Antilles. From Punta de Quemado the faint outline of Hispaniola can sometimes be seen 77 kilometres to the east.

An area of savanna sands lie between the estuary of Guantánamo Bay, where there is a naval base, and the province of Santiago de Cuba. This is the tail-end of the Central Valley, which runs down from Holguín Province, in the north. The road to the neighbouring capital skirts this dry, desert-like region, where many cacti and other exotic flora can be found.

The **Sierra Cristal** offers innumerable hiking and horse riding opportunities. Baracoa is the only region where the insectivorous, living fossil, the **Almiquí** is found, which is very rare and one of the earliest mammals. Take time to travel the 30 kilometre – **La Farola** – The Beacon, highway which bobs and dips around the beautiful Bay of Honey.

Guantánamo

This capital, of the province of the same name, was founded in 1797, and lies north-east of Santiago de Cuba. Contrary to some beliefs, the entire area is not a US naval base, and its fertile plain provides work for almost 200 000 inhabitants. Sugar is the important crop and very few Cubans actually work on the 75 square kilometre, bayside base.

The city itself is situated a good way inland from the Bay of Guantánamo, which creates an almost hourglass indentation in Cuba's south coast. An attractive highway route links Santiago de Cuba, through Guantánamo, around the bay, to Baracoa, on the north coast. In the city there are many charming **Spanish-style houses** and some well-preserved old mansions,

From the mountains of the 'land of song' the peaks of Haiti can be viewed on a clear day.

141

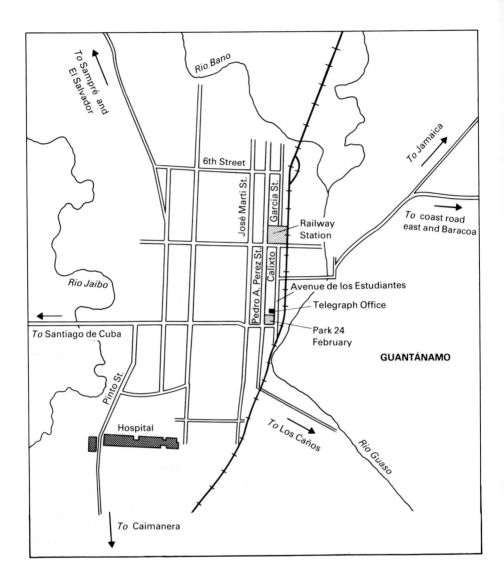

To Sampré and El Salvador

Rio Bano

To Jamaica

6th Street

José Marti St.

Garcia St.

Railway Station

To coast road east and Baracoa

Rio Jaibo

Pedro A. Perez St.

Calixto

Avenue de los Estudiantes

Telegraph Office

To Santiago de Cuba

Park 24 February

GUANTÁNAMO

Pinto St.

Hospital

To Los Caños

Rio Guaso

To Caimanera

from the days of the landowners of the mid-19th century. Most visitors find little more of interest in the city, which serves as a transit town, between north and south coasts.

The history of the US base goes back to December 1903 when the section of bay was ceded, under a lease – which still has to be paid – as a coaling station for US ships. No ships are coaled here now, and no external dealings are permitted. The base remains a 'thorn in the side' and a demonstration of obstinacy – even the marines dub it the 'country club base'.

Baracoa

Named Puerto Santo by Christopher Columbus during his north coast explorations in 1492, the conquering Diego de Velázquez established the cove as Cuba's first settlement in 1512, renaming the first capital Baracoa. After he moved the administration of the territory to Santiago de Cuba, some two years later, the Atlantic coast city became prey to pirate raids. Its isolated position and rocky environment gave it no economic value, and it was largely ignored by the government, until the triumph of the revolution when housing, education, and health projects, improved the conditions of the inhabitants. This town, of almost 60 000 inhabitants, lies just 120 kilometres from Guantánamo.

There is little evidence now of the great Spanish period, but one of its oldest buildings is **La Punta Fortress**, built in 1803 to guard the port, now a restaurant/cabaret specialising in Cuban food – taste the local sweetmeat, cucurucho.

A little older, though not well preserved, is the 1802 **Fortress of Matachin**. What is now left forms part of the city's museum – just a crumbling wall and remnants of towers, located at the entrance to the city.

The **Cathedral**, which originally was located further from the Independence Plaza, is around 160 years old, but the first Cathedral building, of which nothing remains, was built during the city's foundation year.

Two small restaurants, apart from La Punta Fort, the **El Tropical** and **El Caracol**, serve local food, and afford good views of the city and bay. In Plaza Marti, the **Hotel Plaza** serves good meals, but the best view and dining location, is the **Motel Sanguily**, on the hill overlooking the city and its port. The remains of an old defensive position, **El Castillo**, served as the basic construction material for the motel atop a terraced mount.

EXCURSIONS FROM BARACOA

Moa in the north; Maguana; the Yunque de Baracoa which Columbus described as a high, square mountain which looks like an island; Toa River raft trip; the Cuchillas del Toa; the obelisk at Duaba Bay, which marks the point of landing in 1895 by Antonio Maceo; Viaducto la Farola; Maisi Point and; Playitas Beach on the south coast.

Granma Province

'Our Granma Province can awaken the interests of the historically minded tourists.'

FIDEL CASTRO RUZ

This province lies in the south-west corner of southern Cuba. Its capital city is Bayamo, located near the centre of the province. It is connected by major highways and rail routes, to Santiago de Cuba in the south-east, Holguín in the north-east, and the eastern coastal ports of Manzanillo and Niquero. Manzanillo has the province's only other airport.

Granma has a total population of about 750 000 and is important for the production of tobacco, sugar, vegetable and fruit crops, mainly for local consumption. Fishing is also a major industry (in the Caribbean

143

waters of the Gulf of Guacanayabo), from Manzanillo and other, smaller ports. The area has also become one of Cuba's major tourist attractions, particularly because of the history connecting the province with the early revolutionary hero, Carlos Manuel de Céspedes. Visitors are particularly attracted to Bayamo City for its fascinating history and architectural significance.

To the south of the city of Bayamo are the tourist attractions of the **Sierra Maestra** mountain resorts, **Las Coloradas**, on the shoreline, where Fidel Castro's yacht, *Granma* landed to inaugurate the revolution, and nearby the beach resort of Las Coloradas. Fishermen and hunters are attracted from all over Cuba, and abroad, to the famous grounds of the **Laguna Virama** hunting club. Deepsea fishing and diving is catered for, both off the eastern and southern shores. One most interesting location of natural beauty, is the area around Demajagua, Céspedes' plantation.

The Rio Cauto, Cuba's largest river, cuts across the north of the province, with its mouth in the marshy swamplands of the Bay of Guacanayabo. The Bayamo River is a large tributary of the Cauto, and flows from the high sierra, south of the city. The province's other large river is the Yara which has its source above the large reservoir of Paso Malo.

Historical points of interest are legion. Generally, most follow either the routes of Carlos Manuel de Céspedes' army, from Demajagua, through Bayamo, or Fidel Castro and his comrades, after landing at Las Coloradas, along the southern coast of the province, towards Santiago de Cuba. **Battlefield sites** from both revolutions including smaller skirmishes, number almost thirty, throughout the province. Places of historical interest also exist in most of the province's towns and cities.

There are three important campsites in Granma Province. Between them they can accommodate 2400 visitors. They are located at Ela Salto de Jibacoa, Los Cantiles and La Sierrita.

Bayamo

Originally named San Salvador de Bayamo, the city is one of Cuba's oldest settlements and a national monument. Bayamo and its citizens took a fiercely active part in the formation of Cuba's history. After he had followed Columbus' route to found Baracoa in 1512, Diego de Velázquez established the settlement of Bayamo the following year. Its chequered history, of Spanish conflicts with local Indians, landowners challenging Spain's authority and the earliest documented revolt of black slaves, all indicate a staunchly patriotic nucleus in the stategically strong city.

This quality was proved when, in 1868, Carlos Manuel de Céspedes, landowner of La Demajagua sugar mill, freed and armed his own slaves and led them against the Spanish. By the time his army had control of Holguín, Spain's troops turned on Bayamo. The women of Bayamo fled to the hills, first burning the city to the ground, saving their heritage in one heroic act.

At exactly the time of the attack by Fidel's forces on the Moncada Garrison in 1953, the people of Bayamo took up arms against Batista's garrison, only for their force to be decimated and many people murdered. This carefully timed attack coincided with several in Granma and in Santiago Province – a co-ordinated uprising planned by the revolutionaries to upset Batista's army.

Passing the Manuel de Céspedes Airport, just outside the city, it is evident that the people of Bayamo take great pride in their streets. Flowering trees line the road, and quaint, pastel-painted cottages on the outskirts, huddle around narrow, cobbled lanes. The buildings begin to get larger as the thoroughfare approaches the main square of the city. A bell in the ancient tower of **San Juan Evangelista** still hangs with its attendant statue, denoting the entrance to an old cemetery. The rest of

In the centre of Bayamo is the birthplace of national hero, Carlos Manuel de Céspedes.

The Church of San Salvador, one of the oldest in Cuba, was the setting for the first rendering of the National Anthem.

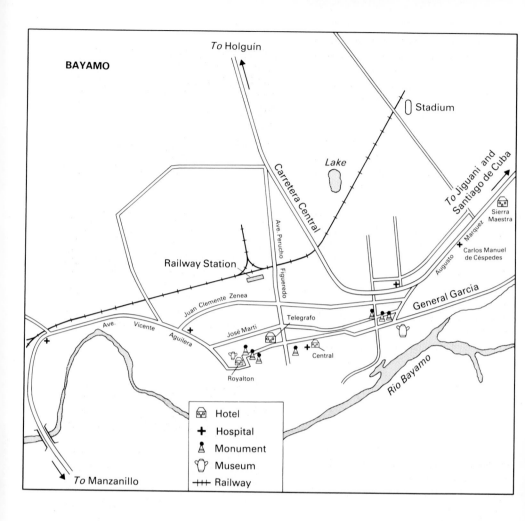

BAYAMO

To Holguín

Stadium

Lake

Carretera Central

To Jiguani and Santiago de Cuba

Sierra Maestra

Ave. Perucho Figueredo

Carlos Manuel de Céspedes

Augusto

Marquez

Railway Station

General García

Juan Clemente Zenea

Ave. Vicente Aguilera

Telegrafo

José Martí

Central

Rio Bayamo

Royalton

	Hotel
+	Hospital
	Monument
	Museum
++++	Railway

To Manzanillo

the church was ravaged in the fire of the 1860s. On the square opposite, is a statue to **Francisco Vincente Aguilera**, flanked by a bas-relief of heroes of the Revolution. Estrada Palma, the first President of Cuba was born in Bayamo, his house is now a monument, but the plinth which held his statue is empty – a testimony to his traitorous actions during office. In the garden, where Palma's father kept slaves, is a magnificent Royal Palm, supposedly

planted by the young President-to-be.

The centre of the city, Céspedes Park, must be one of the most striking in Cuba. Shaded by Royal Palms the square is flanked by well maintained buildings such as the City Hall, Hotel Royalton and the Archives building. Also on the square is the fascinating, authentically furnished, 18th century, Spanish-style **home of Carlos Manuel de Céspedes**, now a museum. The square is the centre of activities for festivals and youth, with wrought iron seats, and little shops. A local inhabitant, Luz Vazquez was once considered the prettiest woman in this city renowned for its beautiful women. Her son erected a window near here in her memory during the last century.

A square adjacent to Céspedes Park is the location of the **Church of San Salvador**, probably the oldest church in the country, founded in the earliest days of the city. In 1702, the church was given the title of Parochial Helper and, according to Padre Rafael Cos, a great historian of the area, its exterior, columns and cupola, on the left of the entrance, date back to 1630. The ornate altar to Signora Dolorosa, with the dagger clasped to her heart, dates from 1733, and a shrine in the baptistry has been dedicated to the town of Céspedes. The church contains a bible stand, formed of two metal cocks, and the original flag of Céspedes, made by his wife. It was in this church that the National Anthem, by Perucho Figueredo, was first played in defiance of Spain. A clock above the cafe near Céspedes' house chimes the tune each hour.

Modern Bayamo is a great contrast to the quaint, traditional Spanish-style houses of the main city. A new city has been created by the micro-brigade, with Homeland Square, cinema, shops, schools, polyclinics, hospitals, baseball stadium and, across the main road, a huge amusement park, **Granma Park**, with the Luanda bar-restaurant.

Nightclub Bayamo is opposite the 204-room **Hotel Sierra Maestra**. Here there is an excellent restaurant, rustic bower barbecue and pool. The hotel was inaugurated by Fidel Castro, and Nicaragua's President Ortega – see the gift of wicker furniture from the Central American state in the foyer.

Although the Sierra Maestra Hotel is the largest in the city, Bayamo has three other hotels in the centre of town. These are the **Central**, the **Telégrafo** and the **Royalton**. **El Vincente Restaurant** is

out near the Sierra Maestra Hotel and Bayamo nightclub whereas on the way into the city one passes **El Viajero, La Fonda** and **La Fresa**. In the centre are the restaurants Manegua, Ching Lai and several cafeterias. Bayamo has three ice cream parlours and the nightclubs Nocturno, Los Recuerdos and, on the outskirts, near the river Bayamo, the Los Caneyes nightclub.

Horse carriages can be taken from outside the Hotel Sierra Maestra or in town near Bayamo station. Located about 127 kilometres from Santiago de Cuba this ancient city has a population of about 125 000.

EXCURSIONS FROM BAYAMO

Manzanillo; Las Coloradas; *Granma* landing site; Sierra Maestra mountain resorts; Celia Sanchez Museum at Media Luna and Demajagua, Contramaestre and Pico Turquino trek.

Virama and Leonero Lakes provide excellent facilities for bird watching or hunting. Hunting, fishing and boating trips can be arranged through Sierra Maestra Hotel reception, or Cubatur representatives.

Of particular interest to the holidaymaker is the black sanded beach resort of Marea del Portillo, at Pilon, on the Marea Highway.

HOTELS IN GRANMA

Guacanayabo
Avenue Camilo Cienfuegos, Manzanillo
Tel: 05–4012
Marea de Portillo
Marea Highwaty, Pilon   Tel: 05–94201
Sierra Maestra
Central Highway, Bayamo   Tel: 4–5013

In Manzanillo, on the Caribbean coast, the only hotel is the **Guacanayabo**. The town has three restaurants, Cayo Confite and Golfo de Guacanayabo plus the Balcón de Guacanayabo outside town near the hostel called Cabañas Stromboli. The Guacanayabo Hotel, in Manzanillo, on the coast can cater for up to 112 visitors.

Holguín Province

A most important region for many reasons, Holguín Province lies on the northern coast of southern Cuba. It has an estimated population of about 930 000 inhabitants and its capital city is Holguín, in the centre of the larger, western sector of the province. Holguín city has one of the island's main airports, other airports in the province, are at Levisa, and Moa on the coast.

The long northern coastline, from Gibara in the west of Moa in the east, surrounds the Bay of Nipe, and provides a multitude of opportunities for beach-loving tourists, at its famous resorts of **Bariay** and **Guardalavaca, Corinthia** and **Arenas Negras**. The Bay of Nipe has many ports used by fishing boats and for the export of a variety of goods. Game fishing here is excellent, as are all the facilities for tourist pastimes connected with the water and beach.

The city is connected by road to the coastal resorts and ports, and to each of the surrounding four provinces. The Central Highway runs through the city, but the railhead is at Cacocum, south of Holguín city. Another railway links the port of Antilla, on the Bay of Nipe, with Guantánamo, passing the central rail-link at Alto Cedro. Cuba's largest river, the Rio Cauto, flows through the extreme southern corner of the province, and several other

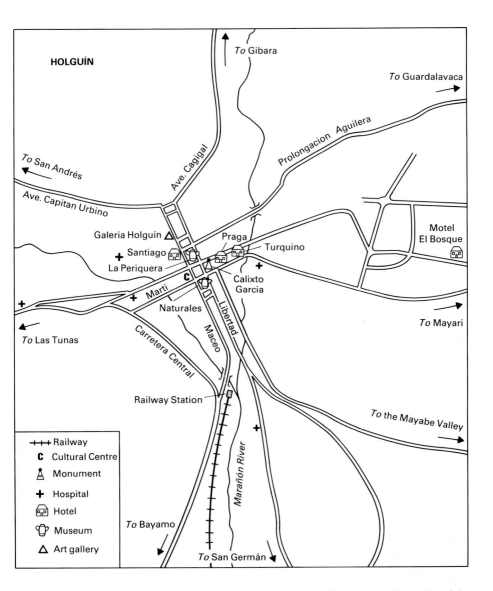

HOLGUÍN

To Gibara

To Guardalavaca

Prolongacion Aguilera

Ave. Cagigal

To San Andrés

Ave. Capitan Urbino

Galeria Holguín △

✛ Santiago

La Periquera

Praga

Turquino

Motel
El Bosque

C

Calixto
Garcia

✛

Marti

Naturales

✛

Libertad

Maceo

To Mayari

To Las Tunas

Carretera Central

Railway Station

To the Mayabe Valley

✛

Marañón River

Railway
C Cultural Centre
A Monument
✛ Hospital
Hotel
Museum
△ Art gallery

To Bayamo

To San Germán

rivers flow into the Atlantic, including the Gibara, Naranjo, the Nipe, the mighty Mayari, the Sagua and the Moa.

The area around the capital is rich in minerals, and oranges, beans, maize, and bananas are grown in abundance. Holguín Province however, is mainly a cattle rearing area in the west, tobacco is grown in the centre, and sugar in the east and around the main bay.

Beauty spots include **Loma de la Cruz** and **Mayabe Valley**, on either side of the city, **Silla de Gibara**, in the north and **Rio Bitiri**, the **Sierra de Nipe, Sierra del Cristal**, and the **Chuchillas de Moa** in the extreme east. Holguín is an historic city and several sites outside the capital are memorials to past events. In the mountainous countryside in the south and centre of the province are the *Edicion del Periodico Cubano Libre*, and the 1878 battle site of **San Ulpiano**.

Holguín

The road from Las Tunas as it enters Holguín is typical of any thriving industrial city in Cuba. Large colourful hoardings promote the region's developments, its history and famous internationalists. Model Farms, a garrison converted into a school, the University of Technology, opposite an agricultural machinery workshop, bus station, provincial radio station, and School of Medicine are the main points of the city, with a population estimated at around 180 000. Across the centre of the city which is made up of three old, main squares and shopping areas, the Hotel Pernick, with accommodation for 202 guests, is situated opposite the vast Calixto Garcia Stadium, and behind the New Communist Party Headquarters.

In new Holguín and Lenin District on the Mayari road, is the brightly coloured, **El Bosque Hotel** and, in the centre of the city, are the hotels **Santiago, Praga** and **Turquino**. Pizzeria Roma, Las Antilles and El Caney, are the main restaurants, but for excellent decor, try the **Polinesio** on the 13th floor of an apartment block. Also in the city there are more than a dozen cafeterias and two ice-cream parlours. A hotel on the outskirts of town which is a good choice for travellers is the **Mirador de Mayabe**, overlooking the fantastic Mayabe Valley, with cabins, terrace bar and a beer-swilling donkey 'Pancho'! **El Bosque Motel**, on the Mayari Highway, in the Pedro Diaz Coello district of Holguín is a fine location. The **José Marti Park**, outside the city, is an interesting area with many facilities for boating and several restaurants.

Holguín is steeped in a history which goes back further than when Columbus' men thought its Indian settlement was the Japanese Emperor's capital city. Behind its main square there are several colonial churches and early monuments.

Just outside the city is the luxuriant Lookout of Mayabe, an idyllic mountain resort. Horse riding here is a popular pastime.

Attractions in this ancient, 1523, city are mainly the new developments, and views from the **Loma del la Cruz**, or Hill of the Cross cafeteria, to the west of town. This hill is thought to be the site of the original Holguín settlement. Spanish-style houses and stately buildings range along the Maceo.

Two old churches in the city centre flank the squares. The oldest with its own plaza, dominated by a statue of Karl Marx, is furthest from the shopping centre and dated 1720. Two very interesting history and natural history museums are situated on **Maceo Square** and well worth visiting. In the **History Museum**, Museo de la Periquera, is the cherished Holguín Axe, a 35-centimetre-long, pre-Columbian, carved axe head, discovered in 1860 near the city. See also the Holguín **Art Gallery**, the

Holguín has more than fifteen notable beaches many with modern, open-plan accommodation. The provinces's best known beach is Guardalavaca.

Sala Moncada, and try to catch some local culture at the **Casa de la Trova**. Do not miss the birthplace of Calixto Garcia, the local hero.

EXCURSIONS FOR HOLGUÍN

Guardalavaca beach and other seaside attractions; Bariay Bay, site of Columbus' landing; Banes; Cayo Naranjo; Moa; Gibara; Mayari Abajo; Valley of Mayabe and; the Sierra de Nipe.

Banes

A small town built on the site of an ancient, pre-Columbian settlement, Banes is a popular place to visit, because of its interesting museum. The **Museum of Indian Civilisation** contains exhibits of Indian artefacts, tableaux and local historical information. Just 60 kilometres from Holguín, this town was founded in 1887.

Gibara

This is a popular north coast town just 30 kilometres from Holguín and with a population of about 58 000.

This bay is commonly believed to be the site of Columbus' first landfall in Cuba.

Established in 1817, the town is centred around the fishing industry on its bay and makes a convenient diversion from the beach resorts. Two museums in the town contain a wealth of colonial art, furniture and examples of local and foreign natural history. Often referred to as *Silla de Gibara*, is the local feature which creates a saddle between two hills.

Guardalavaca beach

This is one of the country's most attractive and popular north coast beach resorts. It provides every comfort and facility for seaside vacationers. The hotel of the same name accommodates 225 guests.

Almost 90 kilometres from Holguín, the area is well located for visits to other northern coastal towns.

Mayari Abajo

This small town was established in 1814, on Nipe Bay about 80 kilometres from Holguín, and has recently developed into a tourist area, because of its lush vegetation, mountain tracks and the vista of the distant ranges of the Sierra Cristal. The town has an hotel, as does the park in the mountains.

Moa

This is a popular north coast resort built around a port. Hotel Moa will soon accommodate up to 120 guests.

Cayo Naranjo

This isolated cay is now a hatchery for the state-controlled fish and shellfish enterprise. The hatchery can be visited by boat, by prior arrangement with the authorities.

HOTELS IN HOLGUÍN

El Pernik Hotel
20 Aniversario and Plaza de la Revolucíon Avenues, Holguín   Tel: (244) 42160
El Bosque Motel
Mayari Highway, Pedro Díaz Coello, Holguín   Tel: 4 – 2188/4 – 2763
Mirador de Mayabe
Mayabe Valley
Villa Cabaña
Guardalavaca beach, Banes

Las Tunas Province

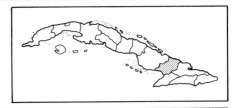

'*For thirty years I have known this land.*'

JUAN FRANSICO MANZANO from his poem
Treinta Años

The population of this south-central province, which forms a band across the island, below Camagüey Province, is made up of about 450 000 inhabitants. Victoria de las Tunas, the capital lies in the centre of the province, on the Central Highway.

The terrain is made up of three parts, with lowland either side of a spur of the Holguín Ridge. The province's south-eastern area borders Granma Province on the edge of Cauto-Nipe plain, and its southern coastal flats are marsh and swamp. Inland, the main crop is sugar, with a certain amount of deciduous scrubland, suitable for cattle farming.

Quique Marina, a restaurant, is not only a by-word for excellent 'caldosa' stews, but has gained international fame for its secret recipes.

Two railways cross the province. One runs through the capital and south of this, a line to Bayamo runs through Jobabo. Two rail links also run to the north coast and one joins Colombia, through Amancio, to the south coast harbour of Guayabal.

Commercial, and the occasional game fishing, is practised off the province's north coast and there are a few areas designated as beach resorts, such as **La Herradura**. On the south coast, past the mangrove swamps, which fringe the Caribbean waters, bone fishing and Tarpon can provide sport, together with deeper-sea fish, in the Gulf of Guacanayabo. The many small rivers serve only to irrigate the cane fields and ground crops, grown for local use.

Many bay inlets on the north coast have led to the development of fishing and general harbours at places such as Puerto Padre, Delicias and Puerto Carupano.

Victoria de Las Tunas

This city was founded in 1759, and has become known as the '**city of sculptures**', as a result of the great number of artworks on the street corners. The city is located exactly in the centre of the province, and relies for its activities on the cattle and sugar fields that surround it. It has a

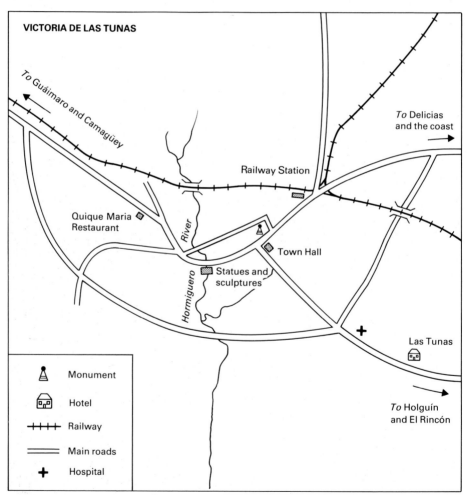

VICTORIA DE LAS TUNAS

To Guáimaro and Camagüey

To Delicias and the coast

Railway Station

Quique Maria Restaurant

River

Hormiguero

Statues and sculptures

Town Hall

Las Tunas

To Holguín and El Rincón

Monument

Hotel

Railway

Main roads

Hospital

population of 100 000.

Approaching Las Tunas from Camagüey in the west, just before the city's entrance, is the little roadside cafeteria '**Quique**

Around the island's coast a variety of craft are available for pleasure or fishing excursions.

Marina'. The couple, Quique and Marina, now well-known personalities nationally, run the pretty little bar and restaurant as a family concern. The basic meal, and one that attracts custom from across the province, is *Caldosa*. This is a thick soup containing chicken, banana, greens, juca, sweet potato, beans, peas, herbs, spices

and a secret ingredient, is served in custom-moulded bowls, and is delicious!

Past a cattle fodder mill, the city's night club is a converted twin-propeller, ex-Cubana aircraft.

The tree-lined main street, covered colonnade and little church add interest to the capital. A small square, with pool, and sculptures of four Indian heads, serves as a meeting place for the local elders.

EXCURSIONS FROM VICTORIA DE LAS TUNAS
El Cornito; Puerto Padre on the north coast; farms or ranches and; sugar plantations or sugar Centrales.

El Cornito
This is a rustic resort, dedicated to relaxation, recreation and particularly watersports. It is an exceptionally good game fishing spot, because of the excellent facilities at the Hormigo River.

The resort is an 18 kilometre drive from the city of Victoria de Las Tunas along the Central Highway.

HOTELS IN LAS TUNAS
Hotel Las Tunas is located on a hill, just out of the city. Few, except local visitors, stay in Las Tunas, as it is bisected by the Central Highway.

Camagüey Province

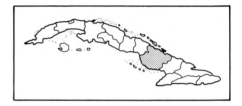

'*Happy is the one that, next to you, longs for you.*'

GERTRUDIS GÓMEZ DE AVELLANEDA from the poem *Imitation of an Ode*

This is one of the largest and most prosperous provinces in Cuba. Its capital, is right in the centre of the, almost square-shaped, region. The province's population is around 700 000, and its main products are cattle, some tobacco and a variety of citrus fruits. *Zebu, Santa Gertrudis, Holstein* and *F1* strains of cattle are used for both beef and dairy farming.

Camagüey city has one of Cuba's four universities and an international airport. It lies at the junction of a railroad from Nuevitas' industrial sector to the north and the Central Highway and its adjacent railway.

Along the north coast are the islands of the Camagüey Archipelago, and some fine tourist beaches like the **Santa Lucia** complex, in the extreme north-east. Out from Nuevitas town the north coast is comparatively barren and marshy, although just inland near Cubitas is a rocky mountain spur, with its caves and beauty spots. The land rises only slightly, to a low plateau in the centre of the province north of Camagüey city.

On the other side of Camagüey city are three more natural attractions, the mountain of **Najasa, Chorrillo** and the hill of **Deseada**. The natural beauty of the

Camagüey is famous for its earthenware water jars. Miniature replicas are made as souvenirs.

Sierra de Cubitas brings both national and international visitors to Camagüey. Fishing and hunting are attractions for sportsmen as there are many dams and reservoirs.

The coasts are well-known for good **game fishing**. Sailing on both coasts is exceptional, especially in the northern cays which were known in the mid-1500s as 'The King's Gardens'.

Many points of interest in the province have revolutionary connotations. In the far south is the monument to the massacre of the *Pino 3*, in 1958, a little further north is the **La Sacra** monument, 1873, and just

west of that, the site of the battle of the **Guasimas** and the fall of **Agramonte** in 1874 and 1873. Near Camagüey city is the assembly point of 1868 and near Minas, the rebellion site of the same year. Further east are the sites associated with the first revolution, and the house where the **treaty of La Yaya** was signed in 1897.

Camagüey

As the province boasts of its leading position in the cattle business, so the city of Camagüey enjoys the nickname the 'Corinth of the Caribbean'. The city was established in 1514, initially named Santa Maria del Puerto Principe or Villa del Principe. The city has a natural situation for a defensive settlement, being on a bluff surrounded by a vast, flat, plain of pastureland called 'Savanna Camagüey'.

After an Indian massacre and a rebellion of the native tribes, at the earlier location of Puerto Principe, far to the east near the coast, the city was relocated. The move was the best thing that could have happened to Camagüey, as far as its agricultural development was concerned, but the city continued to figure heavily in pirate raids, until its almost total destruction by Henry Morgan, in 1668.

Today, the city is a national monument and one of the most impressive in Cuba. Its population is now estimated at just under a quarter of a million. Camagüey is large, and has expanded on all sides into new suburbs. The visitor will prefer to concentrate on the centre of the city, between the Tinima and Hatibonico rivers. It is here that the points of interest and monuments are located, such as the **La Soledad church**, which is decorated with some of the most beautiful fresco work in Latin America. The main church was constructed in 1775, just 50 years before the **Iglesia del Carmen**, at the edge of the city centre. The **La Merced church** on the Worker's Square, 1882, is worth a visit, but the oldest ecclesiastical building is the **Cathedral** on Agramonte Park. Also facing the park, is the **Casa de la Trova** mansion, which gives nightly musical performances. Camagüey's Ballet Company is world-famous and the visitor should also try to see the folkloric group 'Caidije', often visiting the city from its base in Nuevitas.

There are three restaurants on the old city side of the Hatibonico river, between two bridges, **La Tinajita**, the name given to the 'trade mark' of Camagüey – the large red clay water jars, originally used as oil containers, and seen everywhere in the province – **La Volanta** restaurant and the **Nanking**.

There are five hotels in Camagüey, the **Gran Hotel, Florida Hotel**, the **Isla de Cuba**, the **Hotel Colon**, and the **Puerto Principe**. Outside the city are the **Caonao Hotel** to the east, and on the Central Highway, the **Hotel Camagüey**, with 142 places in quite modern rooms, in an hotel with all facilities, and a good pool.

Other places of interest in the city include the **Ignacio Agramonte Museum**, the birthplace of Agramonte, the **Museo del Movimiento** and the beautiful **Principle Theatre**, a superlative triumph of architecture and design. The

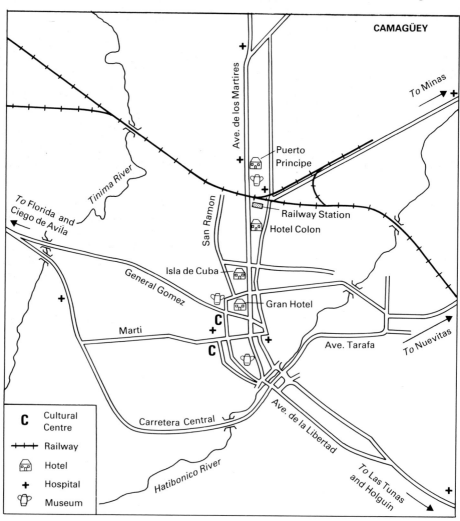

The large port of Nuevitas, on the Atlantic coast, has some interesting architecture dating from early colonial times.

mid-18th century, **Palace of Justice** and the **José Luis Tasende** are worth visiting. Jesús Súarez Gayol, the revolutionary murdered with Che Guevara in Bolivia, lived at 69 República. His home is now a museum celebrating feats of famous Camagüey individuals.

Various crafts, particularly pottery and carving, can be viewed at the **Tienda de Bienes Culturales**, in Avenue de la Libertad, at the Cultural House, where a most interesting shop displays local artefacts, books and trinkets. Miniature pottery *tinajitas*, in typical local red clay, painted with a Cuban scene, are most popular as souvenirs, the full-size jars are a bit unwieldy as gifts or presents as they can be up to 6 metres high and 3 metres wide!

EXCURSIONS FROM CAMAGÜEY

The port of Nuevitas; Santa Lucía, Guardalavaca and Cayo Sabinal beaches; Minas, and its cottage-industry violin factory; Guáimaro and the caves of Los Indio, and Los Generals, Hoye de Bonet, Loma la Deseada, the Sierra of Najasa, and Chorrillo.

Visits to dairy cattle farms and ranches, can be organised through some hotel receptions, or through Cubatur representatives.

There is good inland fishing in the area, where several reservoirs are designated Largemouth Bass reserves.

HOTELS IN CAMAGÜEY

Camagüey Hotel
142 rooms, all modern facilities
Central Highway, Camagüey
Puerto Principe Hotel
Avenue de los Mártires, Camagüey

159

Club Mayanabo
Santa Lucia beach
Villa Tararaco
Santa Lucia beach
Florida Hotel
Town centre, Florida
Hotel Caonao
Nuevitas

Cayo Sabinal

This is a well-known local beach almost 16 kilometres long, with modern facilities and profuse wildlife. Visited from Camagüey, the journey to the beach takes about two hours.

Guáimaro

This is a small country town, with an hotel, recognised because the national flag was first adopted in its main street and Carlos Manuel de Céspedes was named the Republic's first president in the town. Guáimaro is about 80 kilometres from Camagüey.

It is not difficult to see what attracts sunseekers to Santa Lucia's magical resort.

Nuevitas

After a long 90-kilometre drive over flat cattle country, east from Camagüey, the smokestacks and hilly bay of the town, can be seen from a distance. Generally the road has a constant convoy of trucks taking manufactured goods to be shipped and bringing fish, from the industrialised port.

Fertiliser plants, cement factories and fish processing factories, contrast with the new hospital building, on a hill, at the entrance to the town. Neat streets, flower and plant-clad houses, skirt the large bay and busy port. Cuba's second largest power station is located here, built by Czechoslovakian technology.

A pretty hotel, the **Caonao,** named after an Indian who was once chief in the area, commands a view over the bay towards its narrow sea outlet. Few visitors stay in Nuevitas, but fishing from the port is a great attraction. There is an interesting church and museum, near the town's main square.

Excursions from Nuevitas

The cays of the Archipelago of Camagüey – Santa Lucia, Cayo Sabinal and Los Pinos beach, all by sea.

Fishing and boat trips or a visit to Guaimaro town can be arranged.

Santa Lucia

This is a famous north coast beach, 94 kilometres from Camagüey, with excellent facilities for watersports and recreation. The beautiful **Mayanabo Hotel** offers accommodation for up to 225 guests.

Cuban traditional dishes are served at the local **Bahamas** restaurant.

Ciego de Avila Province

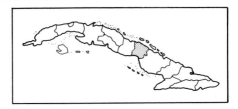

'It was in the afternoon, in the light breeze,
its wings in silence folds
and among the trees and grass it slept.'

JOSÉ MARIA HEREDIA from his
poem *In the Teocalli de Cholula*

With a population of around 340 000, this province has a configuration almost identical to its neighbour, Sancti Spiritus Province, except that its funnel shape saddles the island from a narrower southern shoreline. The province of fruit, land of the pineapple and of sugar, Ciego de Avila is crossed from west to east by two highways and parallel railroads. Two major cities lie halfway along these main routes, Morón, to the north and the capital, Ciego de Avila, to the south.

Along the north coast is a large area of lake and swampland. Two lakes here, **Laguna de la Leche**, and **Redonda Lake**, both offer good hunting and fishing. Much of the province is classified as part of the great Camagüey plain and, along its extreme Atlantic coast, are several beach resorts. The highlands of the **Santa Clara ridge** just project into the low-lying province and the **Sierra Jatibonico** peaks, near the town of Chambas, reveal attractive beauty spots and rocky caves. Another isolated ridge has become a visitor's delight, the **Hill of Cunagua**, between two northern swamps, and near the town of Bolivia. The flat plain becomes marshy along the southern coastal strip.

It is in the south and central part of the province, that the places of historic interest lie. In the far south, is the site of the 1875, shortcut, made by Maximo Gómez, during the early wars. A later site, on the edge of the southern marsh, is the 1958 memorial to the death of **Senen Marino**. North of the capital is the site of Camilo Cienfuegos' 1958 crossing and that of Antonio Maceo, in 1895 is nearby. A memorial to the taking of Morón by Gral Manuel Suarez in 1876, lies near the city, as does that of Enrique Varona Gonzales, (1925).

Tourism is not so widespread in Ciego de Avila Province, but it does have a number of **caves**, and tropical vegetation parks on the Punta de San Juan, in the extreme north-west. The beauty spot of **Loma la Caroline** lies near the city.

Ciego de Avila

Set in undulating, flat countryside positively bursting with orchards and fruit plantations, the city has been dubbed 'the Pineapple Town'. The Central Highway, from Sancti Spiritus, passes a huge cannery, before crossing a bridge over the railroad and a local street, onto the main road.

Established comparatively recently, in 1849, it was previously thought that the site had been a *hacienda* and plantation belonging to the Spaniard, Alonso de Avila, one of Velázquez' commanders. This town, with a population of 73 000 has little of sightseeing value compared with older cities. There is an old Spanish fort in the far north-eastern corner of the city, two small galleries, two classical monuments, and a monument to José Martí in the main square. Towards the main street the **Principal Theatre**, 1927, is well worth a quick visit for its unusual decor.

There are five restaurants in the town, including **Pizzeria Napoles, Mandarin, El Colonial** and **La Confronta**. Seven cafeterias and seven bars offer refreshment.

An entertainment park has been constructed outside the city beyond the **Ciego de Avila Hotel**, and further west is the **Motel Las Canas**. *La Patana Boatel* in Los Jardines de Reina has 12 rooms.

EXCURSIONS FROM CIEGO DE AVILA

Cayo Guillermo; Morón; Loma La Carolina; Playita de Majagua and; trips to the local citrus fruit plantations or cattle and dairy farms.

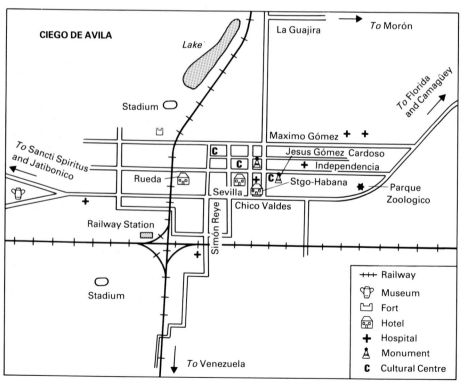

Bottle Brush trees are found in many northern coast gardens.

HOTELS IN CIEGO DE AVILA
Ciego de Avila
Carretera Ceballos   Tel: 4014
136 rooms, all amenities
La Patana
Los Jardines de la Reina
136-room floating hotel, diving and fishing centre
Morón
Centre of Morón city, 136 rooms, all amenities
El Ultimo Paraiso
Los Jardines de la Reina

Cayo Guillermo

Just an 85-kilometre flight north from Ciego de Avila, this 13-square kilometre desert island is a paradise in the **Camagüey Archipelago**. Pelicans, flamingos and sea birds are its only inhabitants and in the Old Bahama Channel the big game fish run. This is a coveted, secluded retreat for divers and fishermen.

Morón

In the north of Ciego de Avila Province 36 kilometres from Ciego de Avila city, this city is separated from the north coast by the **Laguna de Leche**, or Milk Lake. Entering the built-up area, a large placard depicting the fruits of agriculture and industry, announces your arrival in this city of 37 000 inhabitants. Immediately before the main street the **Hotel Morón**, with accommodation for 144 guests, cuts the skyline to the right.

Although it is quite an old city, Morón was established in 1750, most of the development regions on the outskirts, like the hotel, are modern. The **clock tower** in front of the hotel on the broad highway, which once sported an old brazen Spanish, crowing cockerel, now towers over the entrance gardens, with a forlorn cock at its feet.

Several interesting buildings line the colonnaded main street, and horsedrawn, ancient carriages, ply the streets as alternatives to motorised taxi transport.

163

A native of Cuba, Dwarf Poinciana is also common in this province.

The city's main attraction is the hunting and fishing, which can be arranged on the *Laguna de Leche*, (named for its colour – although the calcium content appears to have reduced noticeably in recent years) or the smaller *Laguna la Redonda*. Interesting reclamation schemes, have transformed the marshy landscape around the city, and excellent roads link the quaysides at the two lakes. **Motel Turistica** is on the lake road to La Boca.

EXCURSIONS FROM MORÓN
The beaches at La Tinaja and La Boca; the Sierra Jatibonico; caves at Barbites and on Punta de San Juan; the Isla de Turiguano and; the Lomas of Cunagua and Carolina.

Fishing, boating, and hunting trips can be arranged through the reception at Hotel Morón and through representatives of Cubatur.

Turiguano

This recent development, is purely a cattle breeding station (the prized *Santa Gertrudis* strain), on an island which can, by appointment, be visited. It is conveniently near to the little resort of **La Tinaja Beach**, 28 kilometres from Morón and 64 kilometres from Ciego de Avila.

Sancti Spiritus Province

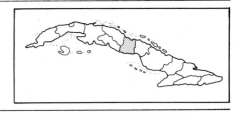

'I loathe the facade and depravation
of the labyrinths in my lodgings:
I turn to the gentle rustlings
of my laurel mountain.
With the poor of the earth

I am happy with my lot:
The mountain stream
pleases me more than the sea.'

JOSÉ MARTÍ from his
poem *The Temple of the Mountain*

Straddling the centre of the elongated island, this province has a population of around 410 000. From a narrow northern coastline on the Atlantic, the province widens towards the Caribbean shores where three major rivers, the Manati, Zaza, Jatibonico del Sur, together with may others, enter the ocean. The Jatibonico del Norte emanates from almost the same source as del Sur, in the highlands, above the town of Yaguajay, and runs into the sea, just over the border, in Ciego de Avila Province.

The edge of the **Sierra Escambray**

Plaza Mayor, in the centre of Trinidad, is the centre of an ancient settlement which dates back to 1514, the oldest in Sancti Spiritus Province.

just stretches into the south-western corner of the province, and the mighty Manati river has carved a wide valley, isolating an outcrop near the city of Sancti Spiritus.

Sancti Spiritus is the capital of the province. It lies on the Central Highway and railroad, near the huge dam of **Zaza**. The great plain of Camagüey extends to the point where the city is built, just at the edge of the Santa Clara Highlands and Escambray Mountains.

Sugar is the main product of the province, but ground root crops are also cultivated. In the south there is a thriving fishing industry, and the production of honey, along the mangrove-choked shores of **Tunas de Zaza**, is becoming most profitable. Cattle are farmed in the north. The province is home to the largest paper mill in the country, the Panchito Gómez Toro mill.

Tourism provides a rewarding distraction from conventional industry, and the province has a great deal to offer in this respect. In the north, but particularly on the Caribbean coast, the excellent beaches bring thousands of holidaymakers to the

Ancient cobbles pave the Trinidad streets and antique cannon once prevented the carriage wheels from damaging house cornerstones.

province. A cave system exists on the north coast near Judas Point and there is a spa at San José del Lago. The Zaza reservoir, many rivers and fishing harbours bring sportsmen who also hunt in the mountainous regions. History-lovers also have a treat in store, in the ancient Spanish colonial treasure house of **Trinidad**. In the north, there are monuments associated with the revolutionary exploits of Camilo Cienfuegos, near the capital are the **Steps of the Damas** (the place where General Serafin Sanchez fell), the old sites of the earlier capital, La Reforma (General Maximo Gómez' garrison in 1896), the site of the capturing and burning of El Jibaro, by Gómez in 1875 and, in the Sierra Sancti Spiritus, the monument to Conrado Benitez, and Che Guevara's campsite, **El Pedrero**.

Sancti Spiritus

In early times this major town was known as Espiritu Santo. Today, once over its little, hump-back bridge entrance, the city of Sancti Spiritus is a delight for architectural enthusiasts. Founded in 1514, and constantly the subject of pirate attention, the inland city, located near the shores of the Zaza reservoir, now tends to be overlooked by the visitor. The city's population is around 90 000. As it is situated on the Central Highway tourist attention is diverted to nearby Trinidad, but the provincial capital still has many interesting sites worth discovering, as it is a national monument.

Sancti Spiritus was established first by Diego Velázquez and Fernandez de Cordoba. The **ancient church** has suffered, over the years, the same fate as the city, and, at one time, before the city moved to its present location, was isolated on the banks of the Yayabo river. Alterations and reconstructions, commencing in 1536, and culminating in the building of the church's cupola, during the middle of the last century, has resulted in a most interesting structure. The church

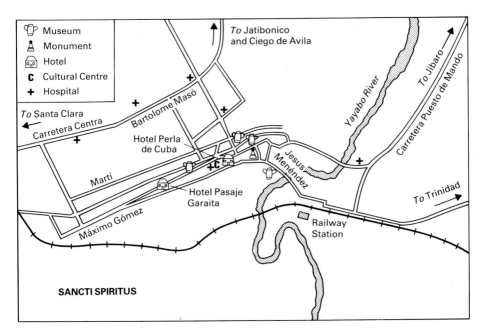

SANCTI SPIRITUS

sports a marvellously carved ceiling and many religious artworks. Sadly, the solid gold cockerel which once adorned the church, fell into pirate hands during repeated attacks in the 17th century.

Two interesting places in the city are the **Decorative Art Museum**, privately owned by artist Erasmo Rameau, and the **Principal Theatre**, 1876. Try to make a booking to hear the *Coro de Claro* or 'Clear Choir'.

The **Museum of Colonial Art** is near the 1850 bridge whilst the **Archaeological Museum**, is on the other side of the city. In the centre near the Sanchez Park, are the Museum of History and Slavery, and the Museum of Art. The house where Serafin Sanchez was born, has also become a museum. On the park, is the **Perla de Cuba Hotel**, next to the Yumuri, Liana and Los Parados cafeterias. The **Las Villas Hotel**, is further out and the city's four restaurants – Pizzeria Sicilia, Pio Lindo, 1514, and Meson del la Plaza, are nearby. Two out-of-town hotels, **Zaza del Medio**, which accommodates 128 guests and **Motel Los Laureles,** are located north, on the route of the Central Highway. Las Cuevas

Motel accommodates 54 visitors. Further out, at the town of Taguasco, is the new hotel of the same name, also **Costa Sur hotel** and the **Zaza hotel**.

The Torre de Iznaga gave the plantation overseers an ideal vantage point from which to supervise the slave field labourers.

167

EXCURSIONS FROM SANCTI SPIRITUS

Trinidad; Casilda; Hanabanilla; Mayajigua; Topes de Collantes; Alturas de Banao; El Boqueron Caves; the Zaza Lake and; fishing trips either on the lake or rivers, or on the sea at El Megano. Horse riding in the surrounding hills is popular and trips can be arranged through Cubatur.

Casilda

Just seven kilometres south of Trinidad, and 76 kilometres from Sancti Spiritus, this 1808 fishing port has a chequered history of pirates and privateering, but is now a pretty Caribbean township popular with scuba divers because of its adjacent coral reefs.

Magajigua

On the north coast road, this lakeside township is an oasis in tropical woodland, best reached from Santa Clara, just 106 kilometres away. The town makes a relaxing stop-over but, although it was founded as early as 1820, does not have much to offer in the way of unusual features.

Trinidad

Trinidad lies about 69 kilometres from Sancti Spiritus and 78 kilometres from Cienfuegos, and today has a population of about 35 000.

In the years after its foundation by Diego de Velázquez in 1514, this charming city, was Spain's richest colony in the New World. The small quantity of gold, which the Spanish mined here, was soon eclipsed when Hernando Cortéz, with men recruited from Trinidad, realised the potential wealth on the Mexican mainland. Sugar, along with the slave trade boomed, as did the city's shipping trade, using the port of Casilda just south of Trinidad.

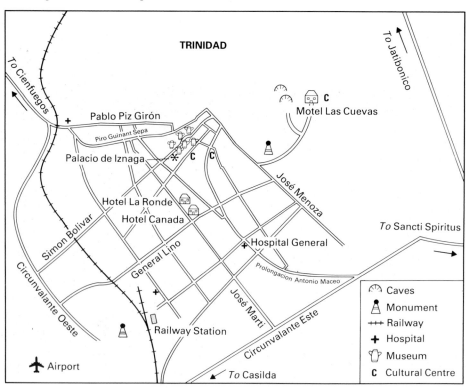

Today 100 small fishing boats operate a collective from here.

The riches made by the inhabitants in past years are reflected in the city's architectural opulence, remaining as testament to the traders of the 17th and 18th centuries. The name Trinidad, derives from the Holy Trinity.

The city almost seeks refuge from the modern world in the folds of the Escambray foothills. Approaching from Cienfuegos in the east – passing the white monument, to the 'man of Maisinicu', (Alberto Delgado, a spy for Fidel in the counter-revolutionary forces, who was discovered and hung on a nearby tree in 1964), the bright orange tiles and white walls of Trinidad, suddenly appear like a mirage over the emerald hills.

The city is now a national monument. Paved with **cobbles** called '*chinas pelonas*' from the local river, with cannon

View of Trinidad from the Museum of Culture balcony

Spanish tiles face some of Trinidad's ancient, patioed homes.

imbedded, muzzle-down, on street corners to prevent carriage wheels chipping the Spanish-tiled walls, the city is a '**time capsule**', blessed by a unique micro-climate. Each house could be a living museum, and the city's pristine condition

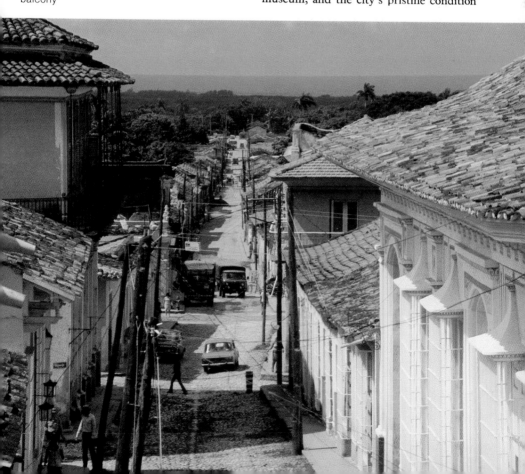

with immaculate streets, bears witness to the care taken by its preservation-conscious inhabitants.

The city's two restaurants are converted houses. **El Pavito** is a beautiful courtyarded, Spanish-style building, with a good size bar and restaurant. Excellent meals are served here and specialities include whole baked fish. The **Pizzeria Tosca** is also good value for money, and the two hotels, **La Ronda** and **Hotel Canada**, also serve meals. All are located on the main José Marti Street.

In the centre of the city is **Marti Square**. This typically Spanish Plaza, is dominated by the Church of the Holy Trinity, dating from the late 19th century. Two, bronze, 'Landseeresque' greyhounds, wrought iron benches, and a raised central patio, are shaded by bowers of Hibiscus, and giant Royal Palms. Palacio Brunet, the **Museum of the Romantic Era**, has been restored, both inside and out, to its pre-1740 glory, and houses a wealth of antiques. Its particularly fine, carved cedar ceiling, in the main hall, is unique. The **Natural Science Museum** houses an unusual collection of Cuban flora and fauna, and the Casa del los Sanchez, nearby, is a rare example of colonial architecture. On the west side of the square is the **Archaeological Museum**, containing artefacts from Indian times, both discovered locally, and nationally. It is a lovely building in itself, with turned, wooden balcony.

Other points of interest, in the centre of the city, are the **Cantero Palace**, now housing the Museum of Decorative Arts. Museum Lucha Contra Bandidos, The Casa de la Trova or **Trova House** for performances of Cuban song, and the **Cultural House**, where dances of Africa and Cuban adaptations are often performed. A ruined church, the 250-year-old Santa Ana and the Inglesia del la Popa, 1726, lie on the city's outskirts. The 1872 Iglesia de Paula is situated on Cespedes Park near a *guarapo* or sugar cane juice bar and bus terminal.

Look out too for the makers of typical Trinidad souvenirs, the bamboo penny whistle and palmleaf hat. Local crafts can be viewed by arrangement with Cubatur.

The **Tower of Iznaga**, once the highest structure in Cuba, 45 metres tall and an old sugar cane watch tower, makes a memorable visit from the city, just 14 kilometres away.

More than a day can be spent viewing Trinidad itself. The **Motel las Cuevas'** stone cabins, restaurant and bar, pool, and natural cavern, provide delightful accommodation, just above the gaily coloured, flower-decked city. **Costa Sur Hotel** is located just outside the city.

Excursions from Trinidad

The beach at Ancon; Casilda port; Iznaga Tower and; San Luis Valley.

Horse rides or treks into the lush countryside can be arranged by Cubatur.

HOTELS IN SANCTI SPIRITUS
Las Cuevas Motel
Trinidad outskirts
Hotel Zaza
Márgenes, Lago Zaza   Tel: 2027–2797
Costa Sur
María   Aguilar   Highway,   Trinidad
Tel: 2107–2208

Cienfuegos Province

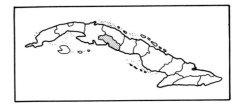

'The light here is wonderful just before the sun goes down: a long trickle of gold and the seabirds are dark patches on the pewter swell.'

from a letter to his sister from Wormold in Cienfuegos – the central character in 'Our Man in Havana' by GRAHAM GREENE

Situated to the south-west of Villa Clara Province, this mainly coastal and mountain province, has an estimated population of 340 000. The capital city is Cienfuegos, located to the east of the vast pocket-bay of the same name, (early maps show the bay as Xagua, or Jagua). This giant port, is one of the most important docking areas in Cuba. Its narrow outlet to the Caribbean sea almost creates an island lake of the bay, which the province surrounds.

The city is linked to its neighbouring provinces by the Southern Highway, and to many towns and cities by rail. It also has a major airport. The road to the south-east, passes many beach resorts, which lie at the base of the striking Escambray Mountains. In these mountains there are numerous beauty spots, and two of the province's major rivers, the Rio San Juan and Rio Arimao. A number of large lakes have been created in the mountains, attracting tourists and sportsmen.

Inland the province is comparatively flat, but undulating, with river basins of the Caonao, Salado, Damuji and Hanabana, which forms the north-western boundary of the province. The main, Havana – Santa Clara highway, follows the same line as the Rio Hanábana, and continues across the province's nothernmost sector. Sugar is the main crop of this south-central province, and the massive port installations of Cienfuegos, testify to the importance of this crop as its most lucrative export.

Apart from the many natural attractions of the **Sierra Escambray**, near to the city are the **Botanical Gardens** with 60 different varieties of endemic palm and a host of floral displays which makes this a very worthwhile visit. The woodland labyrinth is matched, across the bay, by many **caves**, and the historical monument of the **Jagua Castle**. Other important sites include the **battlefields** of Mal Tiempo and Peralejo, and several monuments in and around the city. Cayo Loco is one site of particular naval interest to the north of Cienfuegos, and the monument to Henry Reeve – El Inglesíto – lies far to the west, near the town of Yaguaramas. Ciego Montero is a spa north of the city.

Cienfuegos

This old city port was not established as a harbour until 1819, but its huge pocket-bay, with narrow fortified entrance was in use before 1700. The Bahia de Cienfuegos is almost an inland sea, and provided shelter for fleets plying the Caribbean. **Jagua Castle**, was finished in 1745 after seven years of work by Spanish builders, interrupted by marauding pirates.

Cienfuegos is locally known as the 'pearl of the south'. The French influence on the city, which was rebuilt after storm damage in 1831, derives from its early settlers. It is obvious that the original planners had taken trouble to build an ideal harbour.It has its own lookout point, and a long, wide **Prado**. Running out from Punta Gorda, in the far south of the city, and along the Malecon, the broad boulevard is as impressive as the city's **Parque Martí**. Points of interest include: its pink-domed **Cathedral**, 1870; magnificent **triumphal arch**, 1902; famous **Tomas Terry Theatre** looking out towards the Premier Palace and delicately-fretted bandstand; the **Tomas Acea Cemetery**, with its Parthenon-style gateway, and the **Reina Cemetery**.

Restaurants are international because of the port and naval harbour and include **The Mandarín, El Pollito, La Lagua, La Verja** (a choice of 100 dishes), **El Cochinito, 1819, El Polinesio** and **Pizzeria Giovento**. On Punta Gorda the two restaurants, **Ruben M. Villena** and the seafood restaurant of **Paella Covadonga** vie with the nearby restaurant of the modern **Jagua Hotel**. The Malecon is lined with opulent mansions of the past century. Commanding a fantastic view

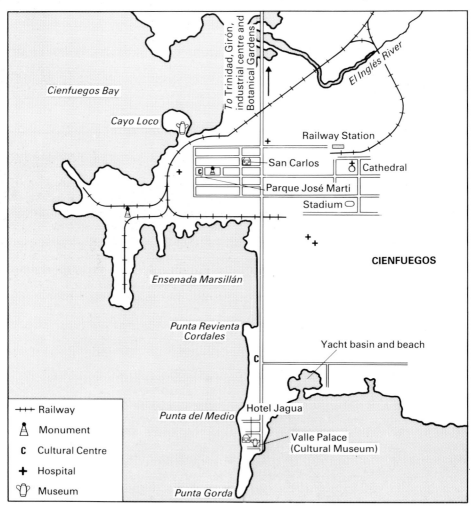

Out on Punta Gorda, past many magnificent 19th century mansions, is the crowning glory – the exquisite Valle Palace, now the Museum of Decorative Arts.

over the harbour, and in itself, a breathtaking edifice, is the oriental-style, **Valle Palace** in whose grounds the Jagua is built. *Jagua* means fountain, wealth or beauty in Cuban Indian. The Valle Palace now doubles as the Museum of Decorative Arts. Take an early evening drink among the roof turrets, after viewing the collection of treasures and rich decorations adorning its intricately lavish interiors.

To the right of the Punta Gorda, is a tiny beach with a yacht and dingy club, children's playground and cafeteria. In the city, the **Trova House** is worth an evening visit, as is the Casa de Cultura and **Conservatory of Music**. Just along from Parque Marti is the **San Carlos Hotel**, and, continuing north around the bay, the road branches off before a flyover, to the industrial area.

Cienfuegos is the third most important Cuban port with a population of about

Constructed in 1902, in Cienfuegos' Marti Park, this commemorative gateway frames the 1870 stone Cathedral on the opposite side of the Square.

60 000, and has a vast industrial complex, including the country's largest cement plant and SIME – the Iron and Steel Machinery Company which makes parts for Giron buses and Tainos trucks. There are also huge cereal storage silos, sugar onloading depots, a canned and bottled fruit and juice handling terminal, a huge

fertiliser plant, wheat mills, and flour plants. Visits to the massive sugar terminal can be made by arrangement with Cubatur. On Jagua Bay is the country's biggest oil refinery, a fishing combine, and a power station.

EXCURSIONS FROM CIENFUEGOS

Jagua Castle; the Soledad Botanical Gardens with 2000 plant species and one of the most prolific flower shows in Cuba, originated by the sugar magnates, the Atkins family in 1852; caves of Verraco La Luz; Murcielago; Jucoral on the Castillo de Jagua Point; the historical Naval Museum at Cayo Loco, behind the city; Laberinte de los Naturales, caves at Sabanita and El Infierno; Pica San Juan, in the Escambray Mountains, at 1156 metres above sea level; El Salto de la Muerto; the Ciego Montero Spring; Loma Cabazaxdel Muerto and; Trinidad is also an attractive day's excursion.

By arrangement with Cubator, trips can also be made to visit the terminals and industrial sector of this, Cuba's major trading port.

HOTELS IN CIENFUEGOS

Pascaballel Hotel
Rancho Luna Highway Tel: 8545
188 rooms, all amenities
Jagua Hotel
Punta Gorda
146 rooms, all amenities plus a cabaret
Motel Rancho Luna
Rancho Luna Highway, 20 kilometres from the city, 225 rooms, beach resort facilities
Ciego Montero Spring
28 rooms, pool and spa baths

Villa Clara Province

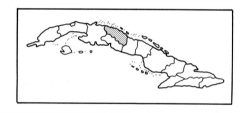

'*Oh, you that say that your country is not so pretty,*
Oh, you that say that the good is not so beautiful,
you are invited to search the world
for another sky as blue as your sky,
another moon that shines so bright . . .'

EDUARDO SABORIT from his song *How Pretty is Cuba*

The capital of this province is Santa Clara city, and its total population numbers approximately 780 000. Although it has a lengthy Atlantic coast in the north, with many fine beaches, the province has no southern seaboard and borders on Cienfuegos Province. Santa Clara city is home to one of Cuba's four universities.

The wide plain of Las Villas is an extension of that in Matanzas Province, but the soil is not so fertile. Sugar is the main crop, in this, the largest producer-province in Cuba, and tobacco is grown on the more sandy soil, to the south of the province. Beans, malanga, juca, and maize, are common vegetables cultivated for local consumption. Caibarien is the main port of the province, and both this northern harbour, and Cienfuegos, in the south, are used to export the main products of sugar, and some industrial manufactured goods.

In the southern part of the province, are the Escambray Mountains, important for their supply of water from reservoirs and rivers. The mountain resort of **Hanabanilla**, has made this part of Villa Clara a popular tourist and fishing area, as is the Indian-style **Caneyes resort**. On the far northern shore, in the many cays of the Atlantic coast, **Cayo Esquivel**, and Isabela de Sagua, provide a wealth of beaches for the sun and sea-loving visitor.

The province's major rivers are the Sagua la Grande, the Sagua la Chica and the Agabama. Between the sources of the last two, is the town of **Placetas** – well known for its extraordinarily mild climate and for one of the widest main streets in Latin America.

Because of its strategic location and its size, the province has been in the centre of turmoil during wars of independence and revolution. **Battle sites** from revolutionary times abound, particularly around the Central Highway, which runs through the city, and bisects the province. Rail connections link most of the northern coastal towns and also link the city with Cienfuegos in the south.

Santa Clara

This city, with approximately 170 000 inhabitants, is situated centrally, between the north coast, and Cienfuegos on the Caribbean Sea. It became a centre of refuge, in the middle of the country, by people plagued with pirate raids.

The city straddles the main highway through the country, and, for that reason became an important stronghold, since its foundation in 1689. Santa Clara now has an important airport.

The twentieth-century square, now forms the focal point of Santa Clara, and here the sights are: in the corner, the old 1797 **Spanish City Hall**; El Pavito restaurant; the **Caridad Theatre**, built in

During a strategic battle in 1958, Che Guevara's troops took the city of Santa Clara and captured Batista's troops attempting to flee in this train, still sporting its military livery.

1885 and; the **City Museum**. The Municipal Palace is now a broadcasting station. The **Santa Clara Libre** hotel, 161 rooms, is proud of the bullet holes in its facade, caused during the battle here in 1958 – the last before Fidel entered Havana. A train carrying Batista's troops, was captured by Ernesto 'Ché Guevara's forces, and still stands near the **Vidal Park** and the **Cathedral**. See the 1748, **Iglesia del Carmen**, the **Buen Viaje Church** and Las Villas University, Cuba's third largest. There are 52 bridges here, more than any other town in Latin America, not all warranting a visit! Listen to local songs at the **Casa de la Trova** in the evenings, and visit the **1878 Restaurant**. with its colonial trappings and typical Santa Claran dishes.

The rustic thatched cabins of **Motel Los Caneyes** which, is just outside the city, can be a unique overnight stay. It cannot be missed, with its huge welcoming statue of an Indian at the entrance. Its nightclub, pool, and excellent restaurant are a great attraction.

Lake Minerva, an artificial lake near the city, offers excellent recreational facilities. A new hotel is to be built near the lakeside, with accommodation for 148 guests. At Lake Hanabanilla there is a modern hotel.

Santa Clara has its place among the big

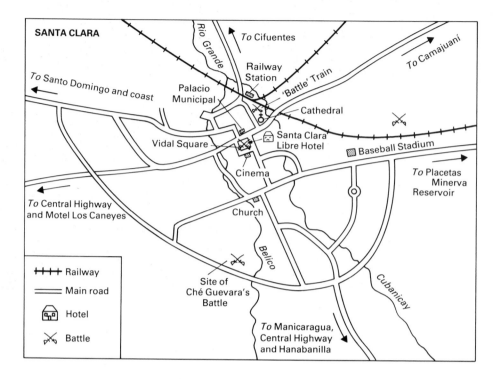

SANTA CLARA

To Cifuentes

To Camajuaní

Rio Grande

Railway Station

To Santo Domingo and coast

Palacio Municipal

'Battle' Train

Cathedral

Vidal Square

Santa Clara Libre Hotel

Baseball Stadium

Cinema

To Placetas Minerva Reservoir

To Central Highway and Motel Los Caneyes

Church

Belico

┼┼┼┼ Railway

═══ Main road

🏠 Hotel

⚔ Battle

Site of Ché Guevara's Battle

Cubanicay

To Manicaragua, Central Highway and Hanabanilla

---

industrial centres of Cuba. The largest factory in the country for the manufacture of domestic products, hardware, refrigerators, kettles and kitchen utensils, is situated just outside the city. There is also a growing textile industry, a huge rail siding for the dispatch of goods and sugar produce, and a thriving agricultural development programme.

EXCURSIONS FROM SANTA CLARA

Remedios Caibarien and Playa Conuco on the north coast; Lakes Minerva and Hanabanilla, for fishing trips; Placetas, the town of the widest streets; La Yaya and; Manicaragua.

HOTELS IN VILLA CLARA PROVINCE

Motel los Caneyes Avenue Eucaliptos y Circunvalacion   Tel: 6193 and 3714
Accommodation for 48 people just outside Santa Clara

Elgea   Tel: 96166
Corralillo
Santa Clara Libre   Tel: 7548/9
161 rooms, centrally located in Santa Clara
Hanabanilla Hotel
Manicaragua, Villa Clara   Tel: 86932
Accommodation for 128 people

Hanabanilla

This beautiful mountain resort, in the Escambray Mountains, just 54 kilometres from Santa Clara, is centred on the game fishing industry because of its lakeside prospect. It does, however, offer all sorts of opportunities for boating, ferry trips, climbing, pony trekking and sailing holidays.

La Yaya

Established in 1972, this modern development, population just over 1000, is based on agriculture, and in particular dairy and cattle farming. It is a model cooperative project just 20 kilometres from Santa Clara.

Some shoreline establishments provide facilities for horse riding.

Manicaragua

Founded in the second year of the last century, this busy town with 75 000 inhabitants is surrounded by green fields of tobacco and rolling hills. An interestingly typical, central Cuban settlement, about an hour by bus from Hanabanilla, the town is 30 kilometres south of Santa Clara.

Mayajigua

An idyllic location, on the shores of a small lake, gives this old town a private situation, in wooded countryside. The town was established in 1820, and good architectural examples remain.

Remedios

Situated just inland from the north coast of Santa Clara Province and 53 kilometres from Santa Clara, this town was built as a completely new settlement, in 1692. Previously, the inhabitants had moved the original location twice, due to pirate harassment and, during this period the town lost its provincial capital status to Santa Clara. The population now is 45 000.

Many beautiful **colonial houses** and mansions, are to be viewed here, but the centre point, is the magnificent square of **Plaza Marti**. Around Plaza Marti are a number of important structures, including the **Alejandro García Caturla Museum of Music**, all shaded by the Royal Palms, and facing the decorative gazebo in the middle of the square. The 1692, **Church of San Juan Bautista de Remedios** is built on the remains of its 1570, original site. It is one of the oldest in Cuba, and contains some most interesting artworks, and a unique, carved ceiling. There is the Buen Viaje Church opposite, and the town also has a small museum.

Remedios is well-known for its festivities and **carnivals**, which date back to the early 19th century, and are known as *Parrandas*. Symbolised by a falcon and a cock, the two areas of El Carmen and San Salvador compete in noisy celebrations. Now there is a festival on 24 July.

Topes de Collantes

A variety of recreational facilities are offered at this forested mountain resort. It is ideal for ambitious families with active youngsters.

Matanzas Province

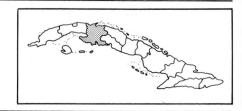

'Is it the sight of the green leaves which excite you?
The fresh streams that invite your bill?
Your call the whispering wind?
Oh! my poor turtle dove, my pretty little turtle dove.

JOSÉ JACINTO MILANÉS from the
poem *Flight of the Turtle Dove*.

To the east of Havana Province, Matanzas has an estimated 570 000 population, and a varied topography, from mountains in the north, to swamp in the south. The city of Matanzas is the provincial capital.

This province is one most frequented by tourists for its differences in terrain and countryside. The internationally famous beach of **Varadero**, in the extreme north, attracts thousands of visitors each year, as does the marsh-bound swamp, and Treasure Lake resort of **Guama**, between the two arms of the Zapata Peninsula. These vast regions of southern Matanzas – Zapata Occidental and Oriental, are fringed with a mangrove belt on their Caribbean coast, and lie either side of the Bay of Pigs.

Stretching almost the width of the province from north to south, is the most fertile plain in Cuba. The Llanura Roja or Llanura de Colon, provides the best sugar crops from its rich, red, soil. Fruit, vegetables and tobacco, are cultivated in the western extremes of the plain, which becomes low-lying and marshy in its most northerly coastal region.

The mountains in the north-west of Matanzas Province, surrounding the excellent natural harbour of the city, are rich in beauty spots. The **Yumuri Valley** to the west of Matanzas, **El Balcon**, the **Cidra Dam**, La Arboleda and the medicinal spring waters of **San Miguel**, all attract visitors from the beaches out into the countryside resorts. Fishing and hunting are provided for in both the Atlantic waters and in and around the southern swamplands. Several **caves** attract tours as do the **spas** at San Miguel de los Baños, Menendez and Elguea.

The **Museum of Girón**, and the surrounding regions of the Bay of Pigs, are rich in the history of recent warfare, as is the sugar Centrale of Australia, once Fidel Castro's centre of operations during the invasion attempt. Earlier sites include the birthplace of Domingo Mujica, the location of the uprising of Martin Marrero, the battlefield of Calimete, Colon's colonial fort, the **Museum of Dr. Mario Munoz**, the battle site of Coliseo and, near Matanzas, **El Morillo** fort.

Matanzas

The city lies 60 minutes, (just over 100 kilometres) east of Havana and straddles the Yumuri and San Juan rivers. Three attractive road bridges, and two rail bridges, link the city west to east at the head of the wide Bahia de Matanzas. Today the city has a population of about 100 000.

Originally thought to refer to a slaughter,

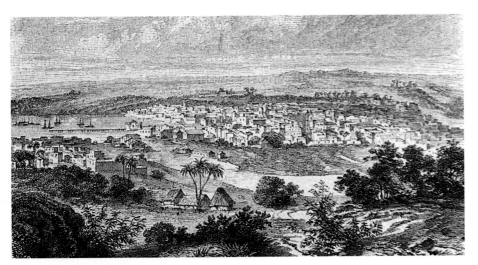

Nineteenth century Matanzas

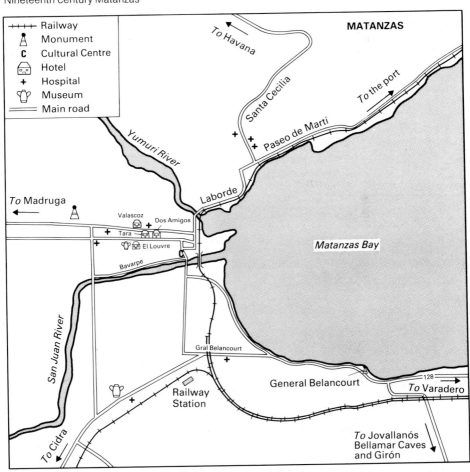

MATANZAS

Railway
Monument
C Cultural Centre
Hotel
+ Hospital
Museum
Main road

To Havana

Santa Cecilia

To the port

Yumuri River

Paseo de Martí

Laborde

To Madruga

Valascoz
Dos Amigos
Tara
El Louvre
Bavarpe

Matanzas Bay

San Juan River

Gral Belancourt

General Belancourt

128
To Varadero

Railway
Station

To Cidra

To Jovallanós
Bellamar Caves
and Girón

179

either of Spanish explorers, or of native Indians, it is now considered that the given name, Matanzas, or massacre, derives from the plundering for food, of herds of pigs, kept near the bay, by local inhabitants.

Matanzas was founded in 1690 and the Castillo de San Severino, a harbour fortress, was built in the 17th century. It is located on the bay, along the northern exit of the city, and was designed to prevent attacks from pirates and enemy fleets.

Approaching the city from Havana, the road runs high over a bluff overlooking the bay and sugar loading wharfs, sulphur mill, and port area. A flowered entrance to the main road passes alongside the railhead, following the line of the bay, over the Yumuri river and past the magnificent **Sauto Theatre**. Matanzas derived its reputation as a leader in the arts from the high standard of culture performed in this 1863 building. Many of the nation's famous poets and writers either originated from this north coast city, or made their homes here. The city is often known as 'The Athens of Cuba' for this reason.

At one end of this bridge, the longest in the Republic, there is a café and bar offering refreshment on a patio with magnificent valley views.

Five restaurants are complemented by seven cafeterias – the restaurants are **Pizzeria Bellamar**, **Bahia** restaurant, **Pio Pio**, **La Gondola** and the **Peking** restaurant. **Hotels Velazco**, **Yara**, **Dos Amigos** and **El Louvre** offer adequate, but not plush, accommodation. These hotels are grouped in the area of **Parque Libertad**, which is noted for the classical architecture of its surrounding buildings – the Casa de Cultura, the 1835 City Library one of Cuba's oldest, the early City Hall and **Art Gallery** whose magnificent carved doors are an added attraction. Just a block away is the **Cathedral**, begun in 1693, but expanded to its present size by 1878.

Following the road out towards the north-east, at a sharp bend, are the bus and rail stations, attractive 1883 constructions. The Matanzas **Museum of History**, (ask about the famous Matanzas mummy), the **Palacio Junco**, and absorbing 1882 **Pharmaceutical Museum**, (supposedly unique in Latin America) are all worth a visit, as is **La Vina**, an early grocery store – now a restaurant/museum.

EXCURSIONS FROM MATANZAS
Bellamar's cave, about 10 minutes from

Rustic cabins and an exquisite restaurant comprise Guama's vacation facilities.

the city; Camarioca; historical Cardenas; Varadero's fantastic beach; Valle de Yumuri; El Balcon and; La Arboleda.

Take a trip to Guama Indian village resort, Girón, and Playa Larga.

Camarioca

This is a stop-over fishing village which has an interesting variety of architecture in the typical wooden fishing hut style. Inland from Varadero, in the opposite direction to Matanzas, the distance is about 22 kilometres. Fine seafood is served in the Boca de Camorioca restaurant.

Cardenas

This little city, population 70 000, is a popular day-trip visit from the vast Varadero resort on the nearby Hicacos Peninsula. A centre for the local sugar trade, the city was founded in 1828, and, 22 years afterwards, was the site for an attempted invasion of Cuba in 1850.

Narciso Lopez failed in his attack, but it was the first time the Cuban flag was raised in the country. Since then Cardenas has been called the 'flag city'. By that time the **Cathedral** in Colon Park had already been erected, four years before. **La Dominica**, in the park, is a national monument. Reconstructed in 1919, it is a local hotel.

A **statue of Columbus** was raised in the park and the birthplace of the revolutionary, Jose Antonio Echevarría, Genes Street, is a most interesting building. The iron dome (built in the US) and colonnade, of the mid-19th century **Molokoff market**, the one art gallery and five museums, are worth visiting, as is the small zoo. 'Molokoff' was the local word for the 19th century crinoline skirts. The market dome was said to resemble these – hence its name!

Cardenas has twin tourist hotels, the **Europa** and **La Aragonesa** hotels. Restaurants **Vanada, El Castillo**, and **Sayonara**, are joined by El Chucho cafeteria, in the provision of refreshments. The city, just a short, 18-kilometre drive from Varadero also has one guarapo

Treasure Lake is the site of Guama's Indian-style retreat. Bass fishing provides excellent sport.

(sugarcane juice) bar, and four nightclubs. This town is famous for its 'Arecha' speciality rum.

EXCURSIONS FROM CARDENAS
Matanzas; Varadero and; the cave at Bellamar.
Fishing in the Bahia de Cardenas and out in the cays, can be arranged locally.
Tours can be made in a relaxing horse-drawn carriage, or by motorised taxi.

Girón

On the Caribbean coast of Matanzas Province, the Bahia de Cochinos or Bay of Pigs, a wild, neglected area suddenly became the focus of world attention. In April 1961 the popular militia under the leadership of Fidel Castro repulsed an invasion attack engineered by US forces.

Today, the **historic site** has become the object of national and international

Girón, on the Bay of Pigs, was a seaside resort until the invasion attempt in April, 1961. Today increasing numbers of holidaymakers throng its historic beaches.

The Museum of War at Girón has many fascinating exhibits and, at the rear, a small display celebrates Cuba's first astronaut.

182

pilgrimage. In the beachside town, a museum commemorates the events of the battle with weapons, artefacts and photo-documentation.

Nearby, the beach's white sand and artificial reef provide a holiday atmosphere with restaurant, cafeteria, bars and pool. At **Villa Playa Girón**, 55 one-room cottages and 115 two-room cabins provide adequate accommodation. New developments and extra room-space are planned.

Playa Larga, surrounded by roadside monuments to the fallen, with its sandy beach, at the head of the Bay of Pigs, provides facilities for national vacationers.

The Zapata Peninsula also attracts its quota of visitors, for the marvellous **wildlife**, swamp regions and **diving** opportunities, across the bay from Girón. **Villa Playa Larga** can accommodate 49 guests. In winter, watch for the flocks of parrots which descend on the area, from the Zapata swamp.

Guamá

About three hours, (about 100 kilometres), south of Havana, lies one of the country's most famous resorts. Guamá, the **Tainos Indian Village**, is not exactly on the

coast, but on the shores of Treasure Lake. This large expanse of water is a Bass-filled lagoon reached, by way of a 2½-kilometre, man-made canal, through pine trees, from a quayside near a **crocodile** breeding **farm**, which is said to contain more than 40 000 specimens. (There are about 20 'corrals' for the crocodiles and alligators). Visit in early evening during feeding time, but take a bite repellant – against insects!

Almost fifty, rustic-style cabins (all with modern facilities), on stilts over the lakeside, offer basic Indianesque accommodation. A thatched restaurant, **Boca de la Laguna**, bar and games are included in the complex. A 40-metre stairway inside gives out to a roundel outside the building with excellent views across the resort. Each cabin has a boat available and fishing is a major pastime. About 25 **sculptures** by Cuban artist Rita Longa, representing Indian village life, dot the area. A small museum houses artefacts from ancient times. The treasures that the Indians supposedly saved from being plundered by the Spanish, have alas, not yet been recovered from the Laguna de Tesora, where they said the treasures were thrown!

Varadero

This is one of the most famous tourist beaches in the world. Founded in 1880,

Varadero beach is world-famous. The peninsula Punta Hicacos, was named after its prolific trees.

and with 20 kilometres of pure white sand, it is built on a peninsula, the Punta Hicacos. It has a history of Indian occupation, and pirate activity – a natural cave here bears evidence of both. Diving, sailing, fishing, and a gamut of watersports are practised here, only two hours from Havana.

A plethora of hotels, motels, cabin and villa accommodation, plus bars, cafeterias, restaurants, amusement activities and nightlife provide everything for the family, single's or double's holiday.

Rentals of all forms of transport and sporting equipment, plus a regular selection of air, road and boat tours, ensure the visitor's vacation is enjoyed to the full. About 10 000 people live in Varadero and most work in the tourism industry. The Du Pont family mansion, now **Las Américas Restaurant**, should not be missed as an example of 1930s opulence.

Industrialist Du Pont could see this view of Varadero from his 1930 villa, now Las Americas restaurant.

HOTELS IN VARADERO
Atabey
60th Street and Thruway   Tel: 63013
Accommodation for 136 in a modern-style hotel with all amenities
Bellamar
17th Street   Tel: 63014
Modern accommodation with all facilities for 291 guests
Hotel Cuba
Calle C, Dupont, Varadero   Tel: 62975
Accommodation for 151 guests

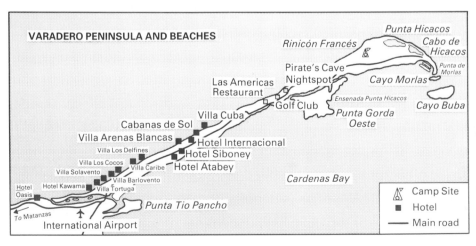

The Internacional is one of Varadero's most popular hotels and its cabaret 'A tableau of Cuba through the ages' is not to be missed.

Internacional
Las Americas Avenue   Tel: 63011
First class accommodation on the beach in modern surroundings with all amenities for 163 guests
Oasis
Via Blanca   Tel: 62902
Accommodation for up to 286 guests in pleasant surroundings
Siboney
64th Street and Thruway   Tel: 63012
Twin hotel of the Atabey with modern accommodation for 136 guests
Tropical Astoria
Accommodation for 44 guests
Kawama
Camino del Mar   Tel: 63113
Beachside accommodation in villa-style, for 142 guests
Ledo
Near the beach, with accommodation for 20 guests
Villa Arenas Blancas

64th Street and 1st Avenue   Tel: 62358
Accommodation for 157 guests
Villa Barlevento
11th Street and Camino del Mar   Tel: 63721
Accommodation for 204 people
Villa Caribe
Playa Avenue and 30th Street   Tel: 63310
Accommodation for 168 guests
Villa Los Cocos
22nd Street and Camino del Mar   Tel: 62552
Accommodation for 89 guests
Cabanas del Sol
Las Americas Avenue Tel: 62828
Accommodation for 274 guests
Villa Herradura
Playa Avenue and 36th Street   Tel: 62648
Accommodation for 179 guests
Villa Punta Blanca
Reparto Punta Blanca   Tel: 63803
Accommodation for 300 guests
Villa Tortuga
7th Street   Tel: 62243
Accommodation for 217 guests
Villa Cuatro Palmas
60th Street and 1st Avenue   Tel: 62251
Accommodation for 155 guests
Villa Los Delfines
Playa Avenue and 36th Street   Tel: 63305
Accommodation for 48 guests
Villa Sotavento
Camino del Mar and 13th Street   Tel: 62953

Accommodation for 198 guests
Villa Solimar
Carretera de las Américas   Tel: 62217
Accommodation for 108 guests

RESTAURANTS IN VARADERO
Albacora
49th Street   Tel: 63811
Superb selection of shellfish dishes
El Legendario Tavern
Antique-strewn with special savoury stews
Las Americas
Las Americas Highway   Tel: 63415
A previous mansion of the Dupont family,
international cuisine
La Arcada
Villa Punta Blanca   Tel: 63803
International cuisine
El Bodegon Criollo
Playa Avenue and 40th Street   Tel: 62180
Typical Cuban dishes
La Cabañita
9th Street and Avenue de la Playa
Shellfish and Meat dishes
Mi Casita
Camino del Mar   Tel: 63787
A curiosity shop of decoration serving
international meals
Castel Nuovo
1st Avenue and 11th Street   Tel: 63787
Italian cuisine
Lai Lai
1st Avenue and 18th Street   Tel: 63297
Prize-winning oriental dishes in splendid
Chinese atmosphere
Meson del Quijote
Villa Cuba, Las Americas Highway   Tel:
62975
Typically Spanish and Cuban-Spanish fare
Ranchon de Solimar
Las Americas Highway   Tel: 63011

Live music with barbecue specialities
Universal and *Antillana*
Internacional Hotel, Las Americas Avenue
Tel: 63011
Both serve international dishes

ENTERTAINMENTS IN VARADERO
Cabillito de Coral Cabaret
Varadero Amphitheatre   Tel: 62169
Continental Cabaret
Internacional Hotel, Las Americas Avenue
Tel: 63011
La Cueva del Pirata
Thruway   Tel: 63224
Eclipse Cabaret
Bellamar Hotel, 17th Street   Tel: 63014
El Legendario Tavern
Villa Sotavento, Camino del Mar   Tel:
62953
Mio Cid Tavern
Villa Punta Blanca, Reparto Punta Blanca
Tel: 63803
La Pecera
Villa Cuba, Las Americas Highway   Tel:
62975
Vertigo Cabaret
Bellamar Hotel, 17th Street   Tel: 63014
VIP Bar
Villa Punta Blanca, Reparto Punta Blanca
Tel: 63803
El Kastillito Disco
Playa Avenue and 49th Street   Tel: 63888
La Patana Disco
Paso Malo Laguna
La Rada Disco
Harbour Dock, Via Blanca   Tel: 62112
Sahara Disco
Oasis Hotel, Via Blanca   Tel: 62902

Isla de la Juventud (Isle of Youth) Municipality

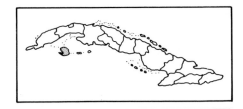

'. . . the Isle of Youth special municipality, an island that went from pre-history to modern times in just a few years.'

FIDEL CASTRO RUZ

Columbus named this island *Evangelista* when he discovered it in 1494 and since then it has been known by various names – Isle of Santiago, Isle of Pines, Island of Parrots and more recently the Isle of Youth.

The island lies off the south coast of Cuba, 97 kilometres from the mainland of Havana Province and has an area of 3000

Lobster beds around this island are a thriving new industry.

square kilometres. It has a total population of about 60 000.

The hill ranges, Sierra Canada (416 metres), Sierra Las Casas (281 metres) and Sierra de Caballos (285 metres) divide the island, and an area of swamp, Cienaga de Lanier, is found in the south. Extensive forests of pine are found in its centre, surrounded by savanna. The 'tail' of this oyster-shaped island is covered in deciduous woodland.

Citrus plantations and fishing provide

the main occupations on the island, apart from the growing tourist industry. A quarry and the forests provide marble and wood for semi-cottage industries including ceramic workshops which use local kaolin to make pottery and souvenirs.

Indians inhabited caves on the Punta del Este, Cueva de Finlay in the south and near the capital. Pirates made the island their base for plundering Spanish treasure fleets and several museums in the capital exhibit historical artefacts. The isolation of the island made it an ideal location for a prison. Today two roads cross the island from Nueva Gerona, the capital, to Playa Roja and Punta del Este.

Hunting, diving, fishing and other outdoor sports are attracting an increasing number of tourists. Boating, on the many lakes or ocean, sailing in the Cays of Canarreos Archipelago and yachting from the two main harbours bring amateurs and professionals to the island from all over the world. Scuba diving around the island is renowned internationally.

Nueva Gerona

The capital lies on the north coast facing the Cuban mainland in an area of flat, dry scrubland. Access to the city from the mainland of Cuba is by air or sea. Micro 70, the capital's model suburb acts as a dormitory town for the city. In earlier days José Martí was imprisoned in **El Abra house** near the city and Fidel Castro and his comrades were incarcerated here in the Model Prison (now the **Museo del Presidio**) during the 1950s.

Visits can be made to the **Museum of the Revolution, Museum of History, Museum El Abra** and the **planetarium**.

There are three restaurants of note in the city, **El Rio, El Coachinito** and **El Corderito**. Hotels include **Hotel Rancho del Tesoro** and **Motel las Codornices**.

Three beaches are found near the city as well as the recreation lake El Abra. On the

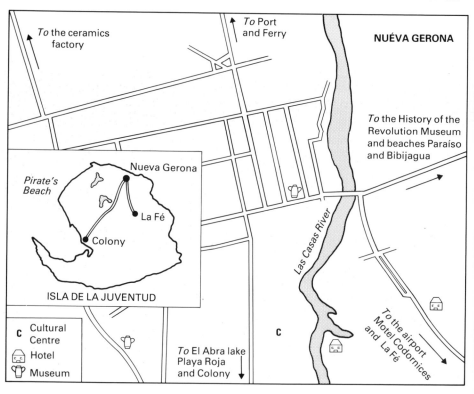

The Isle of Youth, a desert when discovered in 1494, now supports a large citrus industry.

escarpments citrus plantations are propagated by students and the hills are also popular for walking, horse riding and historical trips.

A fantasy island drifting on an artist's palette of aquamarine – this is Cayo Largo.

Other centres on the island

There are three other larger settlements on the island, La Fe just south of the capital, La Victoria and Punta del Este. The latter is particularly interesting for its **Indian caves**, made famous by the 236 wall paintings, and its lovely beach.

Jacksonville, in the centre of the island, is an old English/Scottish community, probably descended from Jamaican exiles.

Near Playa Roja is the most famous hotel on the island, **The Colony**. It has first-class status and every type of activity can be arranged from diving to deepsea fishing and riding.

Cayo Largo (Long Island)

This is a resort dedicated to hedonists, diving and sailing enthusiasts. All types of watersports are available on the island's six beaches. There are excellent reefs, wildlife and marine reserves. At present there are 90 rooms available on the island, but by the end of this decade another 1000 are to be added.

Excursions from Isla de la Juventud

Cayo Largo; Cayo Avalos; Cayo Rosario; fishing; diving and; island tours by car and boat.

HOTELS ON THE ISLA DE LA JUVENTUD
Hotel Colony
Carretera de la Siguanea, Nueva Gerona
Tel: 8182–8282
67 rooms, 7 suites, restaurant, cafeteria, pool and solarium
Hotel Rancho del Tesoro
Nueva Gerona
Motel las Cordonices
Near Nueva Gerona

Habana – Havana Province

'. . . a country which aspires to be a great nation and civilisation stretching out a friendly arm and a true heart to all peoples.'

CARLOS MANUEL DE CÉSPEDES (1868)

Extending about forty kilometres east and west of Havana City Province along the north coast, and south to the Gulf of Batabano, the Province straddles the western 'tail' of Cuba. It has a population of around 615 000 and activities are mostly devoted to agricultural produce. Around the metropolis, however, there is substantial industrial activity, partly concerned with supplying the populace of Havana and partly supplying the export trade through the city's port, Cuba's busiest harbour.

The northern half of the province is quite mountainous and, in the south, the plains, notably those of Güines and the Huerto de la Habana, are under intensive cultivation. The major towns are those surrounding Havana City, Bauta, Santiago de las Vegas and San Jose de las Lajas. In the south-east of the province the most important urban area is around the major township of Güines, which serves as a strategic rail junction. North of this town is the Carretera Central, or Central Highway which runs parallel to the railway diagonally south-east across the province from Havana.

The dozen or so lakes in this province are mostly situated in the mountainous north and serve as reservoirs as well as for sport fishing. The north coast, each side of Havana City Province, is mostly devoted to tourism and resort areas, as it boasts many fine beaches. Two beauty spots in the province are at **Valle Grande**, southwest of the City Province and, to the east of the city, the **Escaleras de Jaruco**. Monuments include the **Ernest** **Hemingway Museum** at San Fransico de Paula, (**La Vigia**), and the commemoration of General Antonio Maceo and Panchito Gomez Toro, at El Rincon.

Three **cave sites** are of tourist interest in this province, Cueva la Virgen, Cueva García Rabiou and the caverns of de Jaruco. **Valle Picadura** is of considerable natural attraction for its vegetation and micro-climate.

Ciudad de la Habana – City of Havana Province

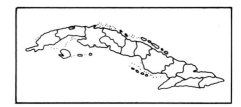

'I could see Havana looking fine in the sun.'

ERNEST HEMINGWAY

By far the most populous province, Havana City, has over two million inhabitants. It is the country's capital and commercial centre. Fifteen municipalities make up the 732 square kilometre area which includes the port around the Bay of Havana, the airport in Boyeros municipality and the beach areas of La Habana del Este and Playa municipality. The most built-up sectors are Habana Vieja, or old Havana, Centro Habana municipality, the Vedado area of Plaza de la Revolucion municipality and Diez de Octobre municipality to the south of the harbour. The Miramar section of Playa municipality is the city's garden suburb and the administrative centre is the Plaza municipality around the central Plaza de la Revolucion.

There are three railheads in the city. One serves the docks, a passenger terminal is located in Nuevo Vedado and, in Casablanca municipality, across the bay from old Havana, another railhead is linked to the main body of the city by ferry. Two road tunnels connect the main marine parade, or Malecon, with the east, under the bay, and with the west, under the Almendares River. The tunnel to the west of the city is divided into two separate streams – in-going and out-going. Bridges also cross the narrow river at certain points. A yacht harbour, the **Hemingway Marina**, is situated in the Santa Fe sector of Playa municipality to the west of the city.

A ring road all but completely embraces the major part of Havana and dormer townships have been constructed on the outskirts of the city to alleviate the problems which might be caused by over-population. Havana is the home city to one of Cuba's four universities; many national museums and art galleries and preserved historic monuments. UNESCO's world heritage programme is now restoring many of Havana's buildings of architectural interest.

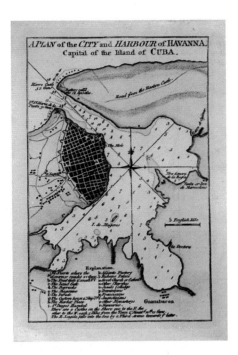

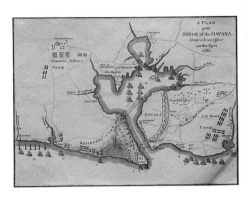

Two rare military maps of Havana from the author's collection, contemporary to the capture of the capital by the English under Admiral Lord Rodney.

Havana – The Old City

It was during the circumnavigation of Cuba, in 1508, by Sabastian de Ocampo, that the natural bay of, what is now Havana, was discovered. The site became known as Puerto de Carenas. By 1514, the Spanish had made several landings near this spot, at Rio Casiguas (now the Almendares River), and it became a regular port of call.

A year later, by the marshy coastline on the Caribbean side of the island, not 55 kilometres from Puerto de Carenas, a small settlement was established. This coastal area was a favourite fishing ground for the native Indians and its swamps were backed by savanna, which made good hunting grounds. The region is still known as Sabana de Guaraguasi. The little township, named San Cristobal de Havana, was near today's Batabano and, in the Indian dialect, was called *Abana*. The founder of the settlement was Panfilo de Narvaez, one of Diego de Velázquez' followers. Diego de Velázquez, during this period, had made and sent several sorties to the Central American mainland in search of gold, from his base at Santiago de Cuba.

Since 1506, the French had been haunting the Caribbean waters, preying on Spanish ships, whose build made them particularly sluggish, compared to the swift barques of corsairs and pirates. The more loot the Spanish were able to plunder in the Americas, the more the French, followed by the English, Dutch and Portuguese, joined in the chase, setting a problem for King Charles V's governor. It was decided to move, in stages, to a location on the western arm of the bay of Puerto de Carenas. This would provide a support, on the north coast of Cuba, and excellent harbour facilities for the treasure fleets, returning from the gold and silver mines of the Americas and in need of an accessible, safe port after crossing the beleagured Yucatan Channel.

On the 16 November, 1519, in the **Plaza de Armas**, the first Mass was said in the new town. Christened 'San Cristobal de la Havana', this was the foundation of Cuba's famous capital. It was in this year, that the entrepreneur, Hernando Cortez, set off from the harbour for Mexico, with a band of conquistadores, on his earliest quest for gold. The new city was also found to be a fine base for the Spanish colonisation of the Bahamas, Florida and Mexico and Honduras on the mainland.

The city, however, attracted a considerable amount of unwanted attention from pirates, privateers and freebooters. In 1538, a French force attacked the poorly defended city, setting fire to its main buildings and looting the little settlement. This prompted the first Governor under the Spanish Crown, Hernando de Soto, discoverer of parts of Florida, to begin fortifying the city as well as rebuilding the devastated quarters. The foundations of the first **Castillo de la Fuerza** were laid, only to be attacked, in 1544, by Francois le Clerc and Jaques de Sores, and reconstructed again, later that year. In 1555, Jaques de Sores again attacked San Cristobal de la Havana, destroying the fortress and burning the city once more. (The first ever drawing of Havana, or La Chorrera City, as artist Teodore de Bray called it, depicted this event 38 years later.)

By this time the city had been laid out in an orderly fashion, and the Plaza de Armas was joined by the **Plaza Vieja**. Diego de

Early nineteenth century engraving of Havana's outskirts

Velázquez, by then Governor of Cuba, had moved to Havana from Santiago de Cuba in 1553, and established the city as the country's capital by the year 1558. In this year, the fortifications of the city were near completion including the rebuilding of the new Castillo de la Fuerza. Havana was declared the official port for all ships in

The remains of Columbus lay in this 1704, doubly consecrated Cathedral until they were returned to Spain in 1899. The great coral-limestone facade dominates its paved square in the old city.

transit to and from Spain and the Americas in 1561, and by 1574, several hundred ships were passing through the harbour annually. This compounded Havana as the 'key between the New World and the Old World'.

The city had become an important commercial centre by 1570, and its first popular election was held in that year. Seven years later, new fortifications were begun, continuing the efforts made in 1568, by the then Governor of the island, Menendez de Aviles. The Castillo de la Real Fuerza was completed in 1577, and five years later the trench-rampart defence system was built. Sir Francis Drake, the notorious English seadog, made an abortive showing off the port of Havana in 1586, and the next year, the inhabitants of the expanding city, began constructing the **El Morro fort**, or Fortaleza de los Tres Reyes del Morro. The status of municipality or official township was granted to Havana by King Felipe II in 1592 and five years later the El Morro fort was completed.

The **Castillo de San Salvador de la Punta** was completed by the year 1600 and the population of the city had crept up to about 4000. Designs for a protective city wall, by the Italian, Cristoforo de Roda, were sent to the King of Spain in 1603. In 1622 and 1623, the English navy attempted attacks on the, by now, heavily fortified Havana. In 1633 the city wall, intended to surround the important sector of Havana, was begun. By this time, a heavy chain barrier, slung between two towers, protected the harbour's narrow entrance. Five years later, the English again were unsuccessful in taking the city and, by 1647, the **La Chorrera** tower, started the previous year, and the San Lazaro tower, were both completed. Two other conical turrets, one with an onion-shaped spire, and a lighthouse, commanded the port. The next year attempts to continue the city's wall were confounded by an epidemic of Yellow Fever and efforts were not renewed until 1654, when fear of attack was rekindled by the English capture of nearby Jamaica.

A comparatively long period of untroubled trade resulted in a slackening off of the attempts to complete the city walls, but, by 1674, the massive task was started again, they were not finished until 1767 – almost a hundred years after they were demolished. By this time the practice of firing a cannon shot, warning of the opening and closing of the gates, was well established.

Havana's Cathedral was constructed in 1704 and, in 1728, the University of Havana was founded.

In 1723, the governor, Dionisio Martinez de la Vega, developed a small area of the Bay of Havana into a shipyard. Some of Havana's oldest existing houses were built around this time and, in 1734, Governor Juan Francisco Guines y Horcasitas established the first post office in Cathedral Square.

In 1740 Britain's Admiral Vernon made an attempt to capture Havana. During 1750 more foundations for' the city's Herculean task of wall building were excavated, and a large ditch divided the houses on the point from the less important dwellings to the west.

The Compania de Comercio de la Habana, took a monopoly on trade throughout the country from 1750 and both the physical outline of Havana, and its economic organisation, began to take on an identifiable character.

On 30th June, 1762, by approaching the fortifications of the capital from the east, and overpowering by sheer persistence and force of firepower the Castillo de los Tres Reyes del Morro, the English finally took Havana. Admiral Lord Rodney, the Earl of Albemarle, and George Pocock, with fourteen thousand soldiers in 44 ships, mined the fortress walls and defeated the 70-gun and garrison force of Captain Don Luis Vicente de Velasco. The spoils, apart from the city itself, consisted of over 100 merchant ships, 100 bronze cannon, the Cathedral bells, the golden statue of Isabel

In contrast to early Havana, the city's skyline
describes an arc along Cuba's Atlantic coast.

de Bobadilla de la Habana, torn from the top of La Fuerza Castle and a vast sum in gold. Added to this was the ransom paid by Bishop Morell de Santa Cruz for not desecrating the holy shrines, and, of course, unlimited tobacco and rum! Meanwhile, in Fort Montego, Jamaica an English gunner died whilst firing a cannon salute, to the taking of Havana. One of the forts' three ancient cannon had exploded!

Eleven months later, the English accepted generous trading rights and the territory of Florida, in return for the City of Havana which was ceded back to Spain. Again, the inhabitants set to, building up the city's defences and beginning construction of the **Castillo de San Carlos de la Cabaña** and the **Atares Castle**. The next year, overseas mail was inaugurated and official permission given for the authorised rum distilleries to go into production legally. By 1767, the **El Principe Castle** was completed as was, six years later, the Castillo de la Cabana, on the opposite side of the harbour's narrow mouth from Old Havana. In 1780, the Palace of **Generals**, in the Plaza de Armas, was constructed.

José del Rio's map, dated 1798, showed that the city had already well overflowed its boundary to the west. The reconstruction of the Principal Theatre was begun in the following year; by 1812 it was completed.

Madrid finally made Havana a free-port in 1818 and the original site of **El Floridita** – La Pina de Plata, was established in the old city walls. Other refreshment houses of the time included, La Columna Egipciana, La Paris and La Bolsa. By this time, the population of Havana stood at around 90 000.

It was really the building of the Templete of Havana, on the east side of the Plaza de Armas, in 1828, that completed the area, known today as 'Old Havana'. This replica of a Doric temple marks the spot of the first Mass, said here in 1519, just over 300 years prior to its building.

EXCURSIONS IN OLD HAVANA

'The bar was on the first floor of a seventeenth-century house and the windows faced the Cathedral where the body of Christopher Columbus had once lain. A grey stone statue of Columbus stood outside the Cathedral and looked as though it had been formed through the centuries under water, like a coral reef, by the action of insects.'

from *Our Man in Havana* by GRAHAM GREENE

La Habana Vieja is bounded by one natural feature – the narrow mouth and portside of the Bay of Havana, and the man-made line created by the location of ancient Havana's city wall. From the **La Punta Fort** (opposite the massive ramparts of **El Morro**) this 1600 squat building is the site of the point where the harbour barrier chain was strung between the two battlements; across the ornate park, with its monument to the hero Maximo Gomez; down the Avenue de las Misiones; along the Avenue de Belgica (Monserrate) and Egido Street; to the Central Railway Station, describes the full extent of the fortifications.

Although La Punta stood outside the city wall, which cordoned off a section of the harbour arm, it is the point where basic trench fortifications were the only protection for the emergent city, against pirates and French fillibusters. The fort was begun after the El Morro Castle and completed around the turn of that century. During the English occupation of 1762, the La Bateria de la Punta was dismantled and, the next year, its reconstruction was ordered by the then Governor Conde de Ricla. The fort was modernised in 1863 and is now occupied by the navy. It contains a small museum.

Continuing into what was once the actual walled city, along the inside of the Avenue Carlos Manuel de Céspedes (Avenue del Puerto), on the street called Tacon, the first point of interest is the **Cathedral Square**. Entering the plaza the heavy, sombre, pitted limestone facade of the Cathedral is to the left, heading the cobbled

Surmounted by the lifesize 'Giraldilla' statue, the Castillo de la Fuerza is the second oldest fort in the New World.

square. Built in 1704 by the Jesuits the two towers, depleted during English occupation of their bronze bells, contain replacements in one tower; one from Spain and the other from Matanzas. With its columned facade, the Cathedral represents one of the finest examples of Baroque architecture in Latin America.

The dually consecrated Cathedral is dedicated to La Virgen Maria de la Inmaculada Concepcion and the patron saint of Havana, San Cristobal de la Habana. Although it was founded early in the 18th century, the building was not completed until 1777. Its impressive embellished, wooden doors lead one into the main body of the church which covers almost 35 metres square. The remains of one of the Columbus family are said to have lain here prior to their removal to Spain. Check opening times in order to view the rich sculptures and paintings setting off the Cathedral's magnificent altar.

The **Bayona Palace** – El Palacio de los Condes de Casa-Bayona, built in 1720, is a fine example of Spanish colonial architecture, and lies directly opposite the Cathedral. The building now houses the Museum of Colonial Art and, unique to Cuba, is the section devoted to stained glass in deliciously rich colours; and ventilation doors, exquisitely designed and containing brilliant glass lights. A wealth of colonial furniture testifies to the opulence of former times. The museum also houses a fine collection of carving and chinaware. Here lived Don Luis Chacon, governor of the island's military forces. Once turned into a College of Literature in the 19th century, the museum is now a national monument.

From here, on the right-hand side of the plaza, is the former house of Marquesses de Arcos. Built in 1741, as the treasure house of the Real Hacienda Diego Penalver Angulo – the title was conferred in 1762. By 1825 the palace had become the country's first post office – set in the wall in 1841, is Cuba's oldest mailbox. In the shape of a tragic Greek mask, with the open mouth

197

Existing fragments of Havana's city walls serve as a reminder that this city was once heavily fortified against all manner of raiders.

the posting slit, this famous carving is used for philatelic and tourist mail as envelopes are specially franked. Part of the house is now a print shop.

Next door is the **Palace of Conde Lombillo**. Built in 1737, by José de Pedrosos y Florencia, and in his family for 175 years, it was also occupied by Gabriel Lombillo, the first Count of Lombillo, brother of José, who formerly shared it with the Pedrosa family. Their earlier 18th century villa is on the Avenue Tacon, opposite the Maestranza sentry box. The magnificent building now houses the experimental print shop specialising in lithography and silk-screen printing.

Immediately across the square is the 19th century **Casa de Banos de la Cathedral**, an art gallery, and next to this, the house of the Marques de Aguas Claras. This is now the delightful courtyard setting for **El Patio Restaurant**, one of the pleasures of this heavy, stone-clad, enclosed square. The land here once belonged, in the 16th century, to Gonzalo Perez de Angulo. In 1760 it was claimed by Sebastian Penalver, who built the initial structure. On his death the relation of the discoverer of Florida, the first Marques of Aguas Claras, Don Antonio José Ponce de Leon, moved in. Much later the house became the Paris Café, and by the time the house had been fully restored in 1963, its present function, as El Patio Restaurant, was designated.

Great columned arches support the covered, wide walkways, called *portales*, surrounding the square, echoing those of the dominant cathedral. Delicate wrought iron adds to the solid stonework and richly-coloured *vitrales* contribute light and art. These flower-design windows are miniatures of the central design on the cobbled square; a flagstone, eight-petalled rose reflecting the emblem above the Cathedral doors.

Take a short detour from Cathedral Plaza, between the main edifice and El Patio, a short walk down Empedrado, to the famous House of Martinez, now known worldwide as **La Bodeguita** (small store) **del Medio** (in the middle of the street). Hemingway's haunting of this tiny bar/restaurant, accelerated the popularity of this charming retreat, now a slice of international art and literature, as each visitor inscribes their comments, names and dates. Cuban food specialities are served plus the inevitable *mojitos* of the Nobel prize-winner's delight. Once the carriage house of the Countess de la Reunion's mansion, next door, this unassuming restaurant has been a magnet for artists, writers, poets, musicians, politicians and film stars. Sit out in the fresh air, or stay inside and take a mojito at its tiny bar and discover the wealth of stories which abound here, whilst reading names scrawled on the walls by the reflected light from multi-coloured bottles and intricate stained glass *vitrales*. Faded photographs and mementoes evoke revelry of past decades. The Havana Bodeguita del Medio now has an imitator – the best form of flattery, the Bodeguita del Medio, Milan, Italy.

Cut round behind the Cathedral, past the 18th century Seminario de San Carlos y San Ambrosio, pass the monument to José de la Luz y Caballro, on the boulevard, and in front, is the 18th century **Palace of Segundo Cabo**, constructed as the Postmaster-General's quarters between 1772 and 1776, and now used by the Ministry of Culture.

The massive structure to the left of the palace, is the **Castillo de la Real Fuerza**. This is Havana's oldest fortress, the original, built on the site by Hernando de Soto to protect the port, was constructed in 1538. This is the New World's second

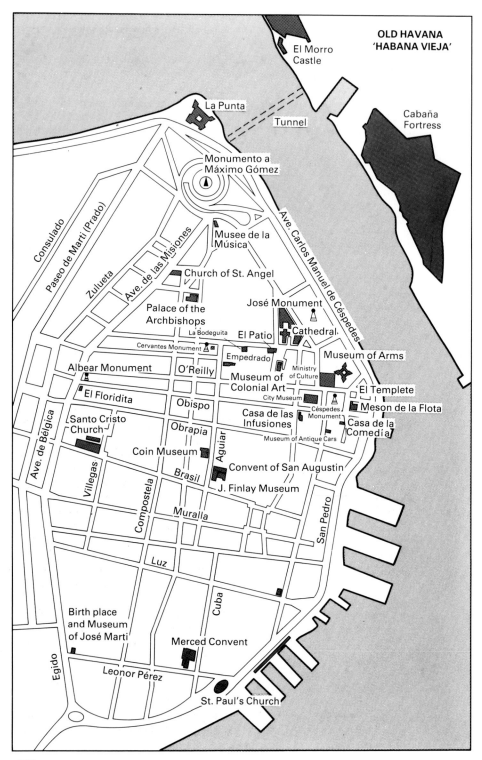

OLD HAVANA
'HABANA VIEJA'

El Morro
Castle

Cabaña
Fortress

La Punta

Tunnel

Monumento a
Máximo Gómez

Ave. Carlos Manuel de Céspedes

Musee de la
Música

Church of St. Angel

José Monument

Consulado

Paseo de Marti (Prado)

Zulueta

Ave. de las Misiones

Palace of the
Archbishops

La Bodeguita

Cervantes Monument

El Patio

Cathedral

Empedrado

Museum of Arms

Albear Monument

O'Reilly

Museum of
Colonial Art

Ministry
of Culture

El Templete

El Floridita

Obispo

City Museum

Céspedes
Monument

Meson de la Flota

Ave. de Bélgica

Santo Cristo
Church

Obrapia

Casa de las
Infusiones

Casa de la
Comedia

Coin Museum

Aguiar

Museum of Antique Cars

Villegas

Brasil

Convent of San Augustin

Compostela

J. Finlay Museum

Muralla

San Pedro

Luz

Cuba

Birth place
and Museum
of José Marti

Merced Convent

Egido

Leonor Pérez

St. Paul's Church

200

Havana's Coat of Arms pictorially underlines the military significance of this 'key to the New World'.

most ancient castle and now serves as the Museum of Arms, with many fine exhibits. It also houses the nerve centre of UNESCO's building preservation force, currently restoring the glorious heritage of Old Havana. On the turret of what is now the new fort, (the old one was destroyed by fire in 1555 by the French pirate Jaques de Sores) is the symbol of the city.'**La Isabel de Bobadilla de la Habana**', is a once golden, bronze statuette replica of the one stolen by English naval officers in 1762. Often referred to as 'La Giraldilla', this representation of Hernando de Soto's wife faces the port across the massive stone walls of the 900 square metre extension to the fort. Its image has been adopted as the logo for Havana Club Rum. On entering the fort notice the many fine cannon in the courtyard, the deep moat and drawbridge, and the 1579 coat of arms above the entrance, carved in Seville.

Directly opposite the Castillo de la Fuerza entrance, is the **Plaza de Armas** or Plaza Carlos Manuel Céspedes, whose statue dominates the square. Surrounded by wrought iron railings, the shrine of El Templete, stands in the shade of an ancient *Silk-cotton* tree, in the corner of the plaza.

This lovely Doric-style temple commemorates the first Mass said in Havana – a plaque nearby locates the exact spot of the historic communion. Inside, a Jean-Baptiste Vermay painting depicts the event and 1754, the governor, Francisco Cagigal y de la Vega, erected a commemorative column celebrating the assembly of the Cabildo. On a plinth in front of the temple is the effigy of Christopher Columbus, crowned by a statue to the Virgin of the Pilar. The building was inaugurated by the then bishop, Don Juan José Diaz de Espada y Landa, and the governor in March 1828. The first Town Council was created here in 1519.

Just across Narciso Lopez Street is the **Mesón de la Flota**, or Palacio del Conde de Santovenia. Now, this impressive ancient building, which was once the abode of the military judge and lawyer Doctor Franciso Martinez de Campo, is a tavern and colonial-style restaurant. Bedecked in flags, including the old Union flag, ancient artefacts, bales, casks, chests and barrels, this early meeting house for traders dating back to the 18th century, recently echoed to the sounds of restoration as the UNESCO scheme lovingly repaired the grand palace. Its name comes from the title of Doctor de Campo's brother, Nicolas, conferred with the Countdom of Santovenia in 1834. During the 19th century the building had doubled as the Hotel Santa Isabel and the restaurant of the commercial market of Havana.

Across the neatly maintained park, laid out in the second decade of the 16th century, with Royal Palms, wrought iron railings and deciduous foliage, is the **Palace of the Captain Generals**. One of the most important and beautiful of all colonial structures in Cuba, this building was started in 1772 and completed in 1776. Its use as a housing for the city council was suggested by Governor Marques de la Torre in 1773. From 1791 until 1898, the large, grandiose structure was the headquarters of the Captains of the Generales of the Spanish Guard. Since

In the centre courtyard of Havana's most
beautiful baroque building, surrounded by
exotic foliage, stands the marble statue of
Christopher Columbus.

then its chequered career has included three substantial reconstructions and a period as the Presidential Palace from 1902 – 1920. It is now the **Museum of the City of Havana**. Its facade consists of Corinthian columns, supporting a first floor terrace over a colonnade. The structure is built in a square format, around a huge courtyard, profuse with exotic palms, *Trumpetwood* and *Yagruma* trees. Terraced inside the central courtyard, with cannon and statue of Christopher Columbus, one of the palace rooms houses, and still remains as it was designated, the King of Spain's chamber – never to be used. The other rooms in the building are part of the Museum of the City of Havana. Nineteenth century luxury decorates and furnishes the ground floor and four rooms contain the carts and carriages of yesteryear. Religious artefacts adorn the Parish Room and the mezzanine floor displays domestic items

from Hispanic Cuba and Sepulchral mementoes.

Louis XV furniture, baroque treasures and rich ornaments are kept on the top floor, together with a wealth of every imaginable everyday utensil and decorations of the aristocracy from the 15th to the 19th century. The great Cuban patriots, thinkers, doers, fighters and heroes are remembered in one gallery and the Hall of the Republic presents the more recent past glories and misdemeanours. Stepping out onto the grand patio entrance, great bronze bells add a sonorous note to the museum which encompasses the entire past of the Cuban peoples and their heritage. Outside, in contrast, school children at play, sport the red kerchief, instigated by Ché Guevara – a symbol of modern youth.

To the left of the Palacio de los Capitanes Generales, is an old 17th century shrine to the 'Mountain of Mercy'. In this small corner of the plaza on Obispo and Oficios Streets are some of Old Havana's restored gems – the Letras Cubanas Publishers, once the Intendencia Palace, the Cafe Habanero and the house of the old stone water jars (*Tinaja*) are located on this corner. Next to the National Bank of Cuba building there is another 17th century colonial residence and Havana's first pawn shop. The fascinating **House of Arabic Culture** nearby includes a traditional Arabic restaurant and a wealth of artefacts, some dating to the times of the Egyptian pharaohs.

Almost opposite is the huge, stable-like building which is now the **Museum of Antique Cars**. This is a sight not to be missed by children and adults alike; it is a most impressive collection of excellently preserved motors. Don't miss, on Obrapia, near Mercaderes, the fascinating African Rooms. Just around the corner, into Justiz Street is the **House of Comedy** – just behind the tiny zoo for fighting cocks, which faces the plaza.

Back to the corner of Obispo Street a short walk takes one past the old residence of Dona Teresa, (La Casa de la Natilla) the Cream Custard Shop, the barbers, an old colonial villa, the 'Cafe' con Leche Bar, La Mina Bar Restaurant, La Casa del Agua where natural drinks are served from an antique cooler, the old silversmiths and the 18th century house of the Marquesses de Casa Torre. On the corner of Obispo/ Mercaderes Streets two columns hold the founding bell of the City University. There is also the herbalist, **El Herbolario**, and pharmacy re-created as in the early 19th century and adjoining, the **Casa de las Infusiones**. These intriguing old shops with coloured jars, flowers, plants and concoctions of every conceivable kind, are full of the aromas and tastes of early medicines, balms, beauty creams and even aphrodisiacs! **La Botica –** the pharmacy, is on the site where the old La Botica Francesa de Santa Catalina once traded. Microscopes, ancient scales, jars and mortars decorate the still operational shop and its neighbour, the **House of Brews**.

Obispo Street itself is one of remarkable colonial atmosphere, ancient gas lamps and old, wrought iron shop signs jut out over cobbled stones, smoothed by the passage of time and almost five centuries of shoe leather and cart, or carriage wheels. (The cobbles are called '*Adoquines*', imported as ballast in ancient galleons.) Look, especially for the typically ornate corner spurs cladding the vulnerable edges of some houses and shops. (The iron corner spurs not only protected rich tiling and decoration from the scraping of carriage wheels, but served as a decoration and have become the trademark of Havana's famous embellishments.) During the 19th century more than 5000 carriages plied Havana's streets, today the striking feature of the traffic in Havana is the number of vintage cars which mingle with modern Ladas or Fiats. Beautiful metal door handles, latches, door knockers and intricate railings also add to the ambience, as do the gaily striped awnings, the carefully reproduced shop signs and café tariffs. Gaslight from ornate bracket lamps

lends a magical, 18th century atmosphere to the historic squares in the late hours. As on many buildings in the Old Quarter, the main features adorning the exteriors are the balconies, wrought iron rails, elaborate curving brackets and ornamented sills. The vitrales are another decorative feature which flood the rooms with light and colour. These are placed above doors and above shuttered windows and are intricately designed with rich blues, reds and greens. Some are half circular and, occasionally, as in the Café Habanero, the full circle, *mediopuntos*, can be seen. *Lucetas* are a similar feature but are square or rectangular in shape and the *mampara* version can be used as room partitioning. The movable wooden slats above, like Venetian blinds, are called *persianas*. In the very old houses, around the window openings, are the *rejas* or wooden screens made of turned wooden rods – *barrotes*, later often replaced by wrought iron in flowery patterns, both serving as decoration and protection. The little rejas, or half-size window guards, are known as *antepecho*. Look for the most common of all architectural additions to the older houses. Often the main doors of houses leading on to the street, large enough to let a carriage through, some built for pedestrian entrance, were overtly grand, and naturally heavy to open and close. Therefore, about head height, cut into the main doors, was a tiny peephole door, large enough generally to lean out of, and small enough to observe the daily traffic without using the cumbersome gate-like doors. These apertures are called *postigos*.

So many of the famous streets contain a wealth of unusual buildings and architectural curiosities that one should at least take the following walk: the length of Obispo, past the Ambos Mundos Hotel (from 1932–1940, room 511 was the retreat for writer Ernest Hemingway), from there to the **Modern Poetry Library**; a stroll along O'Reilly Street, turning at the junction with Aguiar; to enter the grand square **Vieja** past the **Restaurant Lafayette**, with its statue of Miguel de Cervantes y Saavedra. On the corner is the neo-classical baroque and art nouveau-style, Palacio Cueto Hotel. This plaza, Vieja, is flanked by streets containing an exceptionally beautiful collection of colonial masterpieces of architecture.

Continuing down Obrapia Street, the huge structure in front will be the **Convent of Santa Clara**, famous for its carved wood interior and now used as the headquarters for the conservation and restoration of antiquities. Just after San Felipe, anyone who has read *Our Man in Havana*, by Graham Greene, will have recognised the sign, Lamparilla Street. This was the fictitious location of the hero, Wormold's, carpet cleaner store.

Between here and the next, Amargura Street is the Numismatic or **Coin Museum** on the right, and a little way down is the Church of San Augustin (San Francisco el Nuevo) and its convent with the Charles J Finlay **Museum of Medicine and Natural Science** behind. Continue round the square of the 1635 Santa Clara Convent and exit from Luz Street into Cuba Street, the location of O'Farrill House. Two churches passed on the right will be the 18th century **Espiritu Santo**, known for its stained glass, and the **Merced Church** and convent, the frescoes of which are a national treasure. Turn left at Leonor Perez (Paula) Street and this will bring you to the beautiful St Paul's Church on an island in the centre of the main boulevard. Look for the obelisk to Captain General Leopoldo O'Donnell, governor until 1847.

From this point the best move is to make a taxi or car journey around the entire Old Havana area – Havanatur can provide special trips or self-drive cars. Continue around the boulevard into Egido Street. It is here, on the right hand side, that the road passes the birthplace **Museum of José Marti**, a most interesting little memorial to the great leader. Also on the right, after entering Monserrate Street, take a short detour down Brasil (Teniente Rey) to the **Plaza del Cristo**. This most attractive square is adjacent to the **Church of Santo Cristo del Buen Viaje**. This 1693 edifice, with two impressive towers, tiled roof and striking cross-beam ceiling, is one of the city's most restful church areas. Returning back to Monserrate, and the line of the ancient city wall, continue north towards the sea and, a short distance on the right, is the internationally famous, **El Floridita Restaurant**. The Floridita has been called 'Birthplace of the Daiquiri', which was Ernest Hemingway's favourite frappé tipple. This superb location on the corner of Obispo, and in its own small parking square, once the Monserrate Gates in the old city walls, was also the original site of the 'Silver Pineapple' or 'La Pina del Plata'. Now it is the excellent El Floridita, one of the world's most celebrated seafood restaurants and bars.

Just nearby, in this favoured region of the Old Quarter, is the monument and statue to Francisco del Albear. Keep following Monserrate until it becomes the Avenue de las Misiones and, on the right side, turning a short way down Chacón Street, to the corner of Habana Street, is the early **Palace of the Archbishop**. Also in this small area of the old city is the 1672 **Church of St Angel Custodio**. Its spectacular Gothic spires compete with the nearby monument to Cirilo Villaverde. Back to the main avenue, and the road leads out, past the **Music Museum** on the right and the **Maximo Gomez Gardens** fronting on to the Bay of Havana, on the left. Follow the gardens round and out to the Port Road or Avenue Carlos Manuel

de Céspedes, and carry on along the harbour wall. In doing this the sightseer will be encircling the whole of Habana Vieja – Old Havana. Passing the **Castillo de la Real Fuerza** and its 1558 preserved sentry box on the right, there are eight monuments opposite the three, big dockside warehouses on the bay. The first building is the old site of the commercial section and, on Amagura Street, just behind the commerce building, are the houses of the Marques of San Felipe and Santiago and another 18th century villa, Aguilera. In front of the towered Church and Convent of San Fransisco, is the Plaza San Fransisco and the statue Fuente de los Leones. To the rear of the church is the Old Square or Plaza Vieja. The large building behind the convent and facing the dock offices, is the Arco de Muralla and next door the 19th century villa of Los Condes de la Mortera. Not far from here is the 18th century house of the Condes de Barreto.

Only five other important 18th century buildings are recommended for visiting. Behind the Plaza Vieja is the house of the Counts of San Juan de Jaruco; further back from the port area is the Church and Convent of Las Teresas and also on Compostela Street, is the Church of Belen and its convent next to the Arco Belen. The last famous residence is that of Martin Calvo de la Puerta.

Probably the oldest mailbox in the New World, this mask accepts letters which will receive a special franking mark.

Havana's modern skyline, in the process of renovation, contrasts, in its sparkling white marble, with the heavy coral limestone of the old city.

All these magnificent edifices were once encompassed by the harbour wall and port road on the east, and the massive city walls to the west. A wall of just over 2000 metres long, which took 164 years to construct and then only lasted for 66! In this area of around 15 000 square metres there are more than fifty monuments and historic buildings which are of national and international importance. These places are, and have been, receiving careful restoration and are under a preservation programme which is renovating La Habana Vieja to its former glory.

Two other buildings should be included in the description of the ancient Havana. Firstly, the enormous **Fortaleza de la Cabaña**, built across the harbour mouth from the old city between 1763 and 1774. Although it is not open for public visiting and is now a military barracks, the fort played an important role in the protection of the capital and, every day, makes a token contribution to its continued security. In the morning at 4.30 a.m. and in the evening at 8.30 p.m., the city's gates were announced opened and closed, by the firing of a cannon from the Cabana Fort. Today, the custom is still observed, there are no gates however, and the cannon is sounded at 9.00 p.m. each evening instead of twice a day, reminding the city of the ancient practice.

The second structure, also across the harbour from the city, is the **Castillo de los Tres Reyes del Morro**. Its massive ramparts and huge bulwarks were constructed on a point, overlooking the city and port, between 1589 and 1630. This structure was designed by the Italian architect, Bautista Antonelli, after a similar fortress in Lisbon. He also designed the Fortaleza de San Carlos de la Cabana nearby, several years later. Its twelve cannon initially held back countless raids by pirates, corsairs and privateers until its capture by the English in 1762. Admiral Rodney's fleet of forty-four ships with 3000 cannon and 14 000 soldiers completely overwhelmed the Morro under D. Luis de Velasco, who is remembered on a plaque high on the ramparts. Also inscribed there is the name of the Captain General of the Island, Antonio Caballero

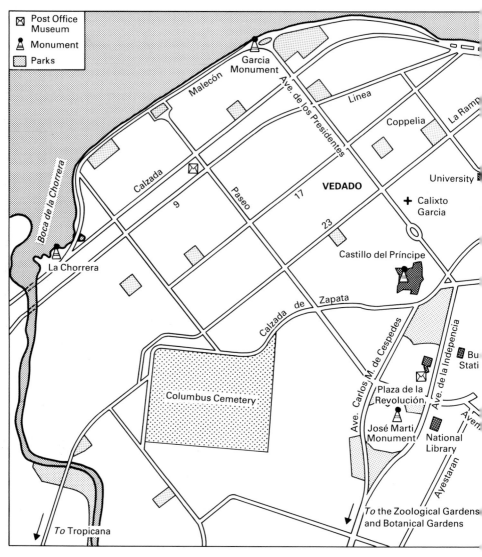

Legend:
- ⊠ Post Office
- Museum
- 🜨 Monument
- ▨ Parks

Garcia Monument

Malecón

Ave. de los Presidentes

Linea

Coppelia

La Ramp

Calzada

9

Paseo

17

23

VEDADO

University

✚ Calixto Garcia

Boca de la Chorrera

La Chorrera

Castillo del Príncipe

Calzada de Zapata

Ave. Carlos M. de Cespedes

Ave. de la Indepencia

Bu Stati

Columbus Cemetery

Plaza de la Revolución

José Marti Monument

National Library

Aven

Ayestaran

To Tropicana

To the Zoological Gardens and Botanical Gardens

de Rodas, 1879. Many cannon, both bronze and iron lie around the fort's entrance, which is made over a drawbridge crossing a deep moat. Down below, on the left, a fine selection of artillery can be seen, pointing out across the harbour mouth. A row of gun slits in the massive walls are visible before entering the giant pair of doors into the heart of the castle. In the archway entrance, look for the ancient candelabra which appears to be older than the building itself! The main fort is built on stepped ramparts and its expansive galleries now serve as a restaurant, a juice bar – try the fresh *toronja*, or grapefruit, and a nightclub. A well-stocked souvenir shop is housed in two large, beamed halls. Restoration work has converted the crumbling walls of dungeons and a sentry post into clean stonework chambers, all to be part of the planned programme of attractions for the Morro's visitors. Walk the battlements and gaze down at the daunting, sombre walls and steep cliff face

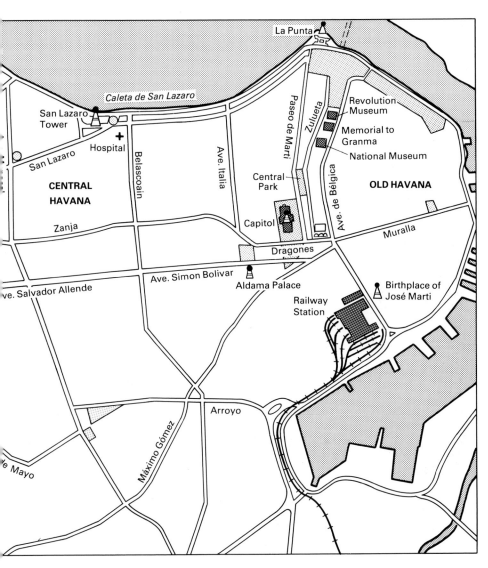

of the headland.

The lighthouse, part of which is occasionally open to sightseers, was constructed during the so-called 'Conspiracy of the Steps' at Matanzas in 1844. The finger of the lighthouse stands sentinel over the great curve of Havana Bay above the coralline cliffs and stout ramparts of the castle, in one, the symbol of the city as much as the gilded statue of La Giraldilla, or 'La Habana'. A formidable fortification for four hundred years, El Morro Castle and its beacon outline appear on coinage, stamps, postcards and trademarks.

EXCURSIONS IN MODERN HAVANA

Although outside the ancient city walls, modern Havana has its share of old monuments and aged structures. In travelling the length of Agramonte, or Zulueta Street, most of these historic buildings and modern edifices can be

The National Museum of Havana

viewed with ease. This avenue runs parallel to the city walls' original location and it is best to take the route from the base of the monument to **Maximo Gómez**, on the point facing the Morro.

In the monument's park, interlaced with highways, are two other important sites. In the uprisings during the early revolution, during 1871, eight young students at the Medical Faculty were shot. Standing in front of the Castilla de la Punta, on the gardens, is an eight-columned monument to these martyrs, erected in 1921. Nearby, is a tiny prison with an appalling history. Captain General Don Miguel Tacon erected this stone structure between 1834 and 1839. Only the basic strongrooms remain, but this was the site of many a torture and garrotting during the Wars of Independence.

Take the Agramonte boulevard south from the sea and, after some pretty park areas, on the left, is the 17th century,

One of the largest theatres in the world, the 2000-seat García Lorca Theatre has hosted famous names from Caruso to Bernhardt.

Bastion of the Angel, the remains of part of the city defences and bulwark of part of the old city gate. Almost opposite is the large building which was the original site of the 'La Corona' Cigar Factory, built early in the last century. A little way down, on the left, are two buildings which complement each other. They are the two most popular museums of recent history. **The Museum of the Revolution** and the **Memorial to the Yacht *Granma***. The older structure, once the Presidential Palace, now houses a magnificent collection of artefacts from Cuba's history, right back to the island's discovery. Called the Museum of the Revolution, this impressive edifice contains documented histories of Independence and Revolution. Its cupola tower is echoed in the foreground by the remnants of the angel gateway, symbolising the historic wars. A nearby military tank, on a plinth, symbolises the recent triumph of the Revolution. The modern building beyond is the last resting place and exhibition hall for the famous yacht *Granma*, in which the revolutionaries, under Commander Fidel Castro, arrived

on Cuba's southern shores to complete the Revolution between 1956 and 1959. The small motor launch is displayed in a glass-surrounded structure with details, maps and relics from the landing.

The **National Museum of Art** is in the following square and houses a unique collection of fine arts and treasures from ancient history. A Cuban gallery with 14 rooms, on the third floor, complements a vast selection of paintings from artists, whose works are priceless, such as Goya, Murillo, Velazquez, Rubens, Reynolds, Gainsborough, Scott and Turner. The ancient Egyptian, Greek and Roman antiquity collections are said to be incomparable in the Americas.

Continuing down past the Hotel Sevilla square on the right, and Hotel Plaza to the left, the boulevard opens out into the **Central Park**. The monument to José Marti is surrounded by majestic Royal Palms, and, on each side, are a host of grand, 19th century buildings. Hotel Ingleterra, a great pastel-shaded, colonial edifice, and its **Louvre Steps**, frame the Marti statue, making an excellent photograph. To the left of the hotel is the spectacular **National Theatre** – dripping in carvings and embellishments, statues and columns. This four-turretted, 1915, 'Garcia Lorca' Theatre, and in 1837, the Tacon Theatre, is now home to the

Along the Malecon esplanade in downtown Vedado, facing what was the United States Embassy, a typically poignant billboard pronounces 'Sĕnor Imperialists – we are not entirely afraid of you!' In the background is the Nacional Hotel.

National Ballet and National Opera. Facing this, across the plaza, is the Supreme Tribunal building next door to the Commercial Centre. On the far side of the square is the Payret Theatre, an ornate cinema, overlooking, to the right side, the grounds of the **National Capitol**. Two blocks along, the Theatre José Marti, built in 1884, overlooks the Capitol's gardens at the south end, although it faces onto Agramonte Street itself.

On Monserrate Street, facing the old city, are several more buildings of interest. The **Prison of the City Walls**, looks down Brasil Street and the **Palace of the Marquesa of Villalba** faces Murella Street. On the next block is the original home of Havana's electricity company and, two blocks on, is the **Balboa Palace**. The park, a little further on, contains the housing for the new Port Guard, and,

coming round, between the park and the railway-station, one returns to Agramonte, or Zulueta Street, leading back, eventually, to the National Capitol.

The **National Capitol** building, on Fraternity Park and inaugurated in 1929, was built of white marble in the style of the North American Congress building. The dome is almost identical to that on their Capitol Hill. Beneath its massive rotunda is a 24-carat diamond embedded in the marble floor – rounding off the cost of this gracious building – an estimated $17 million! The immense *Ceiba* tree in the grounds, was planted in soil brought by delegates to the Pan American conference, held in the city the year before the Capitol was opened.

The Capitol is gauged as being the exact centre of Havana for measurements of distances. It now also houses the **Academy**

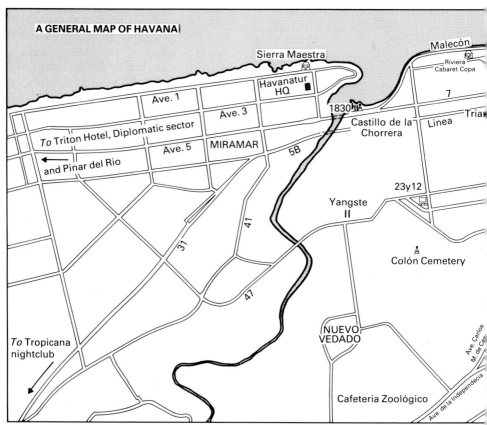

A GENERAL MAP OF HAVANA

Sierra Maestra

Malecón

Riviera
Cabaret Copa

Havanatur HQ

Ave. 1

Ave. 3

7

1830

Castillo de la Chorrera

Linea

Tria

To Triton Hotel, Diplomatic sector

Ave. 5

MIRAMAR

5B

23y12

and Pinar del Rio

Yangste

Colón Cemetery

41

31

47

To Tropicana nightclub

NUEVO VEDADO

Ave. Carlos M. de Cé

Cafeteria Zoológico

Ave. de la Independencia

of **Science** and the **Felipe Poey Science Museum**. Exhibits here include wildlife scenarios and a planetarium. In its grounds, at the bottom of Avenue Maximo Goméz, is the picturesque, 1837, **Fountain of India**.

Further up the street, through park on either side, is the ancient **Palace of Aldama**, now the Institute for the History of the Communist Movement and Revolutionary Socialism.

These buildings and monuments, ruins and antiquities, comprise the more important of all Cuba's historic heritage. They may be Havana's pride, but, on the other side of the city from old and central Havana, is the district of the **Plaza of the Revolution**, also a wealth of buildings, squares, plazas and boulevards, which reflect the city's development and strength since the days of the Revolution.

Today's Havana can be said to lie to the west of the large Boulevard Belascoain. One feature, however, of the Havana past, present and future, is the great sea wall which embraces and protects the city from the ravages of the open Atlantic Ocean. The **Malecon**, over three kilometres in length, stretching from the Castillo de la Punta, to the Chorrera Tower in Vedado, was begun in 1901 and completed by 1926. Its stalwart ramparts are a feature of the city and the wide Malecon causeway continues alongside its attractive walkway so popular with fishermen and sightseers during the day, and romantics and lovers after twilight. One hundred classical buildings, built from the mid-eighteenth century until the present day, stand facing the Atlantic spume across the Malecon drive. This is one of the wonders of the West Indies, its buttressed flank defying

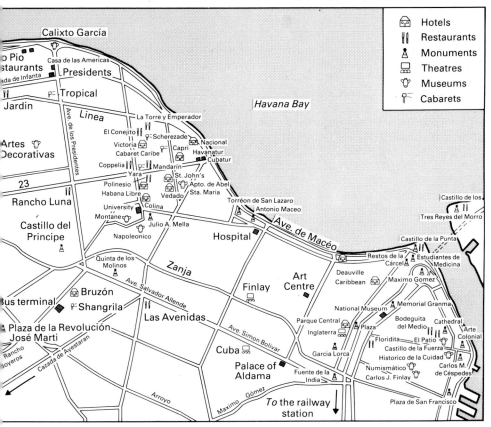

213

even the worst of hurricanes to safeguard its jewel of a city, Havana.

After the Old City area and the fringes of more modern Havana, most streets run parallel to, or at right angles from, the Malecon. Passing central Havana, the Deauville Hotel, the San Lazaro strip with its ancient tower, **Maceo Park** and statue fronting the twenty-five-storey-high Hermanos Ameijeiras Hospital, the Malecon curves round the **Caleta de San Lazaro** towards the Nacional Hotel on a bluff overlooking the ocean. This is the Vedado section of the city. From the Nacional Hotel, with its twin turrets and checkered background, to the 1830 Restaurant on the banks of the Almendares River, this internationally renowned 'city within a city', holds charms and sights unequalled in these latitudes.

From the Malecon, 'La Rampa', (a local name for a very special section of roadway) strikes up from the coast becoming 23rd Street and all but bisecting this part of the city. Restaurants, cinemas, statues, exhibitions, Hotel Havana Libre, Copelia's ice cream park, and a wealth of colonial architecture lie either side. About halfway up, to the left, off D, or E Street, is the 1774 **Castillo del Príncipe**, close to the hospital quarter. Continue past the castle and the road opens out into the magnificent boulevards defining the **Plaza de la Revolution**, and the spectacular monument to José Marti, almost a trompe d'oiel in its towering wizardry. Facing this is the Communist Party Headquarters, the **National Theatre** and the **National Philatelic Museum** where badges, seals and artefacts as well as old letters and stamps are exhibited. **José Marti National Library** is just off Independence Avenue, as is the 'bus terminal for the city.

The park at the north end of Independence Avenue is known as the **Village of Youth** and from this point it is easy to find the imposing points of interest such as the City University, the Montane Museum of Anthropology and the Memorial to Julio Antonio Mella.

Returning to the Malecon via 23rd Street and La Rampa, the causeway carries on round, past the monument to those lost when the US battleship *Maine* blew up in Havana Harbour. Past the ex-US Embassy building and the monument to General Calixto Garcia, near to the Casa de Las Americas, the road sweeps down to the classical lines of the Riviera Hotel. From here, the Malecon curves around the bay and passes a sports ground on the left and the 1647 **Chorrera Tower** and restaurant. Just after the tower, and before the tunnel under the Almendares River, on the right, is the dignified 1830 Restaurant, an early diplomatic residence with a fine aspect of the Boca de la Chorrera.

Two streets should be given extra time in the journey around Vedado, both lead off the Malecon. The **Paseo**, a wide broadway of an avenue, dutifully bristling with trimmed shrubs and dazzling arrays of flowers, is an exquisite example of early boulevard architecture in fine granite, started in 1771. The avenue runs up to the Plaza of the Revolution. Another fine boulevard is the **Avenue de la Presidentes**, from Malecon to the northern tip of the Village of Youth Park. If, however, broad avenues, topiary and horticultural skills are to be found, it is surely in the garden suburbs on the other side of the Almendares River – the Miramar district of Las Playas sector of Havana to the extreme west of the city. Fifth Avenue, with its impressive clock tower, is favourite.

Back in the capital itself, there are three important sights which should not be missed. Apart from the old city zoo, there is now an extensive **zoological park** on the fringes of the city. Its large size enables most of its inmates – elephant, antelope, giraffe, ostrich, rhinoceros and buffalo to wander freely as the 'little zebras' – black and white striped coaches, tour the well-stocked grounds. The three-hectare 'lion gully' is now a famous attraction and the whole setting is made even more spectacular

by the variety of countryside, the wild foreign birds and the tropical climate. Just a short distance away from the zoo is the **Celia Sanchez Manduley Botanical Garden**. Created in the early 1970s, the 600 hectare site is the largest of its kind in the world and sports more than 4000 species. About 15 000 individual plants can be seen and photographed and social areas are designated for the exhibition of orchids, ferns, cacti and typical forest and jungle zones. Nurseries, a library, herb house and experimental areas are features of this carefully nurtured parkland. The last, not to be missed, feature of the western sector of Havana city, lies in the outer part of Vedado, at the furthest end of Zapata Street, where it meets the elbow of 23rd Street. It is the widely acclaimed **Christopher Columbus Cemetery**. This vast, thousand-square-metre grave-yard is an art gallery in itself, with a thousand sculptured 'flights of fancy'

The José Martí monument, created by Cuban sculptor Sicre. This 116 metre obelisk in the Plaza de la Revolucion is a trompe l'oeil.

On La Rampa, Havana's popular promenade which sweeps down to the sea wall, an exhibit celebrates the national women's movement outside a public conference centre.

Colon Cemetery

carved in marble, and architect's dreams created from granite. Replicas of artistic wonders such as Michelangelo's 'La Pieta' and the ubiquitous angels and crucifixions, surround the octagonal, Byzantine-style chapel. A colossal collection of marble tombs is interspersed with mausoleums in the fantastic shapes of Egyptian pyramids, spires and tents. Havana's miraculous saint lies here, the un-recognised 'Saint' Amelia, guarded day and night by an endless stream of silent pilgrims keeping a constant vigil over the flower-bedecked grave. Eighty feet high, the triple gateway is crowned by beautifully carved figures of Faith, Hope and Charity. Since the cemetery's inauguration, when a black slave, Manuela Balido was buried in 1868, over 800 000 memorials have been erected here. Look, particularly for that to the eight medical students, martyred in 1871, the firemen's monument, 1890, and, poignantly, the architect's tomb, inscribed with the date 1872 – he was just 33 years of age.

From the magnificent grandios that man affords himself after death, to the wonders that man can create for himself during his life. From edifices in stone and mortar, to the recreations of sport, art and culture represented in five memorable sites around the outskirts of the city. About twenty kilometres from the centre of Havana is the, around two-and-a-half hectare, **Park Lenin**. Situated on the shores of the giant 'Rebel Army' Reservoir, and with its own 'Path of the Followers' Lake, the vast recreation area is located off 100 Street. It has its own, nine-kilometre long railway with replicas of old locomotives – originals are exhibited at the park's station. Horse riding tours can be taken, as can boating trips. Here, there is an attraction or two for everyone. A huge children's park with a bewildering number of amusements and diversions is not far from the Café 1740, and a nearby snack bar. Near the park entrance is an open air cinema and the theatre/amphitheatre has its own floating stage and Grecian-style seating. The Galapago de Oro café is located near the riding school, and two small restaurants are situated within view of the lake. There are also five swimming pools, one Olympic-size and one expressly for diving. A major attraction is the Las Ruinas Restaurant, reportedly the finest restaurant in Havana and certainly one of the most attractive. With its colonial decor tastefully blended with modern design and reconstructed sections of the ancient sugar mill site, the atmosphere is one of serene elegance in a setting of outstanding beauty. Don't forget the food, dining here is one of the most pleasurable experiences to be found in the province. Further attractions in the park include an art gallery, a small library, a fascinating aquarium, a working ceramic studio, a motocross racecourse and a selection of footpaths and walkways through lush tropical gardens and under the shade of many ancient trees. One particularly exciting addition, is the **Rodeo Stadium**, not far from Las Ruinas, and near the larger lake. This stadium

Author Hemingway's retreat, Finca Vigia, at San Francisco de Paula. Bought for $12,500, this is where 'For Whom the Bell Tolls' and the Nobel Prize winning 'The Old Man and the Sea' were completed.

hosts shows from Mexico and Cuba, including bull-fighting, dancing, horsemanship demonstrations, roping and wrestling steers and the 'Passage of Death' show. This particular venue also hosts boxing, baseball and volleyball tournaments. Another renovated rodeo stadium lies not far from the park, at Rancho Boyeros.

In a similar sporting vein, on the coast, just fifteen kilometres west of the city, is the internationally famous **Hemingway Marina**. Just off 5th Avenue, this giant boating complex is an oasis for deepsea fishermen, divers, yachtsmen and leisure sailors. All forms of watersports are available in this modern setting, developed in memory of one of Havana's most devout disciples, Ernest Hemingway. Inside, the five-kilometre square marina has four, kilometre-long channels for pleasure craft of all sizes. A number of annual fishing tournaments are held from the docks here. There is land-based accommodation in the form of 34 modern villas with all amenities. The Hemingway Marina is almost like a little village, with an aparthotel, cafeteria, duty-free shopping area, tennis courts, swimming pool, canoeing, scuba-diving,

dinghy sailing and organised tours from the marina. Fiesta, Papa's and Gregorio's restaurants offer a succulent choice of dishes from the most appetising lobster to the juiciest steak, from a cutlet of crocodile tail to a slice of shark's fin. Protocol rooms offer the luxury of international first-class standards to visiting dignitary.

Still with Hemingway, but on the academic side of the Nobel Prize-winner's varied interests, a visit to the **Ernest Hemingway Museum**, is an essential inclusion in tours on the outskirts of Havana. It is at the little settlement of San Francisco de Paula, about twelve kilometres from the city that the great writer made his home. **La Vigia** is the residence where many significant literary works were created. Today, the beautiful, white-painted, colonial-style villa, is preserved just as the hunter, fisherman, traveller, adventurer and literary giant, left it. Trophies hang on the walls, reminiscent of African safaris and Spanish bull-fights. Writing equipment and the famous type-writer are exactly where they were always kept and reference books, magazines and

The Nobel prizewinner's portrait hangs on the drawing room wall of La Vigía, now a museum.

posters line the bookcases and adorn the walls. The tower, overlooking the countryside is full of curios and the writer's yacht, *Pilar*, is preserved, as its own small museum, near the family swimming pool. For twenty-one years the famous family lived on this hill, and La Vigia has become

Few visitors leave Havana without seeing the greatest show on earth – Tropicana, an enthralling sensation since 1931.

a shrine to students of the renowned writer's exploits, accomplishments, reports, celebrated literary works and novels. The gardens around the house are as much an enjoyment, as the interior is an education. Palms, vines and ferns shade, climb and drape over marble steps and columned walls. The conservatory to the rear of the house displays more tropical foliage and brilliant flowers bedeck the paved walkways. The setting is an idyllic genius' retreat, similar in location and isolation to those secluded villas of Noel Coward and Ian Fleming on the nearby island of Jamaica.

Ernest Hemingway, however, did not always retire to the privacy of his hilltop homestead, many of his ideas and inspirations came from his love of hunting, fishing and sailing, his fondness for bars, good company and excellent cuisine. Hemingway enjoyed life to the full and was rarely seen without the company of his Cuban comrades. In the bars of modern Havana, or the eating places of the old city, Hemingway would be found enjoying the companionship and, later in the evening, he would often retire with friends to the city's spectacular nightspots such as the world-famous, **Tropicana**. A cabaret has been showing on this four hectare site since 1939. Nowhere in the world is there a cabaret show which can compete with the extraordinary Tropicana of Havana. It is known locally as 'the Paradise beneath the Stars', here, there are stars above and around you as artists whirl in colourful performances, both on the stage and on platforms, which are spotlighted many metres up in the forest of palms surrounding the audience. The cast of hundreds changes costumes so many times that almost fifty wardrobe assistants are required and the entire enterprise costs over a million dollars a year to maintain. More than 1000 guests can be accommodated in the outside arena, or about 500 inside. The performers are hand-picked from the cream of Cuba's dancers, models, ballet performers, folkloric artists, singing stars and instrumentalists. Supper is served during the stunning evening of colour, music and light which leaves the audience clamouring for more. The show's super-productions are directed by Joaquin Condal, one of the most imaginative experts in the world. Two shows are held, five nights a week, in the most exotic surroundings the Caribbean has to offer.

Returning to the cultural aspect of the city which has thrived on discovery, the arts, sports, entertainment and learning, an important feature of the country's egalitarian aspirations is that of sharing knowledge. Here, in Havana, they have been put into practice with the opening of a unique conference, exhibition and cultural exchange centre. The **Palace of Conventions** is located in the luxurious suburb of Miramar. Set in exquisite gardens and shaded by flowering trees, this ultra-modern structure, with adjoining hotel, just across the Qibu River, hosts a hundred or more conventions, exhibitions, conferences, trade markets, displays and seminars annually. Delegates, exhibitors, speakers, artists, businessmen, experts and leaders in every field, now choose, as their venue in the Americas, the Palacio de las Convenciones de Cuba, Havana. Its many halls, exhibition rooms, film and lecture studios, and variety of international facilities, give the delegates unlimited scope for marketing products, exchanging ideas and sharing knowledge.

These ideals are not just those of the convention palace, they are those of Havana, and Cuba, the exchange of understanding and the forming of judgements through the aquaintance made with the people of Cuba. Havana is a city of live expression, of lively sport and entertainment, of interesting historical heritage and of dedicated learning and education, business and trade.

EXCURSIONS FROM HAVANA CITY
Arroyo Naranjo; Artemisa; Batabanó; Cabanas; Cojimar; Guanabacoa; Guanabo; Las Terrazas; Mariel; Rancho Alto; San

219

Jibacoa beach is well equipped with the most modern sailing and diving gear - two ancient wrecks in one small bay are an added bonus.

Francisco de Paula; Santa Maria del Rosario; Valle Grande; the Escaleras de Jaruco and; the beaches to the east and west of the city.

Arroyo Naranjo

Just on the outskirts of the city, this little settlement typifies the semi-rural life of those living in the suburbs of the capital city. There are several interesting houses in this 1845 town.

ARTEMISA

In the far western corner of Havana Province, this small town was constructed in 1818. It stands on the main rail route to the west and Pinar del Rio, also on the arterial road from Havana. The town's broad high street sports neo-classical, colourful buildings with balconies and doric and ionic-style facades and columns.

Artemisa's heritage is closely linked with the origins of the Revolution, as a monument here attests. The town's heritage is also celebrated at its Cultural House and in exhibitions, or at fiestas on National Holidays.

Batabanó

Immediately south of Havana, on the Caribbean coast, this ancient town was the first location of modern-day Havana, established in 1515. Its chequered history, involving Spanish settlers and raiding pirates, is now long-gone, and the peaceful little village now thrives with its sponge and fishing industry. Its connection with the metropolis and tourism is through the sea again, as this is the mainland port for boat and hydrofoil to the Isla de la Juventud (Isle of Youth) out in the Archipelago de los Canarreos. The town is about one-and-a-half hours drive from the centre of Havana and the crossing to the island can take between 3 to 5 hours by the regular ferry.

Havana's Playas del Este are a great attraction for local residents and tourists alike.

Cabañas

Founded in 1812 this pretty settlement lies in the foothills of the Sierra del Rosario and looks out over Hemingway's 'Great Blue Stream' off Havana's north coast.

Cojimar

Established in 1646, this town's name comes from the Indian word for the local river. Indian settlements have been discovered here and this small settlement, before becoming a proper town, was a target for pirates and raiders from the mid-16th century.

Cojimar has its own Morro fortress, La Cabana, a now-ruined watchtower, over-come when the English raided Havana, and an ancient mill, part of the San Pedro sugar cane business, built in 1603. Primarily a fishing village, Ernest Hemingway's fishing exploits from here culminated in his Nobel Prizewinning novel *The Old Man and the Sea*, written around the lifestyle of pre-revolution Cojimar fishermen. The fame afforded the town by its connections with the celebrated writer, has popularised the, now inter-nationally renowned, La Terraza Restaurant, a former sailing club, and its wide bar.

A trip around the town, walking up its cobbled paths, between ancient buildings, affords some beautiful vistas across its harbour and Morro castle. The sea-folk here, stripped brass fittings from their fishing boats when Hemingway died, and had the memorial bust cast, and placed overlooking his 'Great Blue Stream', the gulf waters.

Guanabacoa

This early town is generally visited for its unique folklore museum, performances of ancient dances and architectural beauty. Although the area had an earlier history going back to the Spanish use of Indian labour and later the prevalent slave trade, its official foundation year is 1743. Evidence of its earlier history can be found in the museum and even its church.

Being only a very short drive from Havana City, the town offers a special attraction in the form of re-enactments of African and Cuban folklore songs and dances. The performing group of this unique display, the Conjunto Folklorico Guanabacoa, perform in the Casa de Cultura area, which also encourages literary and artistic participation in the town's heritage preservation. At the Historical Museum exhibits show costumes dating from the times of slavery and before, ritualistic implements, musical instruments, tableaux and jewellery, magical signs and weapons. Other displays show antique furniture, clothing and Cuban artefacts.

Guanabo

This little fishing village made history during the 1812 uprising against the Spanish. It was founded in 1800 and is just a few minutes drive from Havana.

Las Terrazas

Located in the foothills of the Sierra de los Organos, this new town was founded in 1969 when a forestry enterprise started to develop the surrounding hillsides. The region is a popular camping and rustic-style holidaymaking area and there is an excellent restaurant here with rural views across the broad, terraced, terrain of the town and surrounding valleys.

The houses are now a little dated, but present an unusual picture on the green slopes, supported by legs reminiscent of the European landscape of the Alps.

The good road out of Havana makes it easy to reach this little resort.

Mariel

This small, semi-industrial township lies on the north-east coast of the province, by a small bay. Having developed as a fishing village from its establishment in 1762, the town now thrives on its industrial complex, including sisal processing factory, cement and thermo-electric plants, port and light industrial enterprises. The naval academy here is a result of the town's origins as an English naval post during the eleven-month occupation.

Rancho Alto

A recent, favourite resort and eating place is the Rancho Alto. Located just 30 kilometres from Havana, to the south-east, near Guines, and the beauty-spot of Loma de Amores (Lovers Hill), the motel commands stunning views over rich, forested hillsides. The restaurant is well-known for its Mexican specialities.

San Francisco de Paula

This charming town, just off the capital's ring road, to the south-east, is only a short drive from old Havana. Built on a small hill, its town square is surrounded by attractive, tiled houses and a little chapel.

The town is world-famous now as the location of Finca Vigia, Ernest Hemingway's residence from 1939. The villa stands as a museum to the great writer, overlooking the surrounding countryside from its cliff-top perch, surrounded by a little wood and a short drive from the town centre.

Santa Maria del Rosario

Located just a few minutes east of the capital, this 1732 settlement and its main buildings are fine examples of architecture spanning two-and-a-half centuries.

Dominating the skyline, however, is the vast, baroque church, started just one year after the founding of the city, enlarged in 1760, and beautifully preserved both inside and out. It has been dubbed 'the Cathedral of the Countryside'. A small park holds the attractive buildings in a uniquely charming 18th century perspective.

Valle Grande and Escaleras de Jaruco

Although on opposite sides of the capital, and several kilometres from central Havana, these are the two most important country locations for photographic visits.

Valle Grande lies to the south-east of the city near Punta Brava. This deep cleft contains a wealth of foliage and attractive walks with spectacular views.

Hotel Nacional, Vedado, Havana

Escaleras de Jaruco is a little further from the city, to the south-east, near Jaruco, and these natural 'stairs' provide a number of look-outs over fascinating countryside. Riding horses here is a particular pleasure as is the excellent food at the new motel.

HOTELS IN HAVANA
Havana Riviera

Malecon and Paseo, Vedado Tel: 30–5051
Considered the most exclusive hotel in Havana, with 410 rooms, 26 suites, all with balconies, every convenience and the use of two restaurants, two bars, cabaret, solarium, pool, Turkish bath, hairdressing salon, shops etc., this hotel is one of the most luxurious.

Havana Libre
L Street and 23 Street, Vedado Tel: 30–5011
This hotel rates almost on a par with the

Hotel Havana Libre, Vedado, Havana

Riviera, formerly the Havana Hilton, it has the most rooms of all the city's hotels – 576, all with balconies and every modern extra. Two restaurants, cabaret, pool, Turkish bath, conference rooms, underground garage.

Nacional de Cuba
O Street and 21 Street, Veldado Tel: 7–8981
This colonial-style hotel is known the world over and has the most magnificent views across Havana harbour. It has 461 rooms, two bars, two restaurants, cafeteria, La Parisienne cabaret, two pools, excellent shopping facilities, hairdressing salon, tennis courts etc.

Capri
N Street and 21 Street, Vedado Tel: 32–0511
In a central position, with all modern facilities, two restaurants, good shopping,

Hotel Capri, Vedado, Havana

Hotel Triton, Miramar, Havana

Hotel Comodoro, Miramar, Havana

Hotel Riviera, Vedado, Havana

cafeteria, bars, superb rooftop pool, snack bar, shop and conference rooms. Good service with all requirements in 216 rooms and 23 suites, tastefully decorated with views of the city.

Triton

70 Street and Mar Street, Miramar   Tel: 22-5531

Built in 1979, this hotel is in the exclusive area known as Miramar and has 273 rooms, with one suite. A restaurant, cafeteria and two bars, a shop, hairdressing salon and all facilities make this a good location even if it is not in the centre of the city.

Hotel Sevilla

Trocadero 55, between Prado and Zulueta   Tel: 6-9961

Built in the twenties and made famous by author Graham Greene, this salubrious, but not top-class hotel, is popular with Cuban visitors to Havana and has 189 rooms and an excellent restaurant.

Deauville Hotel

Avenida Italia, between Malecon and San

Lazaro   Tel: 61-6901

With rooftop pool and all basic facilities, this centrally located hotel has good dining facilities, bar, shops, nightclub and hairdressing salon. 134 rooms with good service and reasonable prices.

St John's Hotel

O Street, between 23 Street and 25 Street, Vedado   Tel: 32-9531

Basic requirements in this centrally situated hotel in 96 rooms with cafeteria, bar, restaurant and nightclub/cabaret.

Victoria

19 Street, No 101, corner of M Street, Vedado   Tel: 32-6501

All requirements in 32 rooms in a central

location and with restaurant, cafeteria, two bars and a shop. Good food, garden and ambience.

Vedado
O Street, No 244, between 23 and 25 Streets, Vedado   Tel: 32-6501
All facilities in the 120 rooms, shared pool with Flamingo Hotel, good facilities and central position. Restaurant and bar used by organisations and Cuban promotion seminars.

Colina
L Street and 27 Street, Vedado   Tel: 32-3535

Comodoro
84th Street, Miramar
On the coast of the luxurious Miramar district of Havana, this hotel has 124 rooms, a 96-seat restaurant and all facilities especially sporting, such as squash, volley-ball, basketball and beach sports.

Bruzón Hotel
Bruzón Street, Rancho Boyeros

El Arab Restaurant in old Havana offers Middle-Eastern cuisine in authentic Moorish surroundings.

MAIN HOTELS ON HAVANA'S EAST BEACHES

Bacuranao
Carretera Via Blanca y Celimar   Tel: 58
Accommodation for 102 guests

Los Pinos
Ave. de las Terrazas, Santa Maria   Tel: 2571
Accommodation for 175 guests

Marazul
Ave. Sur entre Ave. de las Barderas y calle 7, Santa Maria   Tel: 2531
Accommodation for 406 guests

Megano
Via Blanca between Santa Maria and Tarará   Tel: 56
Accommodation for 102 guests

Tropico
Via Blanca, Santa Cruz
Accommodation for 102 guests

RESTAURANTS IN HAVANA

Arabe
Oficios, between Lamparilla and Baratillo Streets   Tel: 62-8715
Authentic Middle-Eastern cuisine in a genuine Arabic atmosphere overlooking a courtyard and unique museum.

Los Andes
21 Street, No 52, corner of M Street   Tel: 32-0383
Latin American and Cuban fare at reasonable prices in pleasant surroundings.

La Arboleda
In the Hotel Nacional, 21 Street and O Street   Tel: 7-8981
With a view across the harbour of Havana, this garden-style restaurant serves mesa-buffet at moderate prices.

La Bodeguita del Medio
Near Cathederal Plaza, Empedrado 207   Tel: 6-6121
A rustic, barbecue-type restaurant with tiny bar. Good Cuban food, delightful atmosphere spiced by Hemingway nostalgia and mellowed by the famous mojito. Join the famous in signing the walls.

Situated in beautiful Lenin Park, Las Ruinas Restaurant is Havana's most luxurious. It is constructed around the ruins of an ancient sugar mill. The international cuisine is unsurpassable.

Las Bulerias
L Street, between 23 and 25 Streets   Tel: 32-3225
Good class Bulgarian cuisine in a pleasant atmosphere with rustic-type decor.

La Carreta
21 and K Streets, Vedado   Tel: 32-4485
Genuine Cuban fare at reasonable prices in a popular part of the city, near to the Copelia ice-cream gardens.

La Casa de los Vinos
Esperanza 1, corner of Factoria   Tel: 61-0073
Early this century a wine exchange did a brisk trade here, and now the bar is a popular spot with locals who also flock here for the Spanish dishes and to read the proverbs on the tiled walls.

Centro Vasco
3 and 4 Streets, Vedado   Tel: 3-9354
Fine, genuine, Spanish fare in a pleasant atmosphere with interesting decor.

El Cochinito
23 Street No 457, between 1 and H Streets   Tel: 40-4501

West of Havana City is the Marina Hemingway and Viejo y el Mar aparthotel offering a choice of three excellent restaurants.

Mostly pork dishes done in crillo style at moderate prices.

El Colmao
Aramburu No 366, between San Rafael and San José   Tel: 70–1113
Traditional Spanish music and cuisine. Excellent entertainment, nights only.

El Conejito
M Street, No 206, corner of 17 Street   Tel: 70–5001
Rabbit dishes are a speciality at this tastefully furnished, moderately priced restaurant. Good music and helpful service.

El Emperador
17 Street, No 55, between N and M Streets   Tel: 32–4948
Intimate bar-restaurant – evenings only. Excellent shellfish, meats and game-fowl dishes at relatively high prices.

El Restaurante Floridita
Avenida de Belgica, No 353, corner of Obispo   Tel: 61–2932
Another of Hemingway's haunts and undoubtedly the 'cradle of the Daquiri'. Elegant colonial-style decor with a huge wooden bar reminiscent of the Wild West. Possibly the best seafood in the Caribbean.

El Mandarin
23 Street, No 314, between N and M Streets   Tel: 32–0677
Chinese cuisine is served in this elegantly decorated environment which includes artefacts.

Monsenor
O Street, No 120, between 21 and 0 Streets   Tel: 32–9884
On the corner opposite the entrance to the Nacional Hotel this French-style bar-restaurant serves international cuisine with a musical background provided by local artistes.

Moscu
P Street, between 23 and Humbolt Street Tel: 79–6571
Russian dishes are served here in a typically eastern-European setting. A favourite evening restaurant for Cuban people.

227

La Bodeguita del Medio, also a famed haunt of 'Papa' Hemingway, offers a wonderful selection of Cuban fare in bohemian surroundings – mojitos a must!

El Patio

San Ignacio, No 54, Cathedral Plaza Tel: 61–4550

Courtyard design with a marvellous balcony with plants and fountains. Excellent Cuban fare in a quite Spanish atmosphere just a step away from the busy plaza. Outdoor terrace for drinks.

Polinesio

In the Havana Libre Hotel, L Street and 23 Street   Tel: 32–3753

Interesting South Sea decor, rustic bar and tropical atmosphere. Good Polynesian dishes and cocktails.

Rio Cristal

In the park on Rancho Boyeros, south of the city

Two restaurants here serve Cuban dishes in a lush tropical environment. Elegant garden vista whilst enjoying an aperitif.

La Roca

21 Street, No 102, corner of M Street   Tel: 32–8698

International and Cuban fare.

Las Ruinas

In Lenin Park   Tel: 32–4630

Havana's most exclusive restaurant, set in the ruins of an ancient sugar mill, carefully blending the stonework into its semi-indoor ambience. This elegantly furnished retreat offers an international cuisine befitting Paris tables.

Sierra Maestra

In Havana Libre Hotel L and 23 Streets Tel: 30–5011

Mesa buffet in modern surroundings at the top of the hotel, spectacular views of the city from window tables.

Sofia

O Street, on the corner of 23 Street, Vedado Tel: 32–0740

Bulgarian fare a speciality, good service and interesting menu, a good place to order the excellent Bulgarian wine!

Taberna de San Roman

Oficios 404 Street   Tel: 6–4460

Typical Spanish cuisine, such as paella, in neat surroundings.

La Taberna Tres Reyes

Castillo de los Tres Reyes del Morro   Tel: 6–5129

Fantastic setting for this, recently extended, restaurant which serves traditional food. It has its own unique juice bar.

La Tasca Espanola

Boulevard Matri and Carcel Street   Tel: 6–4460

Spanish favourites are served here with

good drinks, as the name suggests.

Taberna San Salvador
Malecon and Paseo de Marti Tel: 6–6001
Traditional Cuban fare served in historic surroundings, nights only.

La Torre
17 Street, No 55, corner of M Street Tel: 32–4630
One of the most favoured restaurants in the centre of Havana at the top of the Fosa building, stunning view across the city and bay from both the large bar and glass-fronted dining area, first-class service and excellent menu.

Yangtse
23 Street, corner of 26 Street Tel: 32–0677
Chinese fare served in authentic Chinese ambience.

1830 Restaurant
Just before the Almendares tunnel, Calzada Tel: 3–6954
One of the most elegant and highly-rated restaurants in Cuba. Set in a large bay-side mansion the four dining rooms have views out to the gardens, fort, river or bay. Patio and gazebo bars, Cuban and international cuisine.

1647 Restaurant
Castillo de la Chorrera
This meson serves traditional Cuban food in the Spanish fort. Surrounded by arms and cannon, on wooden benches the 17th century style is a favourite with Cubans. Interesting wooden screen near the long bar.

21 Club
21 Street and N Street, Vedado Tel: 32–9602

23 Club
23 Street, between N and O Streets, Vedado Tel: 30–3461

Other eating places include:
La Cecilia; El Carmelo; El Gato Tuerto; Varsovia Restaurant; Lafayette; Potin; El Jardin; La Zaragozana; La Mina and *El Bucan.*

Also, further out of the city the Escalera de Jaruco or Steps of Jaruco, a small town, is an excellent spot for Middle-Eastern fare. There are no taxis back from this town to Havana.

Try the recently established **Motel Rancho Alto** for the most excellent Mexican cuisine. A good look-out spot from the terrace.

Barlovento is the area to the west of Havana where the Hemingway Marina offers a choice of three restaurants, **The Fiesta, Papa's Restaurant** and bar and **Gregorio's**. All excellent fare and particularly good for seafood dishes – naturally!

NIGHTLIFE IN HAVANA

Caribe and also *Turquino*
Havana Libre Hotel   Tel: 30–5011
Copa Room
Havana Riviera Hotel   Tel: 30–5051
Jardines 1830
1830 Restaurant   Tel: 3–4504
Parisién
Nacional Hotel   Tel: 7–8981
Pico Blanco
St John's Hotel   Tel: 32–9531
Rincón del Bolero (Salon Rojo)
Capri Hotel   Tel: 32–0511
Rincón Español
Vedado Hotel   Tel: 32–6501
Rincón del Tango
Bruzón Hotel, Rancho Boyeros
Tropicana
Playa district   Tel: 2–4544/2–6224

THEATRES IN HAVANA

Hubert de Blanck
Modern and classical plays by Cuban and foreign dramatists.
Calzada between A and B Streets, Vedado
Tel: 30–0111

García Lorca
Opera, ballet, musical comedy and operetta.
Prado and San Rafael Streets, Old Havana
Tel: 62–4902
Karl Marx
Foreign artists, national music and dance and special shows.
Mella
Folklore and modern dance, plays and shows.
Linea and A Streets, Vedado   Tel:3–8696
Musical
Musical comedies by Cuban and foreign writers.
Consulado and Virtudes Streets, Central Havana   Tel: 62–2869
Nacional
Foreign and domestic artists, national and international festivals, concerts and plays, in two halls.
Revolution Square   Tel: 79–0611
Sótano
Plays by Cuban and foreign dramatists.
K between 25th and 27th Streets, Vedado
Tel:32–0630

Pinar del Rio Province

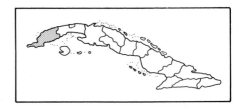

'Pinar del Rio was one of the last provinces to join the wars of independence. It was there that Maceo waged one of the most brilliant campaigns of his life. Once again Pinar del Rio is demonstrating that enthusiasm, that militancy, that patriotic spirit, that intelligence and wisdom to tackle problems and to advance!'

FIDEL CASTRO RUZ

At the far 'tail end' of the island, the extreme western tip of the Cuban Occidente, this province has a population of about 600 000. Originally dubbed the 'Cinderella' because of its less privileged position in relation to its wealthier 'sister' provinces, Pinar del Rio has now bloomed into a prosperous region both agriculturally and industrially. This is Cuba's third largest province.

Rich lowlands surrounding the central, mountainous 'spine' of the province are intensively cultivated with root crops and tobacco, maize and fruit. Its interesting topography has done much to improve the province's lot in tourism and the network of lakes in the far south-west, provide excellent grounds for fishing and hunting. Along the edge of the province's northern plain is an attractive coast which has been developed, in areas, for beach and boating holidays.

The world-famous Havana tobacco emanates from Pinar del Rio Province and the areas of Vuelta Abajo and Semivuelta are said to produce the finest crops. Tobacco here is grown on small-holdings and in very carefully tended little fields. This has created a patchwork effect across the plains. Out of the tobacco season the farmers grow maize on the same land. Some sugar is cultivated in the province, as is rice and a little cotton.

Copper mines in the north-west and mineral oil plants have brought considerable wealth to the province, which has been opened up with a good communication network linking with the Carretera Central – Central Highway. A parallel railway also runs the length of the province.

Sightseeing spots include the Botanical Gardens of **Soroa, La Güira, Las Tumbas, San Juan y Martínez** and the **Valley of Viñales.** Several locations are of particular historical interest with connections from primitive Indian times. There are five important **cave sites** in the province. In the south-west is the **Cueva Funche –** an Indian location surrounded by ancient settlements. Around the Valley of Viñales are the caves of Santo Tomás, the cave systems of Sumidero and the popular tourist caves of José Miguel, or Las Cuevas disco, and Los Indios cavern.

Three **spas** exist in Pinar del Rio Province. The most popular are at San Vincente and Soroa, but locals prefer that at San Diego de los Baños. At least seven important tourist sites for **naturalists,** three scenic viewpoints and numerous locations of outstanding beauty make this province a naturalist's, geologist's and archaeologist's delight.

Pinar del Rio

The capital of this province is Pinar del Rio city, located 182 kilometres south-west of Havana. Its population is estimated at 120 000. Although the city dates from the late 19th century the original land rights were granted to the Indian inhabitants of this area at the end of the 1500s. The city is the birthplace of the famous Cuban musician, Pedro Junco, composer of 'Nosotros'-Us. It has two notable restaurants, the **Rumayor** and **La Casona.** The restaurant and cafeteria at the **Pinar**

Rural scenes like this are typical of Pinar del Rio's treasured tobacco industry, cultivated in a unique micro-climate.

del Rio Hotel are also popular with visitors and tourists.

As the city is located in what the experts consider to be the best tobacco growing area in the world (the hoyos or Vuelta Abajo), the **Tobacco Museum** in the city

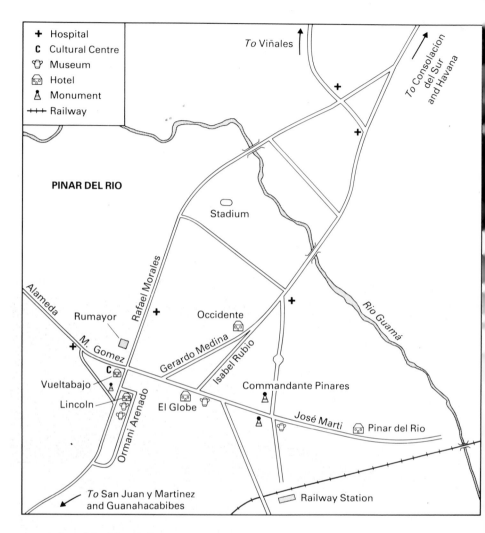

Key:
- **+** Hospital
- **C** Cultural Centre
- Museum
- Hotel
- **Á** Monument
- +++ Railway

PINAR DEL RIO

To Viñales

To Consolación del Sur and Havana

Stadium

Rafael Morales

Alameda

Rumayor

M. Gomez

Occidente

Gerardo Medina

Isabel Rubio

Río Guamá

Vueltabajo

Lincoln

Ormani Arenado

El Globe

Commandante Pinares

José Marti

Pinar del Rio

To San Juan y Martinez and Guanahacabibes

Railway Station

is worth a visit. The city has 18 museums as well as 13 art galleries, including the **Natural Science Museum** in the fantastic **Guasch Palace, Museo Hermanos Saiz,** the **Provincial History Museum** and **Museo Antonio Guiteras Holmes**. The Cathedral dates from 1883 and the José Jacinto Milanes Theatre, originally from 1838, but re-structured in 1845 and in 1898. Information can be found at the **Casa de Cultura** which is also library and art gallery. Visit also La Taberna Café for the local drink – Guayabita del Pinar, a liqueur made from a special variety of guava found here.

EXCURSIONS FROM PINAR DEL RIO
Viñales Valley; Soroa Botanical Gardens; La Güira National Park; Los Portales; El Morillo beach; Cuyaguateje; Miguel Salude lake; San Diego de los Baños; Las Tumbas; Playa Luchana; Verracos beach; Playa Puerto Esperanza; La Altura; Levisa Cays; La Cana beach and; Playa Oceana.

Hunting and fishing trips, climbing, horse riding and nature trails to spectacular viewpoints can be interesting diversions.

Visit also the tobacco fields. Tobacco factory tours are an important draw for the city and are arranged through Cubatur agents.

La Güira

This delightful, lush, rustic forest retreat is set in the mountainous area, with all the facilities for climbing, walking, horse riding and other countryside activities.

Rancho Mundito

An attractive township and resort set in the forest area plantations. Facilities are available to take exploratory trips into the surrounding woodland and to join horse riding treks.

Cigar manufacture is a skill now equally shared by both men and women.

San Diego de los Baños

This retreat is a mineral water spa, but is also popular for its unique micro-climate and scenic beauty. A legend of the waters at Templado Springs, concerning the curing of a leprous slave, spread the famed qualities of this spa during Spanish occupation. Qualified medical staff now supervise the spring's resort.

Soroa

The 'rainbow' of Cuba, a colourful, vivid, botanical resort in the mountains with all facilities and **Villa Soroa** which caters to almost 50 guests.

Soroa's luxuriant botanical garden, set in mountain rain forests, attracts both botanists and lovers of beauty.

Viñales

A fantastic and uniquely weird, lush valley hidden in the folds of the mountains strewn with rocky 'mogotes' surrounds the tiny town of the same name. Hotels **Rancho San Vincente** and **Los Jazmines** can accommodate up to 77 guests.

HOTELS IN PINAR DEL RIO PROVINCE

Pinar Del Rio
Marti Street, at the Thruway Tel: 5071/79
Modern 296-capacity hotel in the provincial capital

Vueltabajo
Marti Street and Rafael Morales Street Tel: 2303
Central city hotel

La Ermita Motel
La Ermita Highway, Viñales Tel: 9–3204
Accommodation in delightful chalets with a marvellous view over Viñales Valley, 18 cabins and all facilities

Los Jazmines
Viñales Highway, Viñales Tel: 9–3205
Accommodation in 30 rooms in Spanish-style hotel commanding views out over the Viñales Valley

Rancho San Vincente
Puerto Esperanza Highway, Viñales Tel: 9–3200
Accommodation for 47 in this modern spa hotel in the mountain resort Villa Laguna Grande

Cuyaguateje Reservoir
La Laguna Grande Tel: 2430
Fishing centre for the reservoir system, club scheme

Villa Maspoton
Granja La Cubana, Los Palacios

Vinãles Valley was formed by the collapse of a gigantic cave. Only the roof's pillars, now worn into 'mogotes' remain, as evidence of pre-historic upheavals.

The Emperor

Book through Cubatur as this is a club for hunting and fishing
Accommodation for 48 sporting guests
Villa Soroa
Soroa Highway, Soroa   Tel: 2122
Fascinating botanical and mountain environment with accommodation plus all facilities for 49 people in chalets and cabin rooms

RESTAURANTS IN PINAR DEL RIO PROVINCE
La Casona
Marti and Colon Streets, Pinar del Rio
Crillo food in colonial-style environment
Las Cuevas de Viñales
Puerto Esperanza Highway, Viñales   Tel: 9–3203

Restaurant, bar, disco, dancing. A huge open cave in the valley
Las Cuevas
Also in Puerto Esperanza Highway, Viñales   Tel: 9–3202
Similar but smaller than above, restaurant, bar near the Indian Cave
Rumayor
Viñales Highway, Pinar del Rio   Tel: 9–3203
Rumayor is famous for its chicken dishes and cabaret entertainment
El Castillo de las Nubes
Soroa
New Spanish-style retreat restaurant, over-looking wooded slopes
La Taberna
103 Ramon Gonzales Street, Pinar del Rio
Relaxing atmosphere and interesting food and aperitifs

Quotations in this chapter are from personalities and notables who were born in or who have written about the provinces of the island in book, poem or song.

CHAPTER 9

Seven Cuban Tours

*'He got into the car and told the chauffeur to go up O'Reilly to the
Floridita. Before the car circled the Plaza in front of the Embassy
building and the Ayuntamiento and turned into O'Reilly he saw the
size of the waves in the mouth of the harbour and the heavy rise and
fall of the channel buoy. In the mouth of the harbour the sea was
very wild and confused and clear green water was breaking over the
rock at the base of the Morro, the tops of the seas blowing white in
the sun.'*
*'It looks wonderful, he said to himself. It not only looks wonderful;
it is wonderful.'*

observations of Thomas Hudson, lead character of
Islands in the Stream by ERNEST HEMINGWAY

This section concentrates on visiting some
of Cuba's most interesting and famous
towns, cities and sites whilst touring the
countryside.

Each point of interest on and by the
roadside is noted and, alongside the text,
the route map indicates on which side of
the road each place of interest or site
occurs.

Havana – Soroa – Pinar del Rio – Viñales

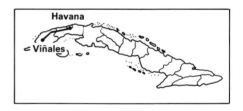

From the city centre, drive out to the
Malecon on Havana's seafront and
continue to the **Fortress el Torreon de
la Chorrera**, housing the 1646 restaurant
on the seaward side. On this headland,
facing the Boca de la Chorrera, there is an
elegant water grotto and temple with a
small cupola. These gardens are all part of
the 1830 restaurant, once an imposing
diplomatic residence and now one of
Havana's more plush eating places.

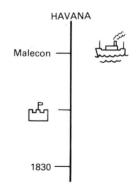

Havana in the sun

Immediately after the 1830 Restaurant, a tunnel under the Almendares River, emerges in the garden suburb of **Miramar**, El Rio nightclub is on the right and in front, on the America Boulevard, is the impressive clock tower surrounded by carefully trimmed topiary. Note the perfection of flower beds and the drum-shaped trees, offset by the little, silver traffic and security control cabins, on stilts, at street corners. A wealth of architectural edifices along the wide avenue testifies to the riches of its past residents. Most of the buildings here are now diplomatic.

Halfway up the boulevard, on the left, is the huge dome of the active church of **Jesus de Miramar**, almost facing the tower of the Triton Hotel, down on the seafront, The massive, missile-like structure, surrounded by glass fronted buildings, is the recently completed, **Soviet Embassy**. After the roundabout and funfair on the right, past the huge ex-sailing club mansion – now a centre of culture – is a Diplomatic Shop, just before the exit onto Avenue 174. Turn *right* at the Provincial Sports School (Manuel Piti Fajardo), past more embassy villas, the Military Academy on the right, and light industrial works, out of Havana City into Havana Province.

Over a small canyon, cattle fields and hills are reflected in a small lake, preceding the large **reservoir** on the left. The six-lane, A4 highway, passes a gully before the reservoir with its pioneer camp, on the opposite bank. On the other side of the motorway is a metal factory, sandy hills and sugar fields interspersed with grazing land.

Directly ahead, over the wooded countryside dotted with cattle stations, are

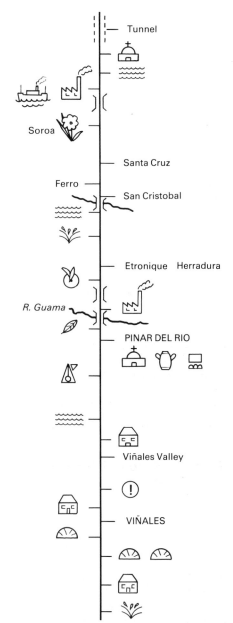

Tunnel

Soroa

Santa Cruz

Ferro

San Cristobal

Etronique   Herradura

R. Guama

PINAR DEL RIO

Viñales Valley

VIÑALES

low mountains. The conical peaks, with deep clefts and rock protuberances, over the road bridge, contrast with the mainly flat land, broken only by the smoke from a sugar centrale. Red earth, malanga fields, sugar crops, and banana plantations, herald Pinar del Rio Province.

After a quarry on the right, a sign for Soroa, and under a road bridge, take a *right* towards the Sierra Rosario Range. These are divided by a river, partitioning the Sierra de los Organos, which is seen later. The road rises through wooded hillside and small hamlets, with spectacular views from the cliff-hugging track to 400 metres above sea level, and the entrance to the resort. A curious signpost surmounted by a model 'plane with rotating propellor, signifies arrival at 'the Rainbow of Cuba'.

Soroa's abundant vegetation, flowering plants mingling with palms, coniferous mammoths dwarfing exotic shrubs and a plethora of orchids, (all 800 varieties) out-blooming the locally prolific trees in full flower, attracts many visitors. Rocky outcrops, cliffs, a beautiful pathway to the

Soroa offers a labyrinth of botanical walks.

spectacular waterfall and botanical trail, are all compensated by the provision of refreshment in the form of bars and restaurants. There are shops here, craft makers – see cigars rolled by hand and hats or decorative objects created from fronds – and cabin accommodation surrounding a huge pool.

It is hard to tear oneself away from the luxuriant surroundings of Soroa, but a half-day visit is enough to take in the main attractions, although an overnight stop is the best way to enjoy the 'Rainbow Gardens'. Don't leave Soroa before sampling the roadside-grown Poma Rosa – like lychees, and the Guayabita del Pinar – a delicious nectar, dry or sweet, made from the locally grown miniature guava.

The winding road down to Pinar del Rio's flat, fertile plain, provides a myriad of vistas through the smooth-barked *Almacigo* and *Jocuma* trees. Take the *right* turn towards the west and the provincial capital. Follow the edge of the mountain range on the right, past wide reservoirs, over dry watercourses and rivers, skirting rice fields in the low, marshy areas until

the A4 highway passes a number of schools and farming installations on the left. The weird bloated trunks of some palms are not an afflicted version of the stately Royal Palm, they are the Belly Palm, or *Barrigona*.

Turn off the road, again *to the right* onto the N1 road to **Pinar del Rio**. On the left are some of the first views of the famous tobacco fields. The curious barn-shaped, thatched huts, are not homes – they are the drying houses for the leaf or *vegas*! Notice that they are all positioned east-to-west, this is designed to make the most of the sun's consistent rays. In the distance can be glimpsed the shiny metallic glints off the modern, aluminium-roofed *vegas*.

The road enters tiny **Santa Cruz** over a little river, and before one has time to notice the one free-market and gas station, the highway is out on the vast plain, and into the little lumber village of **Ferro**. More reservoirs on the right, and the road has passed through **San Cristobal** with its guava plantations, and **Los Palacios'** chicken farms with sacking walls. Here, there are marvellous views of the mountains, as deep river gorges and ravines are crossed. Many of the roadside trees are *Guira* or Gourd Trees, with a huge fruit which is put to so many uses.

Over a girder bridge, drive into **San Diego de los Baños**, with its large mango plantations, and, take the B road *to the right*, bounded by scrub and low, waterlogged land littered with palm stumps. Over to the right, now, are more rugged peaks and across an arm of the **Youth Reservoir**, past a small restaurant, the road improves on reaching a large *majagua* field. This precious wood is part of a reafforestation programme. **La Guira** is on the right, in the foothills. A few thatched cottages, or *bohios*, line the road before a girder bridge, a crossroads, and before passing the **Consolación del Sur and Empressa Pecuria** – a cattle establishment – on the right. A little further on is the giant **Centrale Camilo Cienfuegos** cattle breeding station and **Entronque Herradura** town.

On entering towns in Cuba the roadsign for the town's name is white on blue, on leaving, the sign is crossed by a red diagonal. After the small town, and its gas station, the wooded countryside is dotted with thatched dwellings. Over another girder bridge the patchwork of tobacco fields, and neat *vegas*, are parted by a road to the Central del sur 4. Roadside trees here lean curiously away from the road, and after the avenue of trees, the famous **Captain Thomas Citrus Empressa** looms on the left. This unit processes grapefruit and oranges for juice and pulp.

Rice, citrus and tobacco fields are an indication of the area's prosperity, **The Consolación del Sur township** boasts an impressive statue of José Marti, a fine hospital, school and new apartments, which contrast with the colonial houses and the Hotel la Villa. Orange groves spread on each side of the road, after the town, and across a double girder bridge, over a wide river, and after some tobacco fields, the road passes out of Consolacion Municipality into Pinar del Rio.

Immediately, on the right, and to the front, is a striking view of the, almost primeval, **Viñales Valley**, a rugged profile of the remnants of a huge massif. An attractive avenue, with large Carob trees leaning over to form an archway, shade the road before the **La Conchita Empressa** on the left – a famous international fruit cannery. Initially, **Pinar del Rio** city, was built on the river Guama, where there were pine forests. A few houses by the girder bridge over the river are all that remains of the old city of Pinar del Rio. Another impressive avenue of trees heralds the entrance to the city, with the Communist Party School, huge new hospital and Provincial Faculty of Medicine on the left.

The old Province of Pinar del Rio was terribly underdeveloped before the triumph of the Revolution. It had the nickname *Cenicienta*, or Cinderella, to its richer, sister provinces. Today it has fulfilled the story told in that fairytale and

Pinar del Rio's mountains are lush in tropical vegetation.

become a flourishing region. The city is evidence of the total turnabout in the prosperity of the province. Its interesting architectural mixture combines colonial with neo-classical, gothic with modern. The **Cathedral**, the **Museum of Natural History** – the Milanes Theatre, (built entirely of wood) and the **Rumayor** restaurant, are all well preserved edifices of their day, and add grandeur to the thriving city. The large Pinar del Rio Hotel offers all modern amenities and accommodation in 149 rooms. A smaller hotel, the Vueltabajo, is also in the centre of the city. Turning *right*, past the Rumayor, on the left, the road passes another large hospital, and becomes the *241 route* to Viñales.

Mango plantations, small thatched cottages, and bungalows are left behind as the road winds through lush vegetation, bamboo-lined rivers, deep, green gorges, and palm-fronded banks dividing tobacco fields. Guava fields, on the left, and the **Mango Empressa**, on the right, come

before a **Campismo Popular**, or camp-site, on the left, as the road winds higher into the hills. Passing deep valleys there are fascinating vistas over the low foothills and plains. Woods on slopes get thicker and wilder as the route enters **Viñales**. A marvellous view of the weird valley is possible, just after passing the experimental pine forestry station, and the sign for **Los Jazmines Hotel**.

Just walk out onto the beautiful hotel's patio, around the pool, and catch the breathtaking sight of the unique landscape below – a sight like this can only be seen, in miniature, in two other places in the world, Puerto Rico and China. At sunset it is one of Cuba's most delightfully peaceful experiences. Beyond the Bougainvillea a thousand of the world's richest tobacco fields lie at your feet, in a patchwork of greens, punctuated by the most fantastic rocky pinnacles and cliffs, craggy protuberances and palm-clad spires. This is the eerie **Valley of Viñales**, a gigantic cavern, miles wide, which collapsed millions of years ago, leaving its jagged props as a remembrance of the haunts of

Pteradactyl and Brontosaurus. The musty, thick, winding tangles of lianas and heavy scent of giant ferns, lend to the dank, rich air, an almost prehistoric feel. This valley is now a National Monument, since visited on a field expedition by Fidel Castro and his assistant during the 1960s. Archeological societies and speleology groups come from all over the world to explore its famous caverns and seek ancient secrets.

Visit the isolated township of Viñales, the **Indian Cave**, with its underground river trip, and the **Las Cuevas** disco club, in the side of a mountain. The giant prehistoric mural representation, painted onto bare rock, is a phenomenon of more recent times, but the unexplored caverns of the valley may still reveal knowledge of ancient civilisations. On the roadside fields,

watch the oxen ploughing the red soil, with the ploughman's water barrel resting on the plough as a weight.

A living fossil, the **Cork Palm**, grows only in this valley, and there are several in the entrance to La Ermita Hotel. At the **Hotel Rancho San Vincente** are sulphur baths and a natural spa, also peculiar to this fascinating area. It is in this strange valley that one might possibly find Cuba's National Flower, the **Mariposa** growing wild. Look for it near the tiny streams, its white bloom is a perfect butterfly shape and, if lepidoptery is your forté, the valley swarms with the most brilliant butterfly and moth specimens. These flutter around flowering shrubs and bushes, but the real jewel is the darting, **Bee Humming-bird** – the smallest bird in the world.

Viñales – the ancient valley nursing a new crop, tobacco.

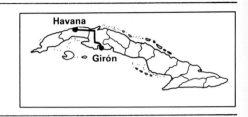

Havana – Matanzas – Guamá – Girón

This journey, of a little more than 200 kilo-metres, is facilitated by the excellent condition of the road, which, although not a highway, is carefully tended as one of the most popular tourist routes from the capital. Take the **Malecon** boulevard east, to the tunnel under Havana Bay and exit at the multi-lane checkpoint, just right of the **Morro Castle**. Continue down Tunnel Avenue, with its gantry-like lamp-standards, and out, past a busy intersection, taking a *left* turning towards the beaches of eastern Havana.

Cojimar port is by-passed as is the huge new apartment development at Alamar, on the left – a dormer town for the city. Apart from weekdays, this route is one of the busiest roads in Cuba when the capital's

Havana

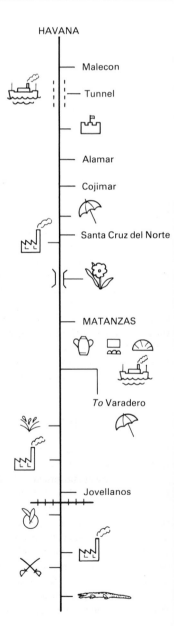

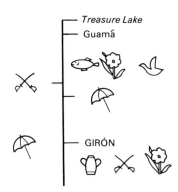

Treasure Lake
Guamá

GIRÓN

Matanzas railway station

residents take to the beaches and resorts of the **Playas del Este**. A swathe of beaches, each with its own accommodation and amenities complex, cut along the shoreline for over ten kilometres, providing magnificent vistas of white sands and blue waters.

However inviting the beaches may be, keep hugging the coast until the coves become more rocky. The road here swings inland slightly, but keeps the sea in view, until the port town of **Santa Cruz del Norte** is passed on the left. On the beach is the old, 1919 rum factory. Up, and to the right, behind you, is the huge sugar Centrale 'Cienfuegos', and on the left, the Santa Cruz refinery of Havana Club rum, producing 19 different varieties. More rocky shore, and the road then turns inland, past a sign for the famous Jibacoa beach resort, and out then into more wooded landscape.

The coastal plain is narrow here, between a steep scarp and flat, oil-rich lands along the sea's volcanic shoreline. Energy is also in evidence along this stretch of Havana's northern coast, with the new electricity generating power station, and its distinctive **lighthouse**, passed as the road keeps to the beach. Towards Matanzas Province the road rises and the countryside becomes more hilly and craggy. Over the deep gorge containing the Yumuri River, Cuba's largest bridge span affords excellent views of the famous valley. Rounding a bend in the road and looking down to the east, the **Bay of Matanzas** can be discerned, and

the freeway dips down to the dock area before entering the town. The smell of sulphur is in the air, mingled with tangs of sugar refining, fertiliser and minerals.

The busy port sector of **Matanzas** is quickly passed and colourful flowered reservations welcome one to the broad avenue leading through the city centre.

Across two pretty bridges, with views of fishing boats riding at anchor on the **Rio Yumuri** and **Rio San Juan**, and one has completed a swift tour of the major sights of the city! A little detour and one could take in the main square and its momuments, a few majestic edifices and cultural houses. Matanzas remains, to the traveller, a stopover for refreshment rather than a place for sightseeing, however a short detour to see the treasures of the museum at **Junco Palace** in old Vigia Square can be rewarding.

Avoid taking the bay-side route out to Varadero and its magnetic beach and turn *right* out past the Central University following the rail track. The road rises now into quite mountainous countryside as it approaches the fair-size township of **Limonar** after crossing the Canimar River by a spectacular gorge bridge. Mahogany and Yagruma trees strike up, metres above the foliage canopy, and Hummingbirds dart in the undergrowth. Still rising high into the wooded hillside, the road keeps meeting the railway and passes the site of the **1895 battle** of Coliseo before entering the pretty township. **Coliseo** represents an important, strategic position as it

243

commands the point of a mountain range, the road to Cuba's 'flag city' Cardenas, on the coast, and the major rail link to Havana.

Keep on the main highway which cuts, straight as an arrow, across cultivated land leaving the medicinal spa resort of **San Miguel de Los Banos** on the right. At **Jovellanós**, another major town, down in the fertile valley of sugar and orange groves, the route *forks to the north*. Routes east and west should be ignored as the more insignificant carriageway heading for **Jaguey Grande**, represents a short-cut across the veritable ocean of citrus plantations.

Country secondary schools and universities or colleges, stand out stark and white, like huge sea-going liners in the deep green of orange, grapefruit, lemon and guava fields. Neat rows of trees become monotonous at just the time that Jaguey Grande, the big railhead for citrus fruit transportation, comes into view. All along the roadside groves one can see young workers tending the oranges and lemons. This is the policy of combining education with agricultural production and an outdoor activity. Students spend half a day picking or attending the fruit trees and the other half-day in the classroom studying. Free education, then, becomes a little less expensive to the State when the national citrus plantations benefit from inexpensive labour from eager students. Passing giant trucks and trailers loaded with delicious juicy fruit, the road approaches a railhead and the major junction with the main **Central Highway** which runs down the 'spine' of the country.

Crossing the highway the route follows the railway for a short distance and branches off, making a 'bee-line' for the Caribbean coast. Not far from the road to Guamá is a national monument. It is the **Centrale of Australia**, which during the Bay of Pigs, Girón, invasion, was the headquarters for Commander Fidel Castro and base for the FAR forces. After more sugar fields and small-scale horticulture the terrain becomes scrubbier and thickets

grow by the roadside. This is the marshy area, part of the giant swamplands of the **Zapata Peninsula** and a region criss-crossed with drainage channels, bogs and low-lying, water-logged ground. Thorn bush, Marabou brush and reeds abound as the road rises up, forming a causeway before reaching the resort lake of the **Laguna del Tesoro**.

Treasure Lake gets its name from the legend of Indian gold cast into the waters to prevent its capture by Spanish colonists. The lake now abounds in a different type of treasure – the bountiful Bass which now inhabit the clear water. Nearby is the **crocodile breeding farm**, with many thousand specimens, and, at the southern end of the lake, is the stilt and artificial island resort of **Guamá village**. Seven islands and about fifty tourist cabins, plus restaurant, café, bar etc. all go to make up one of Cuba's most popular resorts. After the long drive from Atlantic coast to the Caribbean Sea, the inviting boat trip across cool, placid, Treasure Lake, is an invitation not to be missed. The specialities of Guamá restaurant are also a true delight, as are the concoctions devised by its barman. Rita Longa's fine sculptures, in the rustic setting of Guamá model **Indian village**, lend a lifelike atmosphere to the authentic reconstructions. A stroll around the resort's walkways is refreshingly tranquil before continuing on to Girón. The hedgerows here are a delight of pink with the blossom of the curiously-formed Bottle Brush plant which can often grow to a fair-size tree.

The whole region around the Bahia de Cochinos, or Bay of Pigs, is marshy and flat. Scrub and thornbush provide an impenetrable curtain along the roadside and **giant land crabs** scuttle from the seaward side to the swamplands. In places, where the hordes of crustaceans are thickest, the slaughter of crushed crabs can dye the road red or yellow. Vultures wait for cars to speed by before loping into the carnage, with ungainly great wings shadowing their limitless repast.

This area has a long history of bloodshed.

Guamá resort

The Spanish conquistadores are supposed to have slaughtered the scattered Indian tribes living along this coast and, in more recent times, the Bay of Pigs was selected by mercenary infiltrators for their violent invasion attempt in 1961. **Memorials** and gravestone plaques to the fallen, can be seen by the roadside. At the signpost for Playa Larga, the locals favourite, beachside resort, at the head of the long, narrow bay, take the road ahead, past the war monument, towards Girón at the neck of the bay. Part of the beach at Playa Larga can be glimpsed through the pine trees to the right of the road as it hugs the line of the tranquil bay. **Pelicans** love this stretch of water and the comical, brown birds can be seen bobbing across its turquoise surface or wheeling out over the mangrove roots, tangled along its shoreline.

Reaching **Girón**, the site of some of the worst fighting during the invasion attempt,

the kilometre-long sea wall can be seen on the right through pine trees, and the road bears around to the left past a wide plaza. This is the resort centre of Girón, beach, cabins, restaurants, bars and cafés providing for the thousands of tourists who flock here annually.

Girón combines history and tourism with sports and wildlife. There are facilities here for all forms of watersports, entertainment and relaxation. Of particular interest is the abundant natural fauna in this part of the **Zapata Swamp** including **rare birds** such as Dwarf Hummingbirds, Royal Woodpeckers, Parrots, Trogon and Cartacuba. Here also is the haunt of the rare forest rodent, the **Hutia**. Before the area was developed the inhabitants of this region were isolated and made a living from hunting crocodile or burning charcoal. Today, the wide road has opened up the peninsula and both the beach – **Playa Girón** and the **Historical Museum** attract national and international visitors.

Girón – Cienfuegos – Trinidad – Sancti Spiritus

The route out from Girón to Cienfuegos must cross the marshes of eastern Zapata. Although not as impenetrable as those to the west of the Bay of Pigs, the terrain is quite inhospitable and very sparsely populated. Previous inhabitants here eked out a meagre existence from the burning of charcoal for fuel, and hunting the prolific crocodiles. This activity is still practised in the very remote areas and **charcoal mounds** can be seen smouldering at some points along the thicket-lined route.

Leaving Girón, the road passes the National Museum and its collection of **airplanes, tanks** and **warfare machinery,** out into the scrub of marshy wilderness. It is quite possible to take the wrong turning at times. The highway here is not well made up and, although it is being resurfaced, the continual swerving to avoid potholes and the thousands of red, black and yellow land crabs and *Congrejo Ermitano* – hermit crabs, crossing one's path, means the road is best not travelled at night. The occasional palm clump breaks the monotony of **Marabou** and **Mangrove thicket** and road widening has pushed back much of the Jocu scrub which encroached on the roadway. The strange foliage of Yagruma trees, with dark topside and silver underside leaves, gives the wasteland a sinister outline. Here it is possible to spot the lurking **Cotorra,** or Green Parrot in the roadside bushes or giant Traveller's Palm fronds. **Helechal** is a small township just outside Girón, and both here, and at **San Blas,** a little further up the road, there were skirmishes with mercenary invaders during the 1961 Battle of the Bay of Pigs. Further into the swampland the

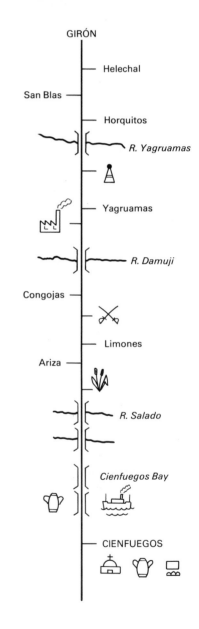

GIRÓN

Helechal

San Blas

Horquitos

R. Yagruamas

Yagruamas

R. Damuji

Congojas

Limones

Ariza

R. Salado

Cienfuegos Bay

CIENFUEGOS

road crosses into the Province of Cienfuegos. Just after **Horquitas**, and after crossing the semi-dried-up river of **Yaguaramas** there is, out on the right hand side, a **monument** to a famous English settler, Henry Reeve – 'El Inglesíto'. Yaguaramas town is a railhead and of no exceptional importance apart from the fact that one should remember to take the *sharp right* turn at the T junction a few metres further on. From here the countryside becomes more agricultural and the usual route is to head for the large town of **Rodas**, a rail, road, the Damuji river confluence and important agricultural centre. The undulating road dipping and diving over rolling hills towards **Congojas** and the battle site of **Peralejo**, resembles a roller-coaster.

The highway suddenly turns south towards the coast as it makes for Limones and Ariza where the terrain begins to take on a hillier appearance. These are the foothills of the large **Escambray Mountain Range**. Here the traffic becomes much heavier as one nears the large industrial centre of Cienfuegos city. Bridges cross the Salado river twice before the great Bay of Cienfuegos is seen in the distance. The road still behaves like a big-dipper through **sugar cane** and other agricultural fields until it joins up with the wide suburban carriageway. Join the *right-hand fork*, the road which enters the city from Palmira, which leads straight into the city centre.

Two bridges cross the inlet of the Bay of Cienfuegos, Ensenada el Ingles, or **English Cove** – the outlet of the Rio el Ingles. Out to the right just out of sight, is the historical **Naval Museum** on Cayo Loco. Stretching out to the right also, are the great **port developments**, sugar terminals – the first sugar mill here was constructed in 1751 – and fertiliser and cattle food plants. Before entering the city centre the road crosses the railway and, if Cienfuegos is not to be visited, one should make a left turning and connect with the Avenue 64, to drive via **Caonao** or, alter-

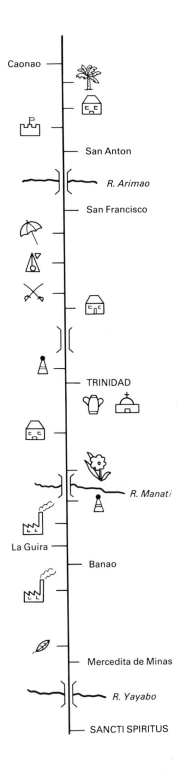

Caonao

San Anton

R. Arimao

San Francisco

TRINIDAD

R. Manati

La Guira

Banao

Mercedita de Minas

R. Yayabo

SANCTI SPIRITUS

247

Cienfuegos Cathedral

natively, for the prettier, but longer route around the bay and coast, turn *left* on the A 46 towards Hotel Rancho Luna, after the city's main shopping street.

The centre of **Cienfuegos** is easy to tour within a morning. The **Cathedral**, massive gateway in the attractive square, **Theatre Tómas Terry, Central Park**, with its statues and monuments and good shopping streets are all worth visiting. The one-and-a-half kilometre boulevard is heavily scented with Hibiscus and Bougainvillea blossom. A short drive should be made south of the city, along the Malecon to **Punta Gorda** and its opulent villas, **Museum of Decorative Arts** in Mogulesque style, Jagua Hotel and tiny marina. Just outside the city are several points of interest such as the famous **Botanical Gardens** and the '**National Labyrinth**', a fascinating valley of local tropical vegetation. One may even want to divert down to Hotel Pasacaballo overlooking the fort called **Jagua Castle**.

The preferable route via **Caonao**, over the Caonao River and up to the Botanical Gardens, is an exciting experience as it heads into the **Escambray Mountains**. The countryside becomes quite forested and, passing **San Anton**, dips sharply into the wide verdant valley of the significant Arimao River. Across the Arimao two more tributaries are crossed and several minor gulleys as the highway follows the river's old course and passes the township of **San Francisco**. Take the *right fork* after the quaint town and the road follows the line of least resistance around the skirting foothills of the mountain range.

With the **Caribbean Sea** coming into view on the right there are several roads leading off to the locally popular beaches of Playitas and La Tatagua. On the right again, an isolated hill is the site of a large **Pioneer Camp** – El Ismaelillo. Along this route also can be seen the roadside **monuments** and graves to those who fought against the counter-revolutionary bandits in the area. The coastal highway hugs the low, narrow strip of land under the towering mountain peaks to the left and passes more beach entrances, coves and little river inlets. Hotel Yaguanabo lies off to the left towards the spectacular valley of the same name. Fawn-grey

Trinidad

Ground Doves bask in the sun on the
metalled road and buzzards wheel above
expectantly.

Past the next river inlet and the **lighthouse** on the point to the right, the
highway crosses into Sancti Spiritus
Province after an attractive, bridged cove.
Here there is a **monument** to Dr. Manuel
Piti Fajardo, who died fighting counter-
revolutionary forces in 1960. More craggy
and jagged seascape follows until the road
crosses a river further inland, heads away
from the coast and bridges a wide, deep
valley before rising through cultivated land
on a more winding road. **La Boca
Anguilla**, a young people's camping ground
includes a local beach resort to the right.

A treasured workhorse

On a sharp bend in the tarmaced road,
to the right, can be seen the track leading
to the **memorial** to Alberto Delgado –
The man of Maisinicu, a spy in the counter-
revolutionary camp, murdered when he
was discovered, and hung from the tree
overshadowing the white monument. On
the hill in front can be seen the roofs of
Trinidad city.

Take the *left fork* just before the railway
to the centre of this gem of **colonial
architecture** with cobbled streets, cannon
as corner posts and ornamental antepecho
or wrought iron window guards. The main
square is a delight of colour with red tiles
and whitewashed walls setting off the
greens of silver-trunked Palms and Pink
Hibiscus blooms. Good restaurants make
this city a **gourmet's haven** and its four
main churches and four museums provide
the historian and explorer with at least a
day's activity discovering the city's background. Two hotels are in the city centre
but the most attractive is Motel Las
Cuevas, set on the hill overlooking the city
and surrounding countryside. Here, in the
evening, the rich scent of Jasmine and
Honeysuckle mingles with the sound of a
million crickets in the patio shrubbery
ushering in the tropical night.

Tearing oneself away from this tranquil
haven, set in the deep folds of the
Escambray Mountains, this miniature of
Spanish colonial history, preserved from

249

the ravages of time and oblivious to modern bustle, with one backward glance, the traveller takes the road out of Trinidad, past the Las Cuevas entrance. Along the edge of the city, the forest-lined highway strikes out past the track leading to the luxuriant **Valle de San Luis** and out into miles of sugar cane fields.

These are the great **plantations** dating back centuries to Spanish times. This broad plain is the fertile **delta** of the vast estuary of the **Manati River**. One gigantic triangle of sugar, watered by a hundred tributaries of the Caburni, Jibacoa, Jicaya, Mabujina, Caracuse and Unimazo Rivers. This cleft between the main Escambray Mountains and an isolated outcrop to the east, is one of the country's largest watersheds.

Don't miss the region's most important historical landmark, the 45 metre-high, **Tower of Iznaga**. This family ran the surrounding plantations of sugar cane and the ruins of their mansion can be seen if one detours left, off the highway, past a tiny hamlet and up towards the great tower. The huge structure was once the highest building in the land and was used as a vantage point from which to watch the slaves working in the 'sea' of cane fields. Fourteen sugar mills were owned here by the Iznaga family – today, further up the road from the ruins, is the newest development in the sugar cane industry, a **sugar pulp mill** which produces wood, chipboard and even building materials from the crop's waste. The new mill on the right of the road is a far cry from the ancient, slave-run presses of Iznaga.

Skirting the outcrop of mountains at the eastern point of the Escambray, the highway undulates across the sugar-clad plateau until the landscape rises to palm and cattle-dotted scrub with its little villages like La Guira. The larger settlement, **Banao**, further on, gets its name from the tall peaks on the left, a popular beauty spot. Well tarmaced, the highway over numerous streams, gullies, dried up streams and miniature canyons passes many **pig farms**. The cafe in **Mercedita de Minas**, a large, busy sugar-based settlement provides much needed refreshment. In this hilly countryside, with its microclimate of a mixed tropical – sub-tropical weather, it is more likely to rain in the afternoon – almost like clockwork. A cement factory and a works for metal component fabrication are passed after fenced in pastures and, like a glinting mirage, especially if it has been raining, the city of **Sancti Spiritus** gleams along the ridge in front.

Over its neat, ancient, hump-back bridge across the River Yayabo, the city presents facade after facade of an intricate assortment of architectural edifices. There must be a building in the large city which represents each minute era or slight change in fashion of building design, over several centuries. Its slightly jumbled aspect and curious city squares, churches and memorials give the place a jostled feel and, apart from these, there is little else to hold the interest of the traveller.

Trinidad Street

Sancti Spiritus – Ciego de Avila – Morón – Camagüey

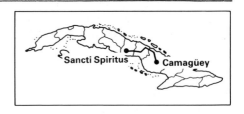

Leaving Sancti Spiritus the wide, tarmaced road stretches, a dusty, bumpy, ribbon, across a plain dotted with palms. The road runs through pastureland and over a flat bridge across the **Rio Zaza** past a cement factory set back off the road. After a cross-roads the target is the group of belching sugar stacks of the distant sugar mills, seen across a sea of cane. Only an occasional political hoarding and tiny, roadside **bohios**, or primitive housing made of palm and thatched with its leaves, breaks the monotony of the high plateau.

Jatibonico lies over the river of the same name and is dominated by the twin-stacked, sugar cane mill. Between the busy township of Jatibonico and Ciego de Avila, the plains are dense with sugar cane and road traffic, which at some times is comprised solely of tractors, trailers, cane lorries and harvesting machines. Today, 60 per cent of all cane harvested in Cuba is reaped by mechanical means. Workers travel to and from the fields in workman's huts carried on the back of trailers, these act as canteens when parked at the work

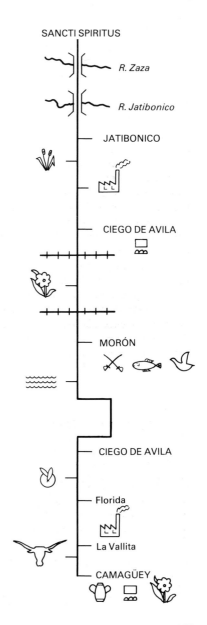

251

This region is famed for its architectural styles.

site. Some sugar cane is burned off before harvesting. This can create clouds of black smoke visible for miles, but it has the benefit of consolidating the sugar crystals in the remaining stalks of cane, making it easier to recover when crushed. The harvest time is known as the Zafra.

Ciego de Avila Province, indicated by a hoarding and undulating countryside with the odd poultry farm, is known as the **'land of the pineapple'**. Agricultural activity here is more diverse because of the change in soil. Banana, maize, juca and palm are common crops and the skyline is constantly punctuated by clumps of Royal Palm and the occasional Date Palm. Apart from the inevitable Vulture and common Dove, the birdlife appears scarce here, but in the oasis-like clumps of palm, hosts of little Finches can often be spotted. Motel Las Cañas and a large ranch are off the Hibiscus-lined route.

Passing a large **fruit cannery**, almost the trademark of this province, the road enters the city of **Ciego de Avila**, passing over a road and rail system. The wide main street is typical of the cities of central Cuba and colonnaded frontages are reminiscent of its mid-nineteenth century heritage. The Hotel Santiago-Havana on the left from the main street, has a good restaurant but is of slight tourist interest, as is the city itself. The **Principal Theatre** may be worth a swift visit but most tours will not hesitate here except for refreshment.

On the other side of town, the crossroads indicate a *left turn* to Morón past new apartment blocks, the city suburbs and the radio relay station. After an arable stretch, the college for training physical education teachers is the large building before the sign announcing Ciro Redondo municipality. The sign also relates to the movements of Camilo Cienfuegos' forces in the area during the 1958 struggles.

La Loma de Carolina – **Caroline's Hill**, is a small settlement in the plantations of **orange** and **lemon trees**. Sugar cane, again, can be seen stretching far out on the right. Like a huge ship riding a sea of green, a secondary school typifies the combination of agricultural activities and educational tution so prominent in rural areas. A railhead for the sugar train has more significance to the traveller than the huddle of small bungalows. Over the crossing is a tiny hut where, for ten centavos one can indulge in the **sweet cane juice drink** called *guarapo*. It is wise to let the ice melt in the yellow green liquor as it is really very sweet indeed! Cane fields dominate the landscape and more lorries, tractors and trucks are passed before entering the township of **Morón**.

The inevitable welcome sign here, proclaims that this is the land of both agriculture and industry, as opposed to the previous municipality which was entirely supported by the agricultural industry. Set in spacious grounds just before the town is Hotel Morón, a modern edifice, typical of twenty other similar hotels throughout Cuba. This small city is popular for its **fishing** and **hunting** exploits on the **Laguna de la Leche** or **Lake Redonda**. A railhead marks the centre of the city and, apart from the station building and a few sadly dilapidated colonial-style buildings there is little else to comment on in Morón. Just outside the Hotel Morón, which has all modern amenities, is a strange **obelisk**. Look closely at its base, in the centre of the boulevard, and one can see the old Spanish **rooster-clock**, which once dominated the spot. Interestingly enough, this is a good spot for a leisurely ride in a **horse-drawn taxi**, some of which appear to date from the mid-eighteenth century, the time of the city's foundation!

From Morón, it is better to take the road *back to* Ciego de Avila and join the Central Highway. Because this area, famous for the crossing from east to west of the revolutionary troops in 1958, is so flat, it is known locally as the **Camagüey Sabana**. The terrain of Carlos Manuel de Céspedes Municipality is scattered with village schools, orange groves and sugar fields before entering the town of Florida.

Florida is heralded by the giant Centrale Argentina, just on the town's outskirts. Off its small square is an INTUR office for travellers assistance. There is a gas station and, just over the hump-back bridge, is the Hotel Florida. **Sugar mills** overshadow the exit road from Florida, a two-stack mill in front and a three-stack mill on the right, just before the small airport. A dairy farm on the right and pig and chicken huts on either side of the road indicate the importance of husbandry in the region. The route passes **La Vallita**

village and the sign, with its giant clay pots, announces Camagüey – the city of the *tinajones*, or water jars.

The **Victory of Girón** cattle insemination breeding installation and **ranch** on the right, is the first real indication that this region is one gigantic pastureland. Another large cattle Empressa on the left is confirmation of the importance to this region of dairy and beef herds. Another two, new, Empressas are passed, after the radio station on the right and before the refinery, gas station and engineering factories on the city's suburban outskirts. **Camagüey's** first municipal structure on this road, is the Maternity Hospital on the right. Then comes the Pizzeria Bentornato almost opposite, a school, new apartments, the Mar Restaurant, a Cubatobacco factory and the Provincial Hospital. Then one is in **Agramonte Park** – the centre of Camagüey. Behind the park is the reconstructed 1530 **Cathedral** and nearby, the **Casa de Trova**, well worth a visit in the evening for its varied performances of local artistry.

A number of impressive structures have given the city the nickname 'the Corinth of the Caribbean' and its columns add great

A typical vaquero from the cattle country.

The 'Volanta' – an old Cuban mode of transport, sometimes known as 'Quitrin'.

architectural wealth to the pleasant city. Camagüey's patronship of the arts has also contributed to its fitting tag. Agramonte Square and its surrounds sport houses from several ages, museums, Ignacio Agramonte's birthplace, the beautiful **Ballet of Camagüey** company mansion, on the exit road, the **Palace of Justice** and the **Principle Theatre**. Hotels include the Colon, Grand and Camagüey, the latter is almost a replica of that at Morón. This prefabricated structure lies just east of the city and has the better facilities. Several interesting local restaurants dot the city. The **Cultural House**, (Tienda de Bienes Culturales, Avenue de la Libertad) is well worth a visit, if only to purchase a miniature of those intriguing **terracotta jars** which abound on street corners and in the quaint Spanish-style courtyards. The origin of these jars dates back to the Andalusians, Catalana and Galicians who lived in the ancient Camagüey in the early sixteenth century. These artisans formed the giant jars to store precious water and later, when the city moved from the dry region of Villa de Santa Maria del Puerto Principe, the jars served as oil containers and water butts.

Near to Camagüey are the famed **Cubitas Mountains** where dry canyons form gorges into the rocky range. **Paredones Passage**, here, is a particular tourist attraction and worth a detour from the highway to enjoy the spectacle of this 150-metre-high and two-kilometre-long ravine.

Camagüey – Nuevitas – Santa Lucia – Victoria de Las Tunas

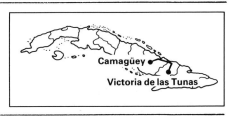

Out of the city of Camagüey the road runs 'as straight as an arrow' across the pastures and plains. On the left can be seen light industrial works, a vocational school and the city's new brewery. Take a *left fork* for the Nuevitas road marked by a large roadside hoarding announcing 'Welcome to the big country'.

Across, on the left, is a modern hospital and the railroad siding with warehousing for grain produce and stockyards. The **Ignacio Agramonte Airport** on the right precedes pastures and tracts of farmland. Watch how the dainty Coco Blanco, or **Egret** carefully follows the innocuous grazing head of its personal grass-beater. Small frogs and a multitude of insects are disturbed by the cattle and picked off by the darting bills of the long-necked white birds. The road follows the line of the railway, crossing it at **Altagracia** and into more wooded countryside. Just before Minas, the plain is dotted with chicken farms and small-holdings. Again the road crosses the rail at **Minas**, passing the famous **violin factory** on the outskirts of

CAMAGÜEY

Altagracia

NUEVITAS

San Miguel de Baga

Carbon

Palo Seco

Guaimaro

R. Jababo

Quique Maria

LAS TUNAS

the town on the left and heads out across more hilly terrain on a long, undulating route.

This is real cattle country and local cowboys, or **vaqueros**, are to be seen herding stock – mostly a **Brahma** cross or the successful FI strain. With their broad-brimmed hats pulled down over weather-beaten faces and long machetes dangling at their sides, the lasso curled on the beautifully groomed horses' flanks; the vaqueros makes a picturesque subject for the camera, typical of this rugged pasture-land.

The straight road continues almost due east until the smokestacks of **Nuevitas** can be seen on the far horizon. Silhouetted on the bluff which surrounds Nuevitas Bay, the busy industrial town advertises its assiduousness with a steady stream of heavy lorries transporting locally fabricated produce. A number of large cement works, light industrial factories and fertiliser plants complement the important fishing industry in this active port. It is not until one has passed **guava plantations** on the right, a large hospital on the hillside and new apartment blocks on the crest of the ring of hills, that one gets a view of the huge **harbour**.

Down a large, wide boulevard, bright with the ubiquitous Hibiscus, the main street heads for the dockside before turning sharply to the right, around the entrance to the Caonaba Hotel. Few travellers stop over at Nuevitas except for refreshment at the hotel's neat restaurant or to go up near the pretty town square with its huge **Baobab** tree. The square also has its neglected old church with gold dome, central cupola monuments, and corner cafe. Nuevitas is well-known for being the site of Cuba's largest thermo-electric power stations and for its plentiful **fishing waters** which attract sportsmen from all over Cuba.

Retracing the route back out of Nuevitas the *left hand fork* towards the resort of Santa Lucia skirts Nuevitas Bay across dry scrubland and cattle pasture. Dry stream beds are crossed and some marshy areas with ponds and waterholes where one can spot an interesting selection of wildfowl and waders, **Herons** and **Hawks**. On the left can be seen the ancient sugar mill which was the site of General Agramonte's extensive plantation. The road forks a little way after the mill ruins and, taking *the left*, towards the coast, a small cemetery is passed on the left with its impressive stone gateway. Here, occasionally, along the roadside, it is possible to find the curious, cabbage-shaped, flabby flower of the rare **Silk Plant**.

The road then runs through the tiny town of **San Miguel de Baga**, past its new apartment blocks on the outskirts and, taking a *left fork* again, the carriageway spins out over a vast plain. The scenery alternates between cattle grazing and small cultivated patches of tomato and squash. Nearing the coast the road becomes dusty and is lined with Marabou scrub and thickets. Bouncing over the potholes and avoiding the little fawn Doves dustbathing in the road, the smell of salt air indicates that the **Atlantic Ocean** is not far away. A sign announces 'Playa Santa Lucia' just before a large pioneer camp on the Punta de Yanado. Many small bungalows indicate that this **resort** is as popular with the Cuban holiday makers as it is with the Canadians and Europeans who flock here year after year. The beach reaches out past Residential la Concha, Tararacos Hotel, and past the Mayanabo Hotel and Villa Bahamas. Its duck-egg-blue sea defies accurate description, as its shades fluctuate through the kingfisher colours. Palms and Hibiscus add an exotic touch to the white sands and greenswards neatly laid out around the cabin-shaped, wood-walled, villas and red-tiled chalets.

Gaily painted tractors towing **passenger trolleys** offer a quaint mode of transport between villas and restaurants along the beach road, and other forms of motorised vehicle or pedal cycles can be hired. The Hotel Mayanabo's Azul Cielo restaurant is famed for its **black bean soup** and its bars offer an exciting selection of tropical refreshments after the long drive. The inviting waters, however, are the main lure and it is guaranteed the traveller will take but a few minutes to check in to the hotel, before plunging into Santa Lucia's warm,

Old US and USSR lorries work together!

languid ocean or limpid green pool.

From this delicious resort one back-tracks, along the dusty road, past wide salt flats tinged with the pink brilliance of flocks of **Flamingos** and waterfowl. Turn *right* at the roundabout at the end of the beach and the road follows the freshwater pipeline through the tiny settlement of *Carbon*, or charcoal-burner's cottages. Goats clamber over everything and from the nearby mangrove swamps come little Pigeons, Doves and the comical, black **Toti Bird**. Past **banana** plantations the route heads out across ploughed country-side dotted with palms and palmetto. Waterholes surrounded by wild-looking cattle and stockyards break the flat monotony until the cross-roads before **San Miguel**.

Leave San Miguel's pink and green apartment buildings on the right and head back on yourself across the plain once again. Two mountain peaks abruptly break the broad, expansive skyline in the distance and the roadside becomes dotted with **mango** plantations and more deciduous growth. The low mountain range of **Loma la Deseada** on the right is scarred by track marks on its sandy flank but the straight highway speeds past its foothills to more orderly pastureland, fenced with **Jocuma** boughs.

After crossing the rail track at **Palo Seco** the area becomes more palmed, and vegetable patches indicate a better class of soil. **Guaimaro** is quite a sizeable town with well kept streets and neat, clean, painted houses. A huge hoarding of

Ernesto 'Ché' Guevara dominates the cross-roads where one turns *left* towards the town centre. At the bus station on the right, refreshments consist of *Chia*, or tea and *pina fria* – a kind of frozen drink made from natural essence of pineapple, served from a roadside trolley – '*sabroso!*', excellent! Down a pretty tree-lined avenue after the bus station, the national Guaimaro Hotel leads off to the right, then the built-up area is left behind for more open pastureland.

Rio Jobabo marks the border of Camagüey Province and the beginning of

La Caldosa soup. Made from a selection of vegetables and chicken, herbs and spices, this dish has become noted throughout Cuba and few can pass by without sampling this savoury sensation and Maria's excellent black coffee. Tear yourself away from the temptation of having an extra bowlful and carry on down the highway into **Victoria de Las Tunas** city immediately in front.

On the left is a nightclub made from a **long-disused aircraft**, just after a charcoal, a cement and a huge cattle fodder factory. Las Tunas is named the 'City of

Las Tunas. Spot the last gigantic clay pot signifying Camagüey and the signpost welcoming the visitor to Las Tunas Province. **Tamarind** trees line the roadside and each settlement appears to cultivate at least one of these attractive and useful giants. The rich arable land makes a rewarding change from the flat, dry pasture plains of Camagüey's savanna and here there are more signs of habitation and farm cottages.

Look out for the famous roadside restaurant – **Quique Marina**, on the right. Pull in to meet the celebrated couple and try a delicious bowl of their secret recipe

Sculptures'. This is endorsed by roadside artworks, especially near the tiny, pretty central park area. The **group of sculptures** shaded by trees, on the right as the road does a sharp turn, is set off by a small fountain and groups of people sitting on benches and strolling in the little park. Hotel Las Tunas is on a hill on the left on the city's outskirts. The city has been known as Victoria de las Tunas in more recent years, a relic, re-introduced, of a famous battle victory. Although attractive, the city itself has no special claim to fame and warrants only a short stop-over.

Victoria de Las Tunas – Holguín – Guardalavaca – Bayamo

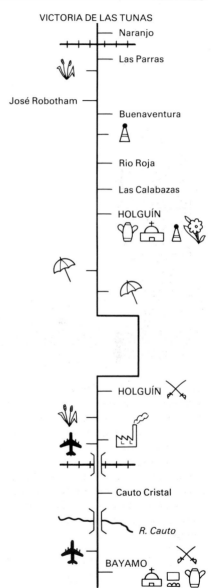

VICTORIA DE LAS TUNAS
— Naranjo
— Las Parras
José Robotham —
— Buenaventura
— Rio Roja
— Las Calabazas
— HOLGUÍN
— HOLGUÍN
— Cauto Cristal
— R. Cauto
BAYAMO

Passing Las Tunas Hotel on the left and the city's industrial centre on the other side of the road, the N1 highway continues past a hospital and busy intersection towards Holguín. The low, flat plain road extends out past a gravel quarry on the right and through a wooded section of countryside into Majibacoa municipality.

After a poultry farm on the left, the tiny town welcomes with a plethora of Bougainvillia and Colonia flowers brightening up its main street. Here, the neat roadside houses are gaily painted and the omnipresent Committee for the Defence of the Revolution building, with unfurled, red, white and blue flag flying from the mast above a bust of José Marti, gleams with a fresh coat of white paint. On the hillside is the little village school and it is here that one might see schoolchildren, 'two-up', on horseback, without a saddle, books clasped under arms, making the long journey from the farmhouse to the new school building.

The lumber mill appears to be the town's only industry until one passes a large asphalt plant, pig and poultry houses and a dairy farm. Sugar plantations with clumps of palm are interspersed with scrub and bush, banana plots and pastureland. After another lumber mill the road enters **Naranjo** with its small-holdings, rail crossing and the huge sugar Centrale of Majibacoa. Further on, the highway passes through good farmland. Fenced pastures vie with pig farms, chicken breeding estates and tiny settlements. After crossing the railway and passing through **Las Parras** there is a vast **quarry** on the hillside called **Cantera**, or the 'Mountain of Stone'. Before one has time to take in the change of scenery the road has taken you through the village of **José Robotham** and into Holguín Province, marked by a huge sign and massive **cog-wheel** from some ancient sugar mill.

More colourful signs promote the various attributes of the province and extoll the achievements of its vivid history. The countryside then becomes quite wooded and hilly. Oxen, their horns minus the pointed, two or three centimetres, as protection against the damaging of hides, graze by the roadside. Tethered to a tree, to a mate or just hobbled, **oxen** are put to graze on every available patch of pasture. Another little settlement, **Buenaventura**, presents the traveller with its boulevard of flowering shrubs, neat, one-storey houses and carefully whitewashed José Marti bust. This village also has a central reservation to its pretty main street, with a large **bronze statuette** to the Independence War hero, Major General Calixto Garcia, native of Holguín Province.

Holguín city from Loma de la Cruz

A large farming cooperative at **Rio Roja** caters for all types of agricultural activity from banana and vegetable production, to dairy husbandry and egg farming. The soil here looks excellent and, considering the patchwork of fields, is heavily worked and put to all kinds of produce. Just after **Las Calabazas** – 'the pumpkin village', the road runs into hillier countryside with pinewoods and small, cultivated valleys to the left. Orchards and small-holdings grace the roadside as the highway nears Holguín city.

More housing, a model farm on the right and warehouses, indicate the city suburbs, then the larger buildings announce the metropolis proper. A sugar cane machinery factory, the old military garrison which is now a technical school, (all military establishments like this at Holguín, were made into educational institutes after the triumph of the Revolution in Cuba), the University of Technology on the left and an agricultural tool store, all indicate the prosperity and importance of **Holguín**, one of Cuba's most influential centres.

Portraits of famous internationalists are emblazoned on a huge hoarding before the bus station and radio installation. On the

left is the School of Medicine and, suddenly, one is in the centre of Holguín city and its busy thoroughfares. Holguín is an attractive city in many ways. Not only does it have its own charm with historic squares, colonial colonnades and ancient sites, but Holguín is the base for enjoying the spectacular surroundings which include mountain and beach, forest and valley.

Many historians believe that Holguín was the original site of the Indian township called, as Columbus relates, **Cubanacan**. This was, supposedly, one of the first settlements to be visited by the Spanish colonists. Evidence has been uncovered on **Loma de la Cruz**, the Hill of the Cross, overlooking the city, of primitive habitation. This also is the location of the mid-nineteenth century find, the Indian **Holguín Axe**, a treasured exhibit of the municipal museum.

A host of interesting sites and spectacular vistas surround Holguín. The **Mayabe Lookout, José Marti Park** and the enticing beaches lie to the north. A day or two can be spent exploring the city and its environs from the modern Hotel Pernik, the Mirador de Mayabe outside the city or Hotel Turquino in the city centre. Everywhere, around the built-up areas, Rhododendron and Magnolia blossom enhance the road side. Holguín boasts an exotic Polynesian restaurant and several excellent cafés and bars. Its heritage is centred on many battle legends and their heros, such as **Calixto Garcia**, whose birthplace is in the centre of the city and whose name is carried by the huge stadium on the outskirts of town.

Driving towards the stadium one passes the Children's Hospital and heads out to the east past the Pernik, the New Red Square and Communist Party headquarters, the new Physical Training Teacher's University below, on the main road and the Vocational Military School. There is no signpost to **Guardalavaca**, but turn *right* at the second roundabout after the Pernik and follow the mainstream of traffic over the crest of a hill until two,

pointed mountain peaks are seen in the distance.

The road undulates through interesting countryside dotted with cattle stations and chicken farms, passing a low, hilly peak to the left and then between two more mountains. Steep pitons, or conical, karst-type outcrops punctuate the landscape before the giant Rafael Freyre Sugar Mill, the municipality sign for **Rafael Freyre** and **Minas de Melones**. The road condition alternates between bad and good as it makes for the coast through rolling hills and to the coastal plain. Out to the left are two sugar Centrale smokestacks and a politico-economic sign fronts a large cattle station before the road crosses the railway. More sugar fields, and picturesque rocky cones, before the sign for Playa Pesquero and the first indication that the sea is near.

Before long, on a small ridge, is the first sign for **Guardalavaca** and, skirting a small wood, the first glimpse of a sea inlet and wooded island below to the left. A few more kilometres of sugar fields and a giant hoarding declares 'Guardalavaca', just after the municipality signpost for Banes. Follow the road down past the wood-clad bay on the left and turn *right*, off the main route to Hotel Guardalavaca where cattle graze with sleek horses, on the smart hotel's greens.

Vivid greens and blues of the palms, shrubs, sea and sky, are a feast for the eyes after the 53-kilometre drive from Holguín. Bright paintwork, tiled roofs and the brilliance of Hibiscus bloom add dashes of primary reds and yellows, contrasting with the gaily decorated signs. Even the restaurant here has a nautical flavour, with waitresses dressed in sailor-type uniforms, and nets, coral and marine ornaments surround the reception desk. The sea, and the amazing, white sand, are the attractions at Guardalavaca and every activity on water as well as land-based sports can be enjoyed at this, one of Cuba's most famous coastal resorts. Take a good, long look at the sea before departing on the next leg of the journey to Bayamo – the next hundred or so kilometres of highway is cross-country.

Returning, from Guardalavaca to Holguín, the landscape seems somehow more craggy from the east-west road. Pocket agriculture clings to the hillside, as do the scanty habitations of local farmers. Through banana and cane plantations the route comes out onto the flat plain with the mountain range near Holguín in the far distance. Serpentine rocks of amazing hue show clear evidence that the region is abundant in **mineral wealth** – chrome, nickel and copper. Here, **cactus fences** protect the small homesteads from straying oxen and cattle.

Across to the right, below a small bluff, the remains of an ancient, abandoned **sugar cane train** can be made out from the shape of the vegetation which has overgrown it. Back in the spectacular, conical mountain scenery the road cuts through gullies and rises and falls over rocky crests and into deep cuttings. Odd-shaped **ox-carts** can be seen plying the side tracks. The curious curved, bark-covered hood on massive wheels appears not to hinder the dual-yoked oxen with their impassive, consigned heads bowed in heavy leather bridles. Chicken dash from beneath the wheels of cars and turkeys strut along the roadsides where more oxen are tethered with saddled horses. The sparse green grass, lies clumped in patches in the shade of Royal Palms or near glinting irrigation channels.

A large hillside, passed on the right, has been decorated with the pebbled words **'No Pasaran' 'Viva Fidel'**, above a little community of huts tenuously teetering on the steep slope. This slogan can be seen the length and breadth of the country – a favourite by-word. If this highway is taken at the week-end the amount of traffic can be staggering as, seemingly, the entire population of Holguín Province heads for the coast. Motorbikes, mopeds, cars and lorries, coaches, trucks and tractors, horses, oxen, bicycles and hitchhikers are passed if one is travelling against the stream on a

Saturday or Sunday!

Arriving again at the outskirts of Holguín the *left fork* must be taken after the Hotel Pernik. A severe **bronze bust** of Maximo Gómez is passed to the right and the ring road carries on past new apartments and the Physical Training College. The University is on the left opposite the Teachers Training School with its tall, white, water tower. Just past the entrance to José Marti Park a tower has been christened *'Feria'*, or 'Fair'. After a new paper mill a roadsign directs to Bayamo, and another factory for manufacturing cane-cutting machinery is passed at a junction where the road doubles upon itself to join the Bayamo highway.

The blue-and-white buildings of the municipal services, with a uniformly painted water tower is on the right, and on the left are the neat cottages of the garden suburb, each with its own huge **water butt** at the base of its neatly-tended frontage. **Frank Pais Airport** is passed on the right and the long wall, stretching for many kilometres, is the boundary of a military training establishment. A semi-built-up area follows before canefields and then a bridge across the railway. Heading almost due south now, the route passes cool-looking, palm-thatched dwellings – each with their own fridge, radio or television, sewing machine and group of framed portraits of family, relations and revolutionary leaders.

During the Zafra, or cane harvest, flocks of white Cattle Egrets can be seen following the great cane cutters as they rumble across the vast sea of sugar, spitting out the measured lengths of stalk and disturbing thousands of insects for the dainty bird to pounce on. Soon, the rock-built sign for **Granma Province** is reached. Its gateway-style arch supporting a large bronze bell, symbol of the Province, and representing the giant sugar estates of hero Carlos Manuel de Céspedes.

At **Cauto Cristo** the highway crosses Cuba's longest river, the **Rio Cauto** – 370 kilometres long, and then follows a small canyon or bed of an ancient, dried-up river. Through the small settlements of Babiney and Cauto Cristo, the vague smudge in the haze to the left is the first glimpse of the jagged backbone of the **Sierra Maestra Range**. Nearing Bayamo, the road skirts the mountain foothills where cattle graze on the yellowing grasslands and the **Brigade of Granma Aerodrome** used for agricultural 'planes in irrigation or fertilising exercises is passed on the right. A flying-training school is also passed before Manuel de Céspedes airport.

Suddenly one is in **Bayamo city**, passing a theatre on the right and taking the *right fork* at the gas station, down through a picturesque boulevard dripping with brilliant flowers from the **Tulip and Flame trees** on the central reservation. Follow the main street past gaily painted, pastel-shaded houses to José Marti Street, the small gardens with statues and the ruined bell-tower of San Juan Evangelista.

This historic city is rich in **monuments and architectural gems**. Since its

Sierra Maestra Hotel, Bayamo

foundation, early in the 16th century, the strategic importance of Bayamo has lent a legacy to the city which is probably unrivalled in any other Cuban city of its size. Most of the names associated with the emergence and development of the nation are commemorated here somewhere. From Carlos Manuel de Céspedes' birthplace to the castellated gates of the city barracks and the ancient **Church of San Salvador**, there is always something new to discover in and around this delightful southern city.

The Hotel Sierra Maestra offers all the comforts for the traveller of the most modern hotel and, apart from the dated Hotel Royalton, is the best base for visits in the town and its outskirts. **Horse-drawn carriages** here allow the visitor to lapse back into the lazy days of the mid-19th century, especially in the environs of the charming **Céspedes Park** in the centre of Bayamo. A little zoo in the park boasts a host of endemic animals and birds, and provides amusements for both adults and children.

Bayamo commemoration

Leaving Cuba's second city, the road, which leads past the Moncada Garrison, hospital buildings, and the University of Oriente, climbs through new apartment developments. Passing more sights, and looking down on the **City Stadium**, one gets a fine view of the metropolis' layout, and its giant harbour. Clefts and ravines near the road, are cut through the rock face of yellows, reds and browns. Through more gulleys, the highway drops down to the bamboo-lined, silver ribbon of a small river, before climbing again to a ridge, affording spectacular views of the **Sierra Maestra** peaks.

Crossing a river gorge over the **Yaragabo**, tributary of the mighty Rio Cauto, the road narrows, and the rock appears chalky, and then becomes similar to a sandstone in the more open countryside. A large bridge crosses the important rail route, where massive **sugar trains** can be viewed, plying the track from the south's huge cane fields to the Santiago refineries. Occasionally, these marvellous old steam engines tote a load of more than 20 of the long cane-piled wagons. Entering **San Luis** municipality the road diverts left, before reaching the town, with its **comical hoardings** of welcome, depicting cartoon sugar trains. Pass a newly-constructed egg farm and cross a small gorge, and the road climbs over low hills scattered with neat little settlements, small-holdings, banana plantations, and ox-grazing pasture. The road begins to wind almost unconcernedly across more hills and over pretty gorges and ravines. **Orange** groves appear alongside the rail track before passing La Gloria bar on the

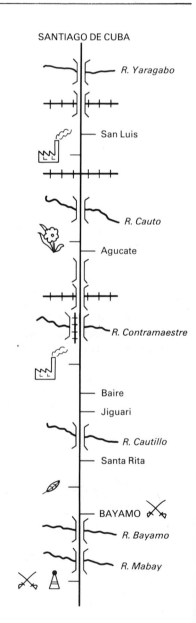

SANTIAGO DE CUBA

R. Yaragabo

San Luis

R. Cauto

Agucate

R. Contramaestre

Baire

Jiguari

R. Cautillo

Santa Rita

BAYAMO

R. Bayamo

R. Mabay

right, and entering the important township of **Palma Soriano**.

Apart from being a centre for sugar, a significant crossroads and rail head, **Palma Soriano** has many claims to fame from the past, during independence struggles. A policlinic is next to the suburban road before a little, quaintly-shaped church, on the right, and the town square. Here, the Praga cafeteria, shops and cinema, offer shade under the watchful gaze of **José Marti monument**. Leaving the square, the pediatric hospital is on the right, as is the giant Dos Rios Sugar Centrale, just after crossing the Rio Cauto, and an agricultural equipment factory is on the opposite side of the road. After a large cattle station to the right, the road passes the turn-off to the famous Motel Mirabel – Motel Valle de Tayaba – a delightful country attraction in the midst of the mountain range.

The following stretch of highway, runs between the two great rivers of the **Cauto** and the **Contramaestre**, and follows a ridge with good views of **orange groves** and palm-forested landscape, before passing through the hamlet of **Aguacate**, over a girder bridge, and out towards more checkered agricultural fields. In **Palma** municipality there are a series of small settlements, sugar fields, and a pretty **gorge**, before a clump of huge **Baobab** trees on the right. After a small hamlet and more sugar cane, a concrete bridge is crossed onto flatter land, continuing on through a culvert and past a large power station. Crossing the railway again, past

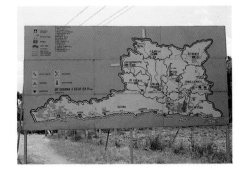

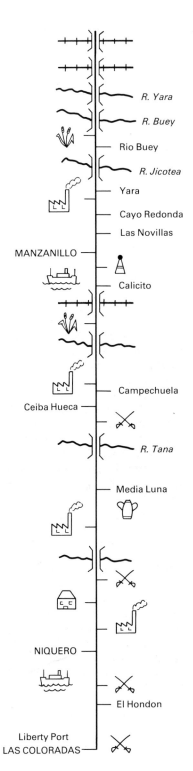

R. Yara

R. Buey

Rio Buey

R. Jicotea

Yara

Cayo Redonda

Las Novillas

MANZANILLO

Calicito

Campechuela

Ceiba Hueca

R. Tana

Media Luna

NIQUERO

El Hondon

Liberty Port
LAS COLORADAS

even more sugar fields, and the road twins with the rail bridge, to cross the deep **canyon** of the Contramaestre River.

Immediately one is in the flowering suburbs of **Contremaestre town**, with its apartment blocks, large new hospital on the hill to the left, and signs to the big Centrale of America Libre. Another girder bridge leads over the river gorge and out, to a straight stretch of highway, through small settlements, orange groves, wooded land, and past a cattle feed factory.

Before **Baire** township, a tiny river precedes the pine-lined avenue through neat rows of houses, and their evidence of historic associations with the second revolution. After a tiny cemetery, the route crosses the railway, passing the micro-brigade houses, and enters palm and pastureland of the Province of Granma. More orange groves indicate the fine quality of the soil as the deep-clefted foothills are reached.

This is the northern flank of the great Sierra Maestra Range and, just inside Granma Province, is the town of **Jiguani** on the Rio Cautillo. Over the river bridge is the Restaurant Cautillo, stop for refreshment before heading out over flattish farmland on the fertile plain. **Santa Rita** marks the site of two 19th century battles. A country school rides, like a stranded ship, on the cooperative farmland, as the railway parallels with the road for the final few kilometres before Bayamo city. The city's industrial suburbs have metal works, prefabricated concrete factory, and textile works near the electrical sub-station and storage depots.

Past the Simon Bolivar School and sports Training College, on the left, the main route should be taken through Bayamo and out past the Cubana Café on the right. Carry on to the Sierra Maestra Hotel if it is intended to view the city with a night's stopover. The streets here are resplendent with **Oleander** and **Azalea blooms**, often shrouded with bright yellow butterflies.

Carrying on to Manzanillo, one should cross the **Rio Bayamo**, a lilly-choked stream at the foot of a deep gorge, following the rail bridge and passing many **pumpkin** fields, heading out to the west. This well-worked, fertile area, obviously supplies vegetables, fruit, beef and eggs for the city – the **municipal nursery** is passed on the left with its radiant display of flowers and shrubs in every hue.

Over the tiny Rio Mabay, the road begins to rise across the plain, past chicken farms and open pasture. The large structure on the left is the **Jorge Dimitrov Higher Institute for Agriculture and Dairy Farming** – an important establishment in agricultural research, and respected world-wide for its international standards. On the right is a small artificial lake and a little hamlet. Look for the roadside **monument** to the hero Antonio Maceo – a brave 'Mambi'. This is the site of a major independence victory for the southern leader – Peralejo.

After the railheads of Julia and Bueycito, the road joins the Manzanillo highway at **Barranca**. Here, at the municipality of Yara, with its star symbol hoardings and many schools, the railway is again crossed, next to a deep canyon. This is the **Yara River**, a most important source of water for this most southerly of Cuba's peninsulas. Many of the country's rivers do not appear very impressive in their narrow gorges, because the headwaters have usually been dammed and reservoirs created for irrigation and electricity. Over another river the Rio Buey, or Ox River, near the girder bridge, turn immediately *right*, past the Technical Training University, and through **Rio Buey** town. Its wide boulevard is covered with flowering Colonia and Tulipanroco shrubs. Busts of General Rabi head the avenue bearing his name, which practically spans the length of the small town. A sugar Centrale, guava plantations, Guanabana trees and more sugar fields, precede the bridge over the **River Jicotea**.

After the large town of **Yara** with its fruit cannery on the right, and the baseball stadium and political square to the left, the countryside suddenly opens out into vast flat fields or **rice** intersected with drainage channels. **Wildfowl hunters** can be seen stalking game birds, and fishermen look 'frozen' near irrigation streams, the only buildings in view seem to be rice packing stations.

Las Novillas is the first town over the border into Manzanillo municipality after passing through Cayo Redondo and its quarry on the small bluff out of town. Las Novillas' signboard proclaims it to be 'the town where independence started – the birthplace of independence'. A Taino machinery spares factory, on the right, precedes **Vuelta del Canyo** town. This has a fish shop – the first sign of nearing the coast, a school, factories and a dairy with hoardings of Camilo Cienfuegos, Ernesto 'Che' Guevara and local heroine, Celia Sanchez who was born in the province. Turn *left* at the next junction, past an agricultural equipment depot, and pass through Blanquizal town, just before entering **Manzanillo** proper.

The University entrance is on the left and, over undulating hillside, the road passes the Polytechnic and the airport. Celia Sanchez Hospital is just before the agricultural airstrip, on the right and, passing the **pioneer camp**, detouring the city to the left, the road affords a magnificent view of Manzanillo town, and its beautiful bay, across **Juca** fields. A stop-over in this town could include overnight at the well-appointed Guacanayabo Hotel or just a meal in its superb restaurant. A wooded area of palms and pines leads down, on the outskirts of the city, to the Demajagua Sugar Mill which once was the property of Carlos Manuel de Céspedes.

After chicken farms and small, enclosed fields on the chalky soil, the hamlet of Calicito is passed, with **stockyards**, railroad and bridge which leads into **Campechuela** municipality. In the distance to the left, is the great Sierra Maestra range again. On the high plateau, the road crosses a small river and the soil becomes reddish before one arrives in **Campechuela** town. A bookstore, baseball stadium, sugar cane juice store and cafeteria comprise the small town's shops. The bookstore, which doubles as a gift shop, is well worth a visit, being just off the main street.

Continuing out of town, the sea comes into view, across **sweet potato** and **banana** fields. To the right is the bulk sugar terminal for sea-going tankers and, at the end of a row of hillocks to the left, the highway passes the entrance to a social club. The one-stack, Centrale San Ramon presents a towering silhoutte after the miniscule port of Ceiba Hueca. As the road turns inland, more **rice** fields are encountered and, on the left, the site of Manuel Marquez murder during the last Revolution. From the plateau, the road drops, to skirt the looming outline of the **Sierra Maestra**. Across a bridge over the **Tana River** one enters Media Luna (Half Moon) municipality. Over the sugar cane, the sea can be glimpsed in the distance, and one can make out another, twin-stacked sugar Centrale, before the radio masts which welcome the visitor to the town itself.

Media Luna is one of the most typical little townships in the region. British technology assisted in the fabrication of the animal foodstuffs factory on the left and, to the right, is a modern baseball stadium. Turn *left* at the road junction in the town and continue past an expanding sugar Centrale, over a small river and into the wide, main boulevard. Right in the

'Gingerbread' house, Media Luna

centre of the town is the old 1908, green painted, chapel-style house which is the **birthplace of Celia Sanchez Manduley**. She was a longtime companion of Fidel Castro throughout the Revolution and in the ensuing peace. Celia Sanchez, 1920–1980, not only acted as lieutenant and secretary to the leader, but also companion on exercises and excursions, reconnoitres and affrays. The house has a superb tiled floor, a garden brimming with Chirimoya, Caimito and Mango fruit, and is now a most interesting museum of the revolutionary period. This town is also the site of the first sugar mill, El Carmen, 1884, and Isabel, 1886, built by the Englishman Beattie Brooks. Bisected by the river, therefore Half Moon, the town has a history going back to Spanish times. It now produces **honey** and **charcoal** products.

Continuing through the town, past a secondary school, the road keeps to the coast past sugar fields and a recently constructed agrochemical works. A small **plaque** on the roadside, commemorates another event linked with the Céspedes uprising, and the large signpost indicates entry into Niquero municipality. A junction on the left leads to Marea del Portillo Hotel, but continue past a sand quarry, on the right, before reaching the port of **Niquero** itself. Here the road forks past a machinery depot and, keeping on the *left*, across a flat plain, the road passes a junction to Alegria de Pio. This is the site of the first **battle** encountered by the occupants of the yacht *Granma* in 1956, three days after the landing. Keep an eye out in Niquero for some really fascinating examples of **stone façades** and elaborate wooden buildings. The little church, just off the main street, is interesting, as are the stores along the central colonnade.

As the road returns to the countryside, with tomato, sweet potato, and sugar fields, the area is known as las Coloradas region, and a little further it becomes Guanito municipality. **El Hondon** is a tiny village with a **thatched church**, neat little roadside gardens and brilliant flower

'Granma' landing memorial, Las Coloradas

beds. Guayaba, with its mango plantations, is a tiny settlement, but sports a large billboard commemorating the landing of the yacht *Granma*. The road now nears the journey's end, and almost the furthest point south in the whole island. Orange, Lemon, Nispero, Guanabana, Tamarind, Mandarin and Banana trees, stress the fact that this region is indeed a tropical garden. The sea-shore road passes a small quarry and a coconut plantation before the sign 'Las Coloradas'.

Turn *left* after the signpost, down to the beachside hotel, with its open-air restaurant, snug bar and ten, fully equipped, bungalow-style cabins. Almond and Uvachaleta Sea Grape, mix with the waving fronds of tall Coconut Palms, and their trunks are knee-deep in flowering plants and Hibiscus blooms. The sea is the colour of a flock of competing Peacocks, the fine sand a brighter white than freshly cut coconut and the sky a paintpot blue.

Cormorants perch on the gaunt 'bones' of an abandoned wreck and Heron stalk the foaming surf.

This is the base for visits to the **Liberty Port**, memorial of the *Granma* landings, just a short drive down the coast. The little, thatched reception unit caters for streams of national and international tourists, who flock to make the pilgrimage to this most revered of modern historical spots in Cuba. Once a tiny fishing hamlet, **Las Coloradas** is now being enlarged to accommodate the anticipated growth in custom. Its idyllic setting contrasts poignantly with the stark devastation in the mangrove swamps of the landing site, where bombers attacked the small band of revolutionaries in early December 1956. Now the **Booby** and **Albatross** wheel overhead, shadowing the **Terns** as they skim the waves, picking off the shoals of **Flying Fish**.

Guide to distances

Bus and taxi travel is the only way to get around the cities and towns, although some areas boast a horse-drawn carriage service and Havana is developing an underground railway system. More information about regions, provinces and towns, plus detailed maps can be obtained from Cubatur representatives in every area of the country.

Travelling around the country is easiest by car. Rentals of all sizes from 'jeepney', to air-conditioned saloon, can be arranged through Cubatur or Havanatur. Bus travel is second choice. The country bus system covers the entire island and long-distance buses are comparatively fast. Train travel is probably the slowest, a network spans the length of the island. The Havana to Santiago de Cuba express takes 18 – 20 hours, to cover the distance of 972 kilometres.

Air travel should be booked well in advance and schedules for domestic flights should be checked with Cubatur.

Boat excursions and regular ferry services are available in most parts of the island.

Long-distance taxis, motorcycles and bicycles can be hired by the hour or day.

The chart gives the distances from Havana to the main towns.

Town or City	Distance from Havana (kilometres)
Pinar del Rio	182
Viñales	210 (from Pinar del Rio 28)
Soroa	89
Nueva Gerona (Isle of Youth)	153
Matanzas	102
Cayo Largo	186 (from Varadero 268)
Varadero	144 (from Matanzas 42)
Guamá	208 (from Matanzas 101)
Girón	253 (from Matanzas 144)
Cienfuegos	296
Santa Clara	301
Sancti Spiritus	381
Trinidad	451 (from Sancti Spiritus 69)
Ciego de Avila	462
Morón	502 (from Ciego de Avila 40)
Camagüey	572
Nuevitas	652 (from Camagüey 90)
Santa Lucia Beach	666 (from Camagüey 94)
Victoria de Las Tunas	696
Holguín	773
Guardalavaca	862 (from Holguín 89)
Moa	945 (from Holguín 172)
Bayamo	845
Manzanillo	910 (from Bayamo 65)
Las Coloradas	1037 (from Bayamo 192
Guantánamo	1058
Baracoa	1178 (from Guantánamo 120)
Santiago de Cuba	972

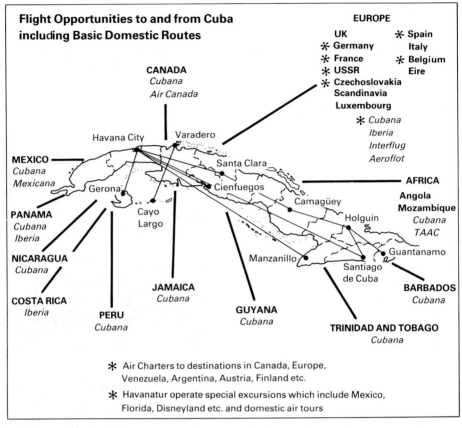

Flight Opportunities to and from Cuba including Basic Domestic Routes

EUROPE

UK   * Spain
* Germany   Italy
* France   * Belgium
* USSR   Eire
* Czechoslovakia
Scandinavia
Luxembourg

* *Cubana*
Iberia
Interflug
Aeroflot

CANADA
Cubana
Air Canada

Havana City   Varadero

MEXICO
Cubana
Mexicana   Gerona

Santa Clara

Cienfuegos

AFRICA

Angola
Mozambique
Cubana
TAAC

Camagüey

Holguín

PANAMA
Cubana
Iberia

Cayo
Largo

NICARAGUA
Cubana

Manzanillo

Guantanamo

Santiago
de Cuba

COSTA RICA
Iberia

JAMAICA
Cubana

BARBADOS
Cubana

PERU
Cubana

GUYANA
Cubana

TRINIDAD AND TOBAGO
Cubana

* Air Charters to destinations in Canada, Europe, Venezuela, Argentina, Austria, Finland etc.

* Havanatur operate special excursions which include Mexico, Florida, Disneyland etc. and domestic air tours

Excursions from Cuba

Trips and excursions can be made from the island, either inclusive of a Cuban visit, or in addition to a pre-paid stay in the country. México, Cancun, Panama, Florida, Miami and Disneyland are among the favourite short-term visits from Havana. These can be arranged most economically through Cubatur, their agents or Havanatur either in, or before arriving in Cuba. Other destinations for sightseeing tours include Yucatán, Jamaica, The Bahamas, The Cayman Islands and even as far south as Barbados and South America.

CHAPTER 10

Information, useful addresses and phrases

'The basic thing is not only to grow, but to know in what direction we are growing and for what purpose.'

FIDEL CASTRO RUZ

Commercial hints and conferences

MINCEX, the Ministry of Foreign Trade, is responsible for the policies followed by the various responsible organisations, or Empresas. Each Empresa deals with a sector of trade. These State Trading Organisations are represented in most countries, and details can be obtained by contacting the Cuban Commercial Counsellor at the nearest Embassy or Consulate.

Correspondence should be in Spanish and the addresses of MINCEX are:
Ministerio del Comercio Exterior,
Ministry of Foreign Trade,
Infanta 16,
Havana,
Cuba.
Telex: 511174–511175

Camara de Commercio de la República de Cuba,
Calle 21 No. 661,
Vedado,
Havana,
Cuba.
P.O. Box 370,
Telephone: 30-3356
Telex: 511174–511175

Palace of Conventions

The Palace of Conventions is the major venue for most conferences and seminars, although arrangements can be made with most hotels. The Palace has facilities for exhibitions, audio-visual aids, and contains 12 halls with a total capacity or more than 3000. Other facilities include office rentals, printshop, photography, translation, typing and photocopying, five snackbars, cafeteria, banquet and reception area, the Bucán Restaurant, communications, press, medical centres and luxury lodgings.

The address of the Palacio de las Convenciones is:
Apartado 16046,
Zona 16,
Havana,
Cuba.
Telephone: 21-9025
Telex: 511609

Useful addresses in Cuba

Baseball stadium
Estadio Latinoamericano,
Ave. 20 de Mayo y Calle Pedrosa
HAVANA,
Cuba.

Bus reservations
Calle 21 y 4,
Vedado,
HAVANA,
Cuba.

Camara de Comercio de la République de Cuba,
Calle 21, No. 661,
Vedado,
HAVANA,
P.O. Box 370,
Cuba.
Tel: 30 3356
Telex: 511 174 – 511 175

Chamber of Commerce of the Republic,
Calle 21, No. 701,
Apartado 370,
Vedado,
HAVANA,
Cuba.

Cubana (National Airline)
Calle 23, No. 64,
entre Infanta y P.
Vedado,
HAVANA 4,
Cuba.
Tel: 7 4911 – 7 4916

Cubatur
Calle 23, No. 156,
Vedado,
HAVANA 4,
Cuba.
Telex: 511 366 TURCU

Cuba TV and Radio
Calle 110, No. 512,
Playa,
HAVANA,
Cuba.
Tel: 22 5893 / 32 1746
Telex: 51 1600 TVC

Havanautos
Capri Hotel,
21 entre N y O,
Vedado,
HAVANA,
Cuba.
Tel: 32 0511

Havanatur
23 entre N y O,
Vedado,
HAVANA,
Cuba.
Tel: 32 2603

Hemingway International Nautical Club
Marina,248 Street and 1st Avenue,
Santa Fe,
HAVANA,
Cuba.
Tel: 22 5591 / 93

Hermanos Ameijeiras Hospital
San Lazaro 701,
Zona Postal 3,
HAVANA,
Cuba.
Tel: 79 8531 / 70 7721

Individual tourism to Cuba
c/o Havana Libre Hotel,
Calle L, entre 23 y 25,
Vedado,
HAVANA,
Cuba.
Tel: 30 5011 ext. 58
Telex: 511 982 TURCU

National Institute of Tourism (INTUR)
Avenida de Malecon y Calle G.
HAVANA 4,
Cuba.
Telex: 511–238 INTCU

INTUR (Santiago de Cuba)
Lacret 701,
Esquina Heredia,
SANTIAGO DE CUBA,
Cuba.
Tel: 20340
Telex: 61210

INTUR (Playas del Este)
Calle 3, No. 111 y Ave. de las Banderas,
Santa Maria del Mar,
HAVANA,
Cuba.
Tel: 087 2551 / 3348
Telex: 511 300

INTUR (Granma)
Parada No. 117,
Entre Pio Rosado y Cisnero,
BAYAMO,
Granma,
Cuba.
Tel: 45105 / 44257

INTUR (Pinar del Rio),
Centro Turistico Soroa,
Caudelaria,
Pinar del Rio.

Ministerio del Comercio Exterior
(MINCEX)
Ministry of Foreign Trade,
Infanta 16,
HAVANA,
Cuba.
Telex: 511 174–511 175

Palacio de las Convenciones
Apartado 16046,
Zona 16,
HAVANA,
Cuba.
Tel: 21–9025
Telex: 511 609 (PALCO)

Parque Lenin
Calle 100 y Cortina de la Presa,
Arroyo Naranjo,

HAVANA,
Cuba.
Tel: 44–3027/44–4344

Medical Centre
Clinica Cira Garcia,
Miramar
HAVANA,
Tel: 709566

Popular camping
Carretera Vieja de Cojimar,
Km. 1, Habana del Este,
HAVANA,
Cuba.
Tel: 65 0822
Telex: 51 1076

Publicitur
Calle 19, No. 60,
M and N,
Vedado,
HAVANA 4,
Cuba.
Aparto Postal 4239
Tel: 32 9881
Telex: 511 955 PUBLIC

Special tours
Suite de la Republica,
Nacional Hotel,
0 and 21 Streets,
Vedado,
HAVANA,
Cuba.
Tel: 79 7001 / 70 8178
Telex: 511 982 TURCU

Telegrams
Western Union,
Calle Obispo, No. 351,
HAVANA,
Cuba.

Theatre García Lorca,
Paseo de Martí y San Rafael,
Centro Habana,
HAVANA,
Cuba.
Tel: 62 2700

Tropicana Nightclub
Calle 72 entre 43 y Línea T,
Mariano,
HAVANA,
Cuba.
Tel: 2 4544/6 6224

Transtur, Vehicle Hire
Santa Catalina No. 460,
Vibora,
HAVANA 5,
Cuba.
Tel: 41 8571/72

Cuba abroad

Cuban Tourist Boards

United Kingdom
Museum House,
25 Museum Street,
London WC1A 1JT
Tel: 580 2942/3
Telex: 26 28 65 CUBTRA – 6

France
24 Rue de Quatre Septembre,
Paris,
France.
Tel: 42963133
Telex: 680791

Germany
Steinweg 2,
Frankfurt,
Main,
BDR.
Tel: 0611 28 8322
Telex: 4185577

Canada
372 Bay Street, Suite 408,
Toronto,
Ontario M5H 2W9,
Canada.
Tel: 416 362 0700
Telex: 0623258

440 Bld. Dorchester Ouest, Suite 1202,
12 eme etage,
Montreal,
Quebec,
Canada H2Z 1V7
Tel: 514 875 8004
Telex: 055 62399

1117 Street Catherine West, Suite 302,
Montreal,
Quebec,
Canada.

Mexico
Paseo de Montejo No. 442,
Mérida,
Yucatán,
Mexico.
Tel: 6-1890 / 6-1365

Argentina
Hotel Le Monde, Apt. 49,
San Martin 839 BS AS,
Buenos Aires,
Argentina.
Tel: 33-2032
Telex: 17012

Selected embassies in Cuba

Austrian Embassy,
Calle 4, No. 101 y 1ra. Avenida,
Miramar,
HAVANA,
Cuba.
Tel: 22 5825 / 22 4394

British Embassy,
Edificio Bolivar, 8° Piso,
Cárcel 101–103 entre Morro y Prado,
HAVANA,
Cuba.
Tel: 61 5681/4
Telex: 511 656 (UK EMB CU)

Canadian Embassy,
Calle 30, No. 518 esquina a 7ma.,
Miramar,
HAVANA,
Cuba.
Tel: 2 6421 / 2 6422

French Embassy,
Calle 15, No. 607 etre B y C,
Vedado,
HAVANA,
Cuba.
Tel: 22 2560 / 22 2569

German Embassy,
Calle 28, No. 313 entre 3ra. y 5ta. Avenidas,
Miramar,
HAVANA,
Cuba.
Tel: 22 2560 / 22 2569

Italian Embassy,
Calle Paseo No. 606 entre 25 y 27,
Vedado,
HAVANA,
Cuba.
Tel: 30 0378 / 30 0390

Netherlands Embassy,
Calle 8, No. 307 entre 3ra. y 5ta.
Miramar,
HAVANA,
Cuba.
Tel: 2 6511 / 22 2534

Spanish Embassy,
Cárcel No. 51 esquina Zulueta,
City of Havana,
Cuba.
Tel: 6 9687 / 6 4741

US Interests Office,
Calle Calzada entre L y M,
Vedado,
HAVANA,
Cuba.
Tel: 32 0551 / 32 9700

Useful words and phrases

Basic conversation

Yes	*Si*	Love	*Amor*	Hello	*Hola*
No	*Non*	Hate	*Odio*	Good-morning	*Buenos dias*
Good	*Bueno*	Like	*Gustar*	Good-afternoon	*Buenas tarde*
Bad	*Malo*	Dislike	*Aversion*	Good-evening	*Buenos noches*
Come	*Venir*	Now	*Ahora*	Goodbye	*Adios*
Go	*Ir*	Later	*Despues*	Sir	*Señor*
Here	*Aqui*	Right	*Derecho*	Madame	*Señora*
There	*Alli*	Left	*Izquierdo*	Miss	*Señorita*
Maybe	*Quizas*	Ahead	*Delante*	Friend	*Amigo/ Companero*
Cheers	*Salud*	Okay	*Esta bien*	Please	*Por favor*
Look	*Mire*	Help	*Ayudar*	Thank you	*Muchas gracias*

Quantifying

Much	*Mucho*	Little	*Poco*	Week	*Semana*
More	*Mas*	Less	*Menos*	Today	*Hoy*
Quickly	*Rapido*	Slowly	*Despacio*	Tomorrow	*Manana*
Big	*Grande*	Small	*Pequeno*	Yesterday	*Ayer*
High	*Alto*	Low	*Bajo*	Minute	*Minuto*
Long	*Largo*	Short	*Corto*	Hour	*Hora*
Old	*Viejo*	New	*Nuevo*	Time	*Tiempo*
Change	*Cambio*	Young	*Joven*	Year	*Año*

Lost	Perdido	Half	Medio	Month	Mes
None	Ninguno	All	Todo	Moment	Momento
Stop	Pare	Go	Pasar	Exit	Salida

Numbers, time, date

One	Uno	Zero	Cero	Monday	Lunes
Two	Dos	Twenty	Viente	Tuesday	Martes
Three	Tres	Thirty	Treinta	Wednesday	Miercoles
Four	Cuatro	Forty	Cuarenta	Thursday	Jueves
Five	Cinco	Fifty	Cincuenta	Friday	Viernes
Six	Seis	Sixty	Sesenta	Saturday	Sabado
Seven	Siete	Seventy	Setenta	Sunday	Domingo
Eight	Ocho	Eighty	Ochenta	Noon	Mediodia
Nine	Wueve	Ninety	Noventa	Midnight	Medianoche
Ten	Diez	Hundred	Cien(to)	Day	Dia

Requirements

I want	Quiero	I am hungry	Tengo hambre
I need	Necesito	I am thirsty	Tengo sed
I am well	Muy bien	I am hot	Tengo calor
I am ill	Muy enfermo	I am cold	Tengo frio
I'm tired	Estoy cansadov	I am lost	Me he perdido

Hotel, dining and shopping

Food	Comida	Meat	Carne
Water	Agua	Fish	Pescado
Eat	Comer	Soup	Sopa
Drink	Bebida	Beef	Rosbif
Breakfast	Desayuno	Cheese	Queso
Lunch	Almuerzo	Salad	Ensalada
Dinner	Cena	Butter	Mantequilla
Snack	Merienda	Bread	Pan
Bedroom	Dormitorio	Shellfish	Crustáceos
Bathroom	Cuatro de bano	Steak	Bistec
Toilet	Servicios	Chicken	Pollo
Pool	Piscina	Bacon	Tocino
Restaurant	Restaurante	Ham	Jamòn
Shop	Tienda	Pepper	Pimienta
Bank	Banco	Salt	Sal
Room	Cuarto	Sugar	Azucar
Soap	Jabón	Egg	Huevo
Paper	Papel	Scrambled	Revoltillo
Glass	Vaso	Boiled	Hervido
Cup	Taza	Fried	Fritos
Money	Dinero	Tea	Te
Cigars	Cigarro	Coffee	Cafe
Cigarettes	Cigarrillo	Beer	Cerveza
Matches	Fósforo	Rum	Ron
Post	Correos	Wine	Vino
Police	Policía	Coke	Cola
Doctor	Médico	Milk	Leche
Manager	Director	Sandwich	Emparedado

276

Waiter	*Camarero*		Omelet	*Tortilla*
Bill	*Cuenta*		Fruit	*Fruta*

Questions

How?	*Cómo?*		I want to go (to)	*Quiero ir*
How much?	*Cuánto?*		How far is it?	*A qué distancia esta?*
What?	*Qué?*		What is the time?	*Qué hora es?*
Where?	*Dónde?*		Do you speak English?	*Habla usted inglés?*
When?	*Cuándo?*		I don't understand!	*No comprendo!*
Why?	*Por qué?*		How are you?	*Comoesta usted?*
Who?	*Quién?*		I am lost	*Me he perdido*
Which?	*Cuál?*		I want to speak with	*Quiero hablar con*
Is there?	*Hay?*		How long?	*Quanto tiempo?*
Open?	*Abierto?*		What is this street?	*Que calle es ésta?*
Closed?	*Cerrado?*		I am looking for	*Busco*

Signs

Abajo	*Down*		Ocupado	*Occupied*
Abierto	*Open*		Oeste	*East*
Alto	*Stop*		Pare	*Stop*
Arriba	*Up*		Pase	*Cross*
Ascensor	*Lift*		Peligro	*Danger*
Avenida	*Avenue*		Prohibido	*No*
Billetes	*Tickets*		No Banarse	*No swimming*
Caballeros	*Gents*		No Pase	*No Entry*
Caliente 'C'	*Hot*		No Estancionarse	*No Parking*
Calle	*Street*		No Fumar	*No Smoking*
Cerrado	*Closed*		Reservado	*Reserved*
Completo	*Full*		Salida	*Exit*
Dames	*Ladies*		Señoras	*Women*
Empuje	*Push*		Servicios	*Service*
Entrada	*Entrance*		Sud	*South*
Entre	*Between*		Tire	*Pull*
Este	*East*		(Calle) 1 y 2	*(Streets) 1 and 2*
Frio 'F'	*Cold*			
Libre	*Free*			
Norte	*North*			
No tocar	*Do not Touch*			

Naturally this short vocabulary list cannot hope to provide the traveller with a comprehensive list of words and phrases in everyday use in Cuba. This little selection is only intended to assist in the most elementary way and act as an introduction to the language.

As earlier suggested, it is wise to carry a pocket phrase-book, and/or a Spanish dictionary with you at all times. In Cuba's cities and larger towns, at most recommended hotels and tourist resorts, at Cubatur and Havanatur offices, at some cultural houses and tourist attractions, there is usually some helpful individual who speaks English.

Another useful hint is for the traveller to take the time to learn just a few words of Spanish to show an interest in the language of the country. Just using the odd word or two can produce a most pleasing reaction when being introduced and making purchases or travel arrangements.

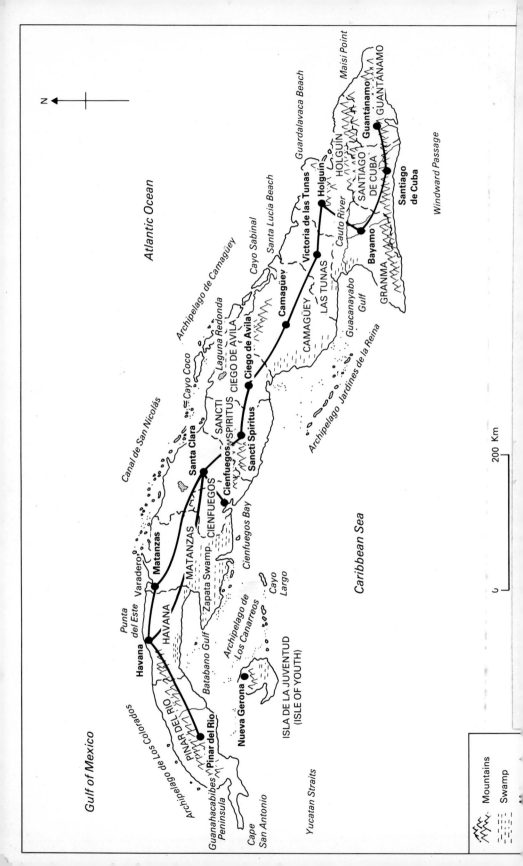